The Saints of Scotland

For my mother and father

THE SAINTS OF SCOTLAND

Essays in Scottish Church History
AD 450–1093

ALAN MACQUARRIE

JOHN DONALD PUBLISHERS LTD
EDINBURGH

The author and the publisher gratefully acknowledge assistance from the
Drummond Trust, 3 Pitt Terrace, Stirling, and from the Hope Trust, 31
Moray Place, Edinburgh, towards the publication of this volume.

© Alan Macquarrie 1997

ISBN 0 85976 446 X

British Library Cataloguing in Publication Data
A catalogue record for this book is available from the
British Library.

Typeset by WestKey Limited, Falmouth, Cornwall
Printed and bound by Bell & Bain Ltd, Glasgow

Preface

These essays do not constitute a history of the Christian church in early Scotland; given the present state of our knowledge, the writing of such a history is not yet possible. They constitute, rather, a contribution towards such a history by examining some of the major names in religious development during the period. They represent, in effect, a survey of the hagiographic evidence. The author has concentrated on written sources, and only deals with archaeology, place-names and art history where these serve as necessary elucidation of the main theme. Some geographical areas and chronological periods receive much attention, others very little; this is largely because of the uneven spread of the literary material.

A number of these essays have already appeared in print, though all have undergone greater or lesser changes to fit the purpose of this work. The Introduction is based on my contribution to *Hagiographies: Histoire internationale de la littérature hagiographique latine et vernaculaire en Occident, des origines à 1550*, ed. G Phillipart, i (Brussels, 1994); Chapter 3 first appeared in *RSCHS*, xxiii (1987), 1–25; Chapter 4 is an expansion of a paper in *RSCHS*, xxv (1994), 188–203, which in turn is a much expanded version of a chapter from my *Iona through the Ages* (Isle of Coll, 1983); Chapter 5 appeared first in *Innes Review*, xxxvii (1986), 3–24, and is here thoroughly revised; Chapter 6 appeared as the Introduction to my edition of *Vita Sancti Servani* in *Innes Review*, xliv (1993), 122–52; the first part of Chapter 7 is vastly expanded from a short article in *Life and Work* (May, 1992), 18–19; part of Chapter 8 appeared in *Pastoral Care before the Parish*, ed. J Blair and R Sharpe (Leicester, 1992), 110–133, while part also came from *RSCHS*, xxiv (1990), 1–17. Part of Chapter 10 is an expansion of an article in *Innes Review*, xlvii (1996), 95–109. I am grateful to all the publishers for permission to reproduce them here. All of them have been revised to a greater or lesser extent in the light of further research and in order to give this collection greater homogeneity.

The remainder of these essays, that is Chapters 1, 2, and 9, the Appendices to Chapter 4, the second half of Chapter 7, most of Chapter 10, and the Conclusion, are here published for the first time.

This book has been more than ten years in the writing, having been begun while I was teaching at the University of Glasgow. A number of scholars have helped me at different times while this work was in progress, too numerous to mention all by name. I will mention, for advice, information and encouragement, the help of Professor G W S Barrow, Dr John Durkan and Dr Richard Sharpe; but no-one helped me more over the years than two sadly missed teachers and friends, Professor Gordon Donaldson and Professor Ian Cowan, and I deeply regret that they have not seen in life the completion of this work. I am grateful to the University of Strathclyde for having given me an academic refuge in my native city. Hazel, John and Andrew have encouraged and inspired when I needed encouragement, and distracted me when I needed distraction. The dedication of this book, however, belongs deservedly to my mother and father.

Glasgow, 1997   *Alan Macquarrie*

Contents

Abbreviations

AASS	Bollandus, J, et al., eds, *Acta Sanctorum* (1643–1910)
Aberdeen Breviarium, Aberdeen Breviary	*Breviarium Aberdonense* (Edinburgh, 1510; reprinted, Spalding and Maitland Clubs, 1854)
AClon	Murphy, D, ed., *Annals of Clonmacnoise* (1896)
AFM	O'Donovan, J, ed., *Annals of the Four Masters*, (1856)
AI	Mac Airt, S, ed., *Annals of Innisfallen* (1951)
Allen and Anderson, *ECMS*	Allen, J R, and Anderson, J, *Early Christian Monuments of Scotland* (1903, reprinted 1993)
Anderson, *ES, ESSH*	Anderson, A O, *Early Sources of Scottish History, AD 500–1286* (1922; new edn 1990)
Anderson, *KKES*	Anderson, M O, *Kings and Kingship in Early Scotland* (1973; 2nd edn 1980)
Anderson, *SAEC*	Anderson, A O, *Scottish Annals from English Chroniclers, AD 500–1286* (1908)
Arbroath Liber	Innes, C, and Chalmers, P, eds., *Liber S Thome de Aberbrothoc* (Bannatyne Club, 1848)
ASC	Garmonsway, G N, ed., *The Anglo-Saxon Chronicle* (1953)
AT	Stokes, W, ed., 'Annals of Tigernach', in *Revue Celtique,* xvi (1895), 374–419, xvii (1896), 6–33, 116–263, 337–420, xviii (1897), 9–59, 150–303, 374–91
AU	Mac Airt, S, and Mac Níocaill, G, eds, *Annals of Ulster* (1983)
Bannerman, *Dalriada*	Bannerman, J W M, *Studies in the History of Dalriada* (1974)
Bede, *HE*	Colgrave, B, and Mynors, R A B, eds, *Bede's*

	Ecclesiastical History of the English People (1969)
Black, *Surnames*	Black, G F, *The Surnames of Scotland* (1946; reprinted 1993)
Bromwich, *TYP*	Bromwich, R, *Trioedd Ynys Prydein* (1961; 2nd edn 1978)
Chron. Bower (ed. Watt)	Watt, D E R, ed., *Walter Bower's Scotichronicon* (1987-)
Chron. Fordun	Skene, W F, ed., *Johannis de Fordun Chronica Gentis Scottorum*, (Historians of Scotland, i, 1871)
Chron. Picts-Scots	Skene, W F, ed., *Chronicles of the Picts: Chronicles of the Scots* (1867)
Chron. Wyntoun	Amours, F J, ed., *Andrew of Wyntoun, The Orygynale Cronykil of Scotland*, (Scottish Text Society, 50, 53, 54, 56, 57, 63, 1903–1914)
CIIC	Macalister, R A S, *Corpus Inscriptionum Insularum Celticarum* (1945)
Cowan and Easson, *MRHS*	Cowan, I B, and Easson, D E, *Medieval Religious Houses: Scotland* (1976)
CS	Hennessy, W M, ed., *Chronicon Scotorum* (RS, 1866)
CSEL	*Corpus Scriptorum Ecclesiasticorum Latinorum*
CSSR	Dunlop, A I, et al., eds, *Calendar of Scottish Supplications to Rome* (1934-)
DIAS	Dublin Institute for Advanced Studies
Diplom. Norv.	*Diplomatarium Norvegicum* (1849–1919)
DNB	*Dictionary of National Biography* (1885–1900)
EHR	*English Historical Review*
Gildas, *EB*	Winterbottom, M, ed., *Gildas: the Ruin of Britain (De Excidio Britanniae) and other works* (1978)
Glasgow Registrum	Innes, C, ed., *Registrum Episcopatus Glasguensis* (Bannatyne and Maitland Clubs, 1843)
Historia Dunelmensis Ecclesiae	Arnold, T, ed., *Symeon of Durham's Historia Ecclesiae Dunhelmensis* (RS, lxxv, 1882)
IR	*Innes Review*
Lawrie, *Early Scottish Charters, ESC*	Lawrie, A C, *Early Scottish Charter prior to 1153* (1905)

LSRB	Mann, J C, and Penman, R G, *Literary Sources for Roman Britain* (1978)
Macalister, *CIIC*	Macalister, R A S, *Corpus Inscriptionum Insularum Celticarum* (1945)
MGH	*Monumenta Germaniae Historica*
Migne, *PG*	Migne, J P, ed., *Patrologia Graeca* (1857–66)
Migne, *PL*	Migne, J P, ed., *Patrologia Latina* (1844–64)
ODCC	Cross, F L, and Livingstone, E A, eds., *Oxford Dictionary of the Christian Church*, 2nd edn (1974)
Paisley Registrum	Innes, C, ed., *Registrum Monasterii de Passelet* (Maitland Club, 1832)
PL	Migne, J P, ed., *Patrologia Latina* (1844–64)
PSAS	*Proceedings of the Society of Antiquaries of Scotland*
PT	Bieler, L , ed., *The Patrician texts in the Book of Armagh* (Scriptores Latinae Hiberniae, x, 1979)
RCAHMS, Argyll, RCAHMS, *Argyll Inventory*	Royal Commission on the Ancient and Historical Monuments of Scotland, *Inventory of Argyll* (1971–92)
Ritchie, *Govan*	Ritchie, A, ed., *Govan and its early Medieval Sculpture* (1994)
RSCHS	*Records of the Scottish Church History Society*
SHR	*Scottish Historical Review*
St Andrews Liber	Thomson, T, ed., *Liber Cartarum S Andree in Scotia* (Bannatyne Club, 1841)
TCWAAS	*Transactions of the Cumberland and Westmoreland Antiquarian and Archaeological Society*
TDGNHAS	*Transactions of the Dumfriesshire and Galloway Natural History and Antiquarian Society*
Trans. Glasgow Archaeol. Soc.	*Transactions of the Glasgow Archaeological Society*
TYP	Bromwich, R, *Trioedd Ynys Prydein* (1961; 2nd edn 1978)
VC	Anderson A O and M O, eds, *Adomnán's Life of Columba* (1961; 2nd edn 1991)
VK	'Vita Kentigerni' in Forbes, A P, ed., *Lives of SS Ninian and Kentigern* (Historians of Scotland, v, 1874)

VMR	'Vita Margaretae Reginae' in Hynde, J H, ed., *Symeonis Dunelmensis Opera et Collectanea* (Surtees Soc., 1868)
VN	'Vita Niniani' in Forbes, A P, ed., *Lives of SS Ninian and Kentigern* (Historians of Scotland, v, 1874)
VS	Macquarrie, A, '*Vita Sancti Servani*: the Life of St Serf', *Innes Review*, xliv (1993), 122–52
Watson, *CPNS*	Watson, W J, *History of the Celtic Place-Names of Scotland* (1926; reprinted 1986)
Watt, *Fasti*	Watt, D E R, *Fasti Ecclesiae Scoticanae Medii Aevi* (Scottish Record Society, 1969)
Zosimus	Paschoud, F, ed., *Zosime, Histoire Nouvelle* (Universités de France, 1971–89)

Introduction

The Hagiography of Medieval Scotland

It is a striking fact which seldom receives comment that the Scots, of all the Celtic peoples, were the only one who developed into a unified political entity in the Middle Ages. The powerful kings of the eleventh century, Malcolm II (1004–1034), Macbeth (1040–1057) and Malcolm III 'Canmore' (1058–1093), presided for long reigns over a kingdom which stretched from the Tweed to the North Cape; this was a situation without parallel in Wales, Brittany, or even the Ireland of Brian Boroma and his Munster successors. When in the twelfth century the descendants of Malcolm III and his second wife Margaret set about converting this Celtic nation into a European feudal kingdom, they built upon a firm foundation of Celtic religious and political institutions and traditions. The reign of David I (1124–1153) has been described as a skillful and successful balance of old and new,[1] and he more than any of his successors showed sensitivity and respect for his Celtic heritage as well as a concern to be involved in the mainstream intellectual and institutional processes of western Europe in his time. In this he followed his mother's example.[2]

One of the main interests of churches in this period was the collection of legends and traditions about their origins. We can detect traces of Christianity north of Hadrian's Wall from at least the fifth century, although the period of conversion and church building on any large scale probably belongs to the sixth and seventh centuries and later. Most of the Scottish 'saints' – Ninian, Columba, Kentigern, and a host of less well-known men and women – belong to this period.[3] Thus there was an interval of some hundreds of years between the careers of the individual missionaries themselves and the drawing up of their *vitae* in a form acceptable to twelfth-century churchmen and their feudalized lay patrons. The fact that most of the 'saints' whom we will be considering in the chapters that follow belonged to the late fifth, sixth and early seventh centuries parallels

1

the corresponding development in Ireland, where the majority of saints for whom *vitae* were composed lived before 650.[4] It is worth pointing out that likewise Irish learned secular tales set in a period after the mid-seventh century are exceptional.[5] Of the full-length Scottish *vitae* to have survived (setting aside such obvious exceptions as *Vita Margaretae Reginae*, which is an example of a different type), the latest chronological setting is found in *Vita Sancti Servani*, set in the period of Bridei f. Derilei and St Adomnán.

Given such a gap, there is little likelihood of strict historical accuracy in such *vitae*, even if that was what the compilers had been aiming for. But twelfth-century hagiographers were usually more concerned to edify, amaze and entertain than to provide historical data, and their sources were usually fantastic and mythological in any case. Where twelfth-century writers had an earlier Celtic *vita* on which to draw, that *vita* usually consisted of a series of miracle stories about the saint which were drawn from a common pool of such stories, many of them based on biblical models from both the Old and New Testaments. These stories are usually located at sites or churches which were claimed as part of the ecclesiastical jurisdiction of the saint's successor, and read at times almost like a collection of the title deeds of the saint's principal church; the twelfth-century *Vita Sancti Servani* is perhaps the most striking example of this kind.[6]

Two examples survive of collections of title deeds of a church which were not worked up into an edifying *vita* for a founder: they are the Gaelic notes in the margins of the Gospel Book of the church of Deer in Buchan, and a collection of notes relating to the church of St Serf of Lochleven in Fife which were translated from Gaelic into Latin and later copied into the register of the Priory of St Andrews. Both of these, although not written up into *vitae*, begin with a foundation legend of typical Celtic type concerning relations between the saint and a local lay aristocrat who at first refuses to let the saint settle in a site of his choice, is stricken with illness, healed by the saint's prayers, and finally grants the site to the saint.[7] Stories of this kind were often the starting point for more elaborate *vitae*, and some of our twelfth-century examples probably originated in this way.

Since the bulk of this chapter was written, the author has become aware of a Latin version of the foundation legend of Laurencekirk in Mearns, embedded in the writings of a prolific eleventh-century Flemish hagiographer working at Canterbury. It contrasts bizarrely with its dignified surroundings, which are drawn mostly from Book II of Bede's *Historia Ecclesiastica*, by transforming the grave Italian monk Laurence into a fearsome Celtic-style miracle worker, walking dryshod over a stormy sea, calling down fire from heaven in vengeance upon those who reject him, raising the dead, and drawing springs of water from dry ground. He had a church near Fordoun (now Laurencekirk) which women were forbidden to enter; Queen Margaret had a chastening experience of the saint's power when she tried to ignore this prohibition. His holy well, mentioned in the story, was at Edzell. The *vita* in which this extraordinary fragment is incorporated can be dated to some time in the 1090s; the story is a fortunate survival from a period from which we have very little else. It has probably been preserved because of the anecdote about Queen Margaret.[8]

These are not the only Celtic foundation legends for Scottish churches which survived into the High Middle Ages. The foundation legend of St Andrews survives in two versions, which although related contain significant differences. These describe how the Pictish king Onuist son of Uurguist (sometimes anglicised as Angus son of Fergus) (fl. c. 727–761) founded a church at a coastal site in Fife in thanksgiving for victory in battle, and dedicated it to St Andrew because the monk Regulus arrived there with relics of the Apostle which he had brought from Constantinople.[9] And the once very important church of Abernethy also had an elaborate foundation legend which locates its foundation in the remote Pictish past and links it with the *familia* of St Brigit of Kildare.[10]

Other *vitae* of the twelfth century support the greatness of individual saints whose churches were becoming centres of pilgrimage. Notable among them are the *Vita Niniani* attributed to Ailred of Rievaulx and the two lives of St Kentigern written for Glasgow Cathedral. In each case these were 'improvements' of earlier *vitae*. The *Vita Niniani* attributed to Ailred, probably written for Bishop Christian of Galloway (and therefore 1154 × 1167), is closely related to an eighth-century Anglian Latin poem, the *Miracula Nyniae Episcopi*, but is not derived from it directly, but from a common, probably ultimately Celtic, original.[11] Part of its objective was to emphasise the catholicity of the twelfth-century Scottish church, stressing Ninian's connection with Rome and personal acquaintance with St Martin of Tours (the former is attested by Bede, but the latter appears to be a twelfth-century fabrication). Just as Bede sought to set up Ninian as 'un contre-Columba' (to use Père Grosjean's felicitous phrase), so did the hagiographers of the twelfth century.[12] In spite of St Margaret's patronage of Iona,[13] that island monastery in the mid-twelfth century remained stubbornly Celtic and unreformed, and under the patronage of the king's enemies Somerled of the Isles and his sons.[14] So the cult of Ninian in the south-west, fostered at a time when the Scottish crown was developing closer relations with the lords of Galloway,[15] provided a counterweight to the cult of Columba, still largely outwith royal control.

The crown had greater success in its revival of the bishopric of Glasgow and the catholicization of the cult of St Kentigern. There was a barbarous and unsound *vita* in use in the cathedral in the twelfth century, and two efforts were made to supplant it. The first was a *Historia Beati Kentigerni* composed for Bishop Herbert (1147–1164),[16] which failed in this objective, since the barbarous *vita* was still in use c. 1180; but the Herbertian *vita* was preserved in fragmentary and anonymous form in order to provide a *vita* for St Kentigern's mother, Teneu.[17] It may be that a complete version of the Herbertian *vita* survived into the later middle ages, because the fourteenth-century historian John of Fordun appears to quote from a part of it which no longer survives.[18]

A second attempt to supplant the barbarous Glasgow *vita* was made c. 1180, when Bishop Jocelin (1170–1199) commissioned the monk Jocelin of Furness to compose a new *Life of Kentigern*. Jocelin combined the *vita* in use in the cathedral with a 'little book of his virtues written in a Gaelic style', full of solecisms.[19] This may not mean that the book was written in Gaelic, since Jocelin's knowledge of that language was probably superficial, but more likely indicates a Hiberno-Latin mixture. Jocelin's *Vita Kentigerni* is of considerable interest, because it is possible to disentangle many of the various threads which went into its makeup, and arrive at an analysis of its composition.[20]

Another twelfth-century *vita* which has survived is the anonymous *Vita Sancti Servani*. This has no dedication, author's name, or other internal indicators, so it is impossible to date with precision; but it may be the *Life of St Serf* which is mentioned by Jocelin in his *Vita Kentigerni*, and therefore be × c.1180. Its localised collection of miracles, set mostly in southwest Fife, Clackmannanshire and the surrounding area, reads like the territorial claims of an early Christian church at Culross; the community of St Serf at Lochleven, probably originally a daughter-church of Culross, was in existence by c.950, but this document represents the 'title deeds' of the earlier house.[21] As such it is of interest in charting the origins of Celtic Christianity in the area where the Anglian bishop Trumwin had been influential 664–685. This *vita* is also of interest because it shares with the *vitae* of St Curetan/Boniface of Rosemarkie and of St Regulus of St Andrews a concern to give these saints exotic eastern Mediterranean origins and a connection with the papacy. It has been suggested that these three *vitae* represent a fashion in eighth- or ninth-century Pictland following King Nechton's pro-Roman decision in the Paschal Controversy in 715; it is perhaps doubtful, however, that these exotic stories can in fact be so early.[22] An allusion to Serf's exotic parentage in an Irish tract 'The Mothers of the Saints' is of great interest, but since this tract is difficult to date with precision and probably contains some *ad hoc* fabrications of various dates, it cannot be used to push these traditions far back into the Pictish period.[23]

In a different category comes a small group of *vitae* of eleventh- and twelfth-century 'royal saints'. Chief among these, and probably setting the pattern for others, is the *Vita Margaretae Reginae* by Thurgot prior of Durham.[24] This survives in two versions. The longer version was written 1104 × 1107, but the shorter version may be an earlier draft composed very shortly after the queen's death in 1093.[25] The fuller version was addressed to Queen Matilda, Margaret's daughter who married Henry I of England and whose brothers Edgar (1097–1107), Alexander (1107–1124) and David (1124–1153) were successively kings of Scots.

Margaret's children were a saintly brood, none more so than her youngest son David, whose generosity to the religious orders became proverbial. Ailred, later abbot of Rievaulx, occupied an important place in King David's household before his conversion to the religious life, and after the king's death he wrote a *Lamentatio* in hagiographic style which he dedicated to the future King Henry II of England (therefore dateable 1153 × 1154).[26] This eulogy contains little information of historical value, apart from the very interesting indication that David wanted to join the Second Crusade (1147) but was dissuaded by his Council; this probably explains why from the mid-1140s until his death in 1152 David's son Earl Henry had the title *rex designatus*.[27]

A third vita of a 'royal saint' is the *Vita Waldeui* of Jocelin of Furness, concerning the life of Abbot Waldef of Melrose (d. 1159).[28]

Waldef was the son of Earl Simon I de St Lis or Senlis, and King
David's stepson. His career and tenure of office as abbot of Melrose
may in fact have been less distinguished than is suggested in Jocelin's
Vita,[29] but the *Vita* certainly supported the pretensions to sanctity of
the Scottish royal house in the same way that the *Vita Margaretae*
and the *Lamentatio* for King David did.

On the whole, the hagiographic legacy of Scotland is slender
between these twelfth-century productions and the end of the fifteenth century. Medieval inventories of the books of Scottish cathe-
drals make references to *Legenda Sanctorum*, but most of these have
been lost,[30] or survive only as fragments.[31] MSS like the 'Sprouston
Breviary' with its *lectiones* and canticles (accompanied by musical
notation) for St Kentigern, or the 'Breviarium Bothanum' or Fowlis
Easter Breviary, with its *lectiones* of Scottish saints, are relatively
rare.[32] Another rarity is a vernacular verse collection of saints' lives,
formerly attributed to John Barbour, 'The Legends of the Saints';
among its apostles, evangelists, virgins, confessors and martyrs,
mostly drawn from the *Legenda Aurea* and the *Specula* of Vincent of
Beauvais, are lives of St Machar of Aberdeen and St Ninian of
Whithorn.[33] The latter appears to be drawn from Ailred's Latin *Vita*.
The attribution to John Barbour, archdeacon of Aberdeen and author
of *The Brus* (c. 1375), is unsupported by any evidence and is no
longer accepted. Other nationalistic chroniclers of the later Middle
Ages such as John of Fordun (writing c. 1385), Andrew of Wyntoun,
(c. 1410), and Walter Bower (c. 1440) made much of earlier Scottish
saints, using hagiographical materials which are now lost.[34] But
Bower in particular may have been conscious of the relative shortage
of writings about Scottish saints, since he felt the need to expropriate
large numbers of Irish saints into his huge *Scotichronicon* and pass
them off as Scots. This was made possible because the words *Scotia*
and *Scotus* were still used to mean 'Ireland' and 'Irish' in the twelfth
century.[35] This has greatly annoyed some modern Irish scholars such
as the late Cardinal Ó Fiaich;[36] but Bower can perhaps be forgiven
for his expropriations, since the hagiographic record of his own
country is relatively sparse.[37]

About half a century after Bower wrote, the task of giving Scotland
a large-scale national hagiography was taken in hand by William
Elphinstone, bishop of Aberdeen, possibly in response to the prompt-
ings of king James IV. His *Breviarium Aberdonense*, published in
Edinburgh in 1509/1510, is the most important collection of Scottish

saints' lives (in the form of short *lectiones* for their feast-days) as well as having the distinction of being Scotland's first printed book.[38] The book is modelled on the English Sarum Breviary, but with important modifications: a large number of English local saints are excluded from the Calendar and their places are taken by Scottish saints, while other English feasts are downgraded in rank and Scottish ones elevated. There seems to have been a conscious attempt to spread the net over the whole of Scotland, to include saints from every diocese and to have a sprinkling of obscure and little-known local saints as well as national heroes such as St Ninian and St Margaret. Saints of the north-east, such as St Machar of Aberdeen, find their place in the *Breviary*, but his feast was not required to be celebrated as a major except in the diocese of Aberdeen.[39]

The sources used by the *Breviary* were various. The historian Hector Boece tells us that Elphinstone made a collection of legends of saints 'sought out in many places' in a single volume, presumably preparatory to drawing up the propers of saints in the *Breviary*.[40] In some cases the source is clear enough; for example, the *lectiones* for St Ninian are drawn, rather slavishly, from the Preface and Chapter 1 of Ailred's *Vita Niniani*,[41] while those for St Moluag of Lismore correspond to a *Vita* printed by the Bollandists in the *Acta Sanctorum*.[42] But it is not always clear whether the compilers of the *Breviary* used a well-known existing *vita* of a saint, or a less well-known local legend.[43] For example, the lectiones for St Fursey mention a 'little book of his life', but this does not necessarily mean that the compilers used it.[44] In the case of St Kessog (10 March), venerated around Loch Lomond and at Auchterarder and elsewhere, the compilers seem to have had access to a *vita* originating at Luss on Loch Lomond, from which they extracted one miraculous episode from Kessog's boyhood, and a reference to his burial at Luss.[45] This *vita* seems to have contained a garbled allusion to a practice of fostering the sons of sub-kings at the court of the over-king of Munster at Cashel, which is suggestive of considerable antiquity; but by the time it entered the *Breviary*, the story was being interpreted in terms of late medieval chivalrous feasting.

An example of the complexity of the source problems of the *Aberdeen Breviary* can be found in its material for the *lectiones* for St Kentigern (13 January). These appear to derive not directly from Jocelin's *Vita Kentigerni*, but from one of its sources, the little volume described by Jocelin as *codiculum stilo Scottico dictatum*; they are

closely related to the canticles in the Sprouston Breviary.[46] There
may be points where the *Breviary* has preserved its 'Scotic' original
more faithfully than Jocelin has done. For instance, the *Breviary*
describes how St Kentigern used to levitate at the *Sursum Corda* while
saying Mass: *Et cum 'Sursum corda' decanteret, corpus eius in aere a
terra elevabatur.* Jocelin says only that while holding up his hands at
the *Sursum corda*, exhorting others to do likewise, he raised his own
[heart] to the Lord (*Dum enim elevatis in modum crucis manibus,
'Sursum corda' diceret, ad quod ceteros ammonuit, suum habebat ad
Dominum*). Jocelin may here have suppressed or misunderstood a
fantastic detail in his original, for his version is relatively tame by his
usual exuberant standard.[47]

For St Columba, the *Breviary* appears to have used a late medieval
legend rather than Adomnán's Life, although this was known in
Scotland and was turned into Latin verses by a later sixteenth-century
commendator of Iona.[48] In the case of St Serf, the compilers of the
Breviary appear to have used a *Life* very closely related to the *Vita*
bound with Jocelin's *Vita Kentigerni* in a (probably) Glasgow MS now
preserved in Dublin, and to the *Life* preserved at Lochleven and
incorporated by Prior Wyntoun into his *Cronykil*. But they claimed
that St Serf was a Scot and a contemporary of St Palladius, while at
the same time they knew of 'another St Serf, of Israelite nationality,
who at the time of the abbot St Adomnán performed many miracles
in the island of Portmoak [i.e., Lochleven in Fife]; as is more clearly
described in the deeds in his *vita*'.[49] For St Margaret of Scotland,
the compilers have used Thurgot's *Vita Margaretae*, but with very
little direct quotation.[50]

There is a tendency in the *Breviary* to claim saints as Scots who
were in fact Irish. A good example here is St Finnbarr, venerated at
Dornoch in Sutherland, the medieval cathedral of the diocese of
Caithness, and at Kilbarr on Barra. The *Breviary* makes him son of
a Caithness nobleman related to the (otherwise unknown) local king
Tigernach.[51] This was presumably a tradition that was current at
Dornoch; it is more likely, however, that these are dedications to a
single saint venerated in Ireland under various guises.[52]

On the other hand, some claims of Scottishness in earlier sources
are ignored. St Constantine, to whom there are important dedications
at Kilchousland in Kintyre and at Govan, is claimed by Jocelin of
Furness as a son of King Rhydderch of Glasgow, granted to his queen
in old age in response to St Kentigern's prayers; but the *Breviary*

ignores this tradition and links him with the (British) royal house of Cornwall, stating that he became a monk in Ireland, then a missionary in Scotland, and was martyred in Kintyre.[53] The *Breviary* compilers seem to have had access here to a Kintyre tradition, and to have discounted Glasgow Cathedral's twelfth-century aggrandizement.

The *Breviary* includes a good deal of local legend and tradition. For example, the *lectiones* for St Patrick (17 March) allude to his supposed birth at Old Kilpatrick on the Clyde near Dumbarton, and also to traditions relating to 'St Patrick's Well' and 'St Patrick's Stone' near the kirkyard. These were important places of pilgrimage in the Middle Ages.[54] Some Irish pilgrimage sites mentioned in the *lectiones*, such as Croagh Patrick and 'St Patrick's Purgatory' in Lough Derg, are relatively late additions to the Patrician 'dossier'.

For many saints the *Aberdeen Breviary* provides our only information. For others it presents variants on traditions which are recorded elsewhere. It is by far our greatest cornucopia of Scottish hagiography. Adomnán of Iona, Baldred of Tynninghame, Baya and Maura, Blane, Boniface (= Curetan of Rosemarkie), Colman, Colmoc, Columba, Constantine, Conval of Inchinnan, Devenic, Donnan of Eigg, Drostan, Duthac of Tain, Ethernan (who also appears disguised as St Adrian of the Isle of May),[55] Fergus, Fillan, Finnbarr, Fotin, Kenneth or Canice, Kentigern, Kentigerna, Kessog, Kevoca, Machan, Machar of Aberdeen, Machutus of Lesmahagow, Madoc, Maelrubai of Applecross, Maioca, Marnoc, Medan, Mirren of Paisley, Moluag, Monan, Ninian of Whithorn, Palladius, Regulus of St Andrews, Serf of Culross and Lochleven, Teneu (whose names still survives in the St Enoch area of Glasgow), Ternan, Triduana, Winnin of Kilwinning; they are all represented, and others besides. And in spite of its late date, the *Breviary* is important because it records many earlier traditions which have otherwise been lost. Some preliminary research into the question suggests tentatively that where the Breviary compilers had earlier materials on which to draw, these are often twelfth-century or even earlier.[56]

The Protestant Reformation came late in the day to Scotland (1560), but when it came it came with a striking comprehensiveness. However much this may be regretted, there can be little doubt that the critical *impasse* which had developed by the late 1550s left no alternative to a radical, revolutionary reform. Devotion to saints and the whole apparatus of shrines, relics and pilgrimages, were outlawed and systematically suppressed during the 1560s and 1570s.[57] Reports of the burning of books and destruction of relics may have been exaggerated; certainly some statements can be demonstrated to be exaggerations, and there was little deliberate dismantling of buildings.[58] But there can be no doubt that, whether as a result of neglect or systematic destruction, the vast bulk of Scotland's liturgical and hagiographic writings have been lost.[59] What survives, chiefly the twelfth-century *vitae* and the riches of the *Aberdeen Breviary*, provides a tantalizing glimpse of what must once have existed in a nation proud of its saintly traditions.

NOTES

1. G W S Barrow, *David I of Scotland (1124–1153): the Balance of New and Old* (1985).
2. See Chapter 10 below, p 211ff.
3. On the date of St Ninian, cf. A Macquarrie, 'The Date of St Ninian's Mission: a Reappraisal', *Records of the Scottish Church History Society*, xxiii (1987), 1–25; revised as chapter 3 below.
4. R Sharpe, *Medieval Irish Saints' Lives* (1991), 8–10.
5. P Mac Cana, *The Learned Tales of Medieval Ireland* (1980), 99–101.
6. See below, Chapter 7, pp 145–59.
7. K H Jackson, *The Gaelic Notes in the book of Deer* (1972). The Lochleven *notitiae* are printed in *Liber Cartarum S Andree in Scotia*, ed. T Thomson (Bannatyne Club, 1841), 113ff, also in W Reeves, *The Culdees of the British Islands* (1864), 242ff, and in A C Lawrie, *Early Scottish Charter prior to 1153* (1905), 4ff.
8. See Chapter 10 below; *IR*, xlvii (1996), 95–109.
9. Printed by W F Skene in *Chronicles of the Picts: Chronicles of the Scots* (1867) (hereafter *Chron. Picts-Scots*), 138–40, 183–93.
10. M O Anderson, *Kings and Kingship in Early Scotland* (1973), 247; Skene, *Chron. Picts-Scots*, 6–7. For discussion, see A Macquarrie, 'Early Christian Religious Houses in Scotland: Foundation and Function', in J Blair and R Sharpe (eds.), *Pastoral Care before the Parish* (1992), 110–133, at 114–20.
11. J MacQueen, *St Nynia* (2nd edn., 1990), 4ff. On St Ninian, see Chapter 3 below.
12. Watson, *CPNS*, 296.
13. Orderic Vitalis, *Historia Ecclesiastica*, ed. M Chibnall (1969–1980), viii, 20.
14. *Annals of Ulster*, ed. S Mac Airt and G Mac Níocaill (1983), s.a. 1164. See A Macquarrie and E Mairi Macarthur, *Iona through the Ages* (2nd

edn, 1992), 13–14; A Macquarrie, 'Kings, Lords and Abbots: power and patronage at the medieval monastery of Iona', *Transactions of the Gaelic Society of Inverness,* liv (1984–1986), 355–75, at 355–8.

15. A A M Duncan, *Scotland: the Making of the Kingdom* (1975), 163–4. But relations between the crown and the lords of Galloway were not always so friendly.

16. *Lives of SS Ninian and Kentigern,* ed. A P Forbes (Historians of Scotland, v, 1874). A Macquarrie, 'The Career of St Kentigern of Glasgow: *Vitae, Lectiones* and Glimpses of Fact', *Innes Review,* xxxvii (1986), 3–24; revised as Chapter 5 below.

17. Edited in Forbes, *Lives of SS Ninian and Kentigern.* See J MacQueen, 'A lost Glasgow Life of St Thaney (St Enoch)', *Innes Review,* vi (1955), 125–30, for a different view. See also J and W MacQueen, '*Vita Merlini Silvestris*', *Scottish Studies,* xxix (1989), 77–93.

18. Macquarrie, 'The Career of St Kentigern of Glasgow', 6–7.

19. Jocelin's Life is edited by Bishop Forbes (n. 16 above). Hereafter referred to as *VK.*

20. Macquarrie, 'Career of St Kentigern'; K H Jackson, 'The Sources for the Life of St Kentigern,' in N K Chadwick et al., *Studies in the early British Church* (1958), 273–357; J MacQueen, 'Yvain, Ewen, and Owain ap Urien', *Transactions of the Dumfriesshire and Galloway Natural History and Antiquarian Society,* xxxiii (1956), 107–31; Idem, 'Reply to Professor Jackson' in ibid., xxxvi (1959), 175–83; D MacRoberts, 'The Death of St Kentigern of Glasgow', *Innes Review,* xxiv (1973), 43–50; see below, Chapter 5.

21. *Vita Sancti Servani* is edited from the Marsh's Library MS by Skene in *Chron. Picts-Scots,* 412–420; a new edition with Introduction, Text, Translation and Notes, appears in A Macquarrie, '*Vita Sancti Servani:* the Life of St Serf', *Innes Review,* xliv (1993), 122–52. See chapter 6 below. It is also discussed by J MacQueen, 'Myth and the Legends of Lowland Scottish Saints,' *Scottish Studies,* xxiv (1980), 1–21.

22. A P Smyth, *Warlords and Holy Men: Scotland, AD 80–1000* (1984); see also Dr Smyth's articles on the saints in question in A Williams, A P Smyth and D P Kirby, *A Biographical Dictionary of Dark Age Britain* (1991), s.n. Serf, Boniface. An argument against this view is that St Adrian of the Isle of May is called a Pannonian in the *Breviary,* whereas he seems in fact to have borne the Pictish name Ethernan or Edarnon; here the claim of exotic origins can be explained simply because his unfamiliar name was corrupted into a foreign-looking form.

23. P O Riain (ed.), *Corpus Genealogiarum Sanctorum Hiberniae* (Dublin Institute for Advanced Studies, 1985), 181, 220.

24. *Vita Margaretae Reginae* is edited in J Hodgson Hynde, *Symeonis Dunelmensis Opera et Collectanea* (Surtees Soc., 1868); it is discussed in

D Baker, "A Nursery of Saints': St Margaret of Scotland reconsidered', in D Baker (ed.), *Medieval Women: Studies presented to Rosalind M T Hill* (1978), 119–41.

25. Baker, 'Nursery of Saints', 130–2.
26. Quoted in *Johannis de Fordun Chronica Gentis Scottorum*, ed. W F Skene (Historians of Scotland, i, 1871), 218ff.
27. A Macquarrie, *Scotland and the Crusades* (1985), 17.
28. *AASS, Augusti*, i (1733), 248–76.
29. Cf. D Baker, 'Legend and Reality: the Case of Waldef of Melrose', *Studies in Church History*, xii (1975), 59–82.
30. For example, in the inventory of the books of Glasgow Cathedral made in March 1432/3; *Registrum Episcopatus Glasguensis*, ed. C Innes (Bannatyne and Maitland Clubs, 1843), ii, 335.
31. See D MacRoberts, 'A Legendary Fragment in the Scottish Record Office,' *Innes Review*, xix (1968), 82–5; see also *Analecta Bollandiana*, lxxix (1961), 343–5.
32. D MacRoberts, *Catalogue of Scottish Liturgical Books and Fragments* (1953). The *lectiones* from the Sprouston Breviary are edited by Bishop Forbes in *The Lives of SS Ninian and Kentigern*. On the music, see J Purser, *Scotland's Music* (1992), 48. The Fowlis Easter MS was published by the Marquess of Bute as *Breviarium Bothanum* (1900).
33. *Legends of the Saints*, ed. W M Metcalfe (Scottish Text Society, 1st ser., 13, 18, 23, 25, 1887–92); C Horstmann, *Altenglische Legenden* (1881).
34. Fordun, *Chronica Gentis Scottorum*; Andrew of Wyntoun, *The Orygynale Cronykil of Scotland*, ed. F J Amours (Scottish Text Society, 50, 53, 54, 56, 57, 63, 1903–1914); Walter Bower, *Scotichronicon*, ed. W Goodall (1759); new edn. ed. D E R Watt (1987-) in progress (hereafter *Chron. Fordun, Chron. Wyntoun, Chron. Bower*).
35. See, for example, *Chron. Bower*, xv, 35. King Henry V of England believed that his fatal illness resulted from having incurred the wrath of St Fiachra, *Scotus* (in fact an Irishman); as he was dying he sourly remarked, 'Quocumque perrexo Scotos tam vivos quam defunctos in barbam meam reperio.' Another example, concerning St Kilian, *Scotus*, bishop of Würtzburg, occurs in xiv, 7.
36. T O Fíaich, 'Irish Monks on the Continent', in J P Mackey (ed.), *An Introduction to Celtic Christianity* (1989), 101–39.
37. Cardinal O Fíaich was not the first to be thus annoyed, nor Bower the last to offer such provocation. It has been stated that much of the scholarly enterprise of Colgan and other Irish religious of the early 17th century in collecting Irish saints' lives was in response to the claims of Thomas Dempster, who 'claimed for Scotland all the saints of ancient

Scotia'; see R Sharpe, *Medieval Irish Saints' Lives* (1991), 41, 48. See also M Dilworth, *The Scots in Franconia* (1974), 214–5, and Chapter 17 in general.

38. *Breviarium Aberdonense* (Edinburgh, 1510; reprinted, Spalding and Maitland Clubs, 1854).
39. See J D Galbraith, The Sources of the Aberdeen Breviary (Aberdeen University, M.Litt. Thesis, 1970); parts of Mr Galbraith's researches are summarised in L J Macfarlane, *William Elphinstone and the Kingdom of Scotland, 1431–1514* (1985), 231–46.
40. Hector Boece, *Murthlacensium et Aberdonensium Episcoporum Vitae* (New Spalding Club, 1894), 99.
41. *Aberdeen Breviary*, PE, f. cvii r.-cix v.; Galbraith, Sources of the Aberdeen Breviary, 199.
42. Ibid., 203–4; *AASS, Junii*, vii, 678–9.
43. There is a good discussion of some possible sources in A Boyle, 'Some Saints' Lives in the Breviary of Aberdeen', *Analecta Bollandiana*, xciv (1976), 95–106.
44. *Aberdeen Breviary*, PH, f. xxxii v.; Galbraith, op. cit., 211–12.
45. *Aberdeen Breviary*, PH, ff. lxvii v. - lxviiir. The *lectiones* refer to St Kessog's Munster origins and to the ancient Irish practice of fostering sons of sub-kings at the court of an over-king; so the Luss original may have been of some antiquity.
46. Macquarrie, 'Career of St Kentigern of Glasgow', esp. 4–6, 9; Boyle, 'Some Saints' Lives', 100; see below, Chapter 5, pp. 125–7.
47. Macquarrie, 'Career of St Kentigern of Glasgow', 9; *VK*, 186–7; see below, Chapter 5, p. 126.
48. McRoberts, 'Legendary Fragment in the Scottish Record Office'; R Sharpe, 'The Life of St Columba in Latin Verse by Roderick MacLean (1549)', *Innes Review*, xlii (1991), 111–32.
49. *Aberdeen Breviary*, PE, ff. xv r. - xvi v.; on *Vita Sancti Servani*, see n. 21 above. See also Galbraith, op. cit., 210–15.
50. Boyle, 'Some Saints' Lives', 106.
51. *Aberdeen Breviary*, PE, f. cxv r. - v.; A Macquarrie, *Cille Bharra: the Church of St Finnbarr, Barra* (1984).
52. D Dumville, 'Gildas and Uinniau', in *Gildas: New Approaches*, ed. M Lapidge and D Dumville (1984), 207–14.
53. *Aberdeen Breviary*, PH, f. lxvii r.- v.; See A Boyle, 'Notes on Scottish Saints', *Innes Review*, xxxii (1981), 59–82, at 67–8; A Macquarrie, 'Early Christian Govan: the historical Context', *Records of the Scottish Church History Society*, xxiv (1990), 1–17, at 10–14; A Macquarrie, 'The Historical Context of the Govan Stones', in A Ritchie (ed.), *Govan and its early medieval Sculpture* (1994), 27–32.
54. *Aberdeen Breviary*, PH, ff. lxx v. - lxxir. See *Registrum Monasterii de*

Passelet, ed. C Innes (Maitland Club, 1832), 166–8 and *passim* for references to the pilgrims' hostel beside the kirkyard of Kilpatrick.

55. G W S Barrow, 'The Royal House and the Religious Orders', in *The Kingdom of the Scots* (1973), 186, n. 100.

56. A Macquarrie, 'Lives of Scottish Saints in the *Aberdeen Breviary*: some problems of sources for Strathclyde saints', *RSCHS*, xxvi (1996) (forthcoming).

57. See, for examples of this, *Stirling Presbytery Records, 1581–1587*, ed. J Kirk (SHS, 1981).

58. E.g., the popular statement that the reformers threw 100 stone crosses into the sea at Iona. Five high crosses survive, complete (St Martin's) or in fragmentary form (St John's, St Oran's, St Matthew's, and one unnamed). This number is comparable with that at Clonmacnoise or Kells, where there is no suggestion of mass destruction of crosses. There is evidence that both St John's and St Oran's crosses on Iona collapsed, possibly more than once, long before the Reformation. See the *Royal Commission on the Ancient and Historical Monuments of Scotland, Argyll Inventory*, v: *Iona* (1982); on the Reformation on Iona, see M Dilworth, 'Iona Abbey and the Reformation', *Scottish Gaelic Studies*, xii (1971–1976), 77–109; A Macquarrie, 'Kings, Lords and Abbots: power and patronage at the medieval monastery of Iona', 371–3; and Macquarrie and Macarthur, *Iona through the Ages*, 19–23. The number at Govan may have been similar; cf. I Fisher, 'The Govan cross-shafts and early cross-slabs', in Ritchie, *Govan and its early medieval Sculpture*, 47–53.

59. This presents a seemingly massive contrast with Ireland, from which survive more than 100 Latin *vitae* and about half as many composed in Irish; but most of them survive in, or were collected from, MSS outwith Ireland. Within Ireland 'almost all early manuscripts have disappeared'. Cf. Sharpe, *Medieval Irish Saints' Lives*, Chapter 1, esp. 4–7.

1

Before the Saints

One of the most important factors in the shaping of early society in the land we now call Scotland was religion, and in particular Christianity. In origin this was only one of a number of obscure oriental mystery cults which spread through the Mediterranean world in the early centuries of our era, and which competed with, and sometimes co-existed with, classical paganism. The emperor Commodus (180–92) encouraged Mithraism, an oriental cult which appealed to soldiers, while the third-century emperor Alexander Severus (222–235) is said to have had a bust of Christ in his private pantheon alongside those of Abraham, Apollonius, Orpheus, and other deities.[1] Christianity was ultimately more successful than Mithraism and other cults;[2] whatever the reason, Christianity was already by far the most successful faith within the Empire long before Constantine's victory at the Milvian Bridge in 312.

The situation on the fringes of Britain, the imperial province furthest from the Mediterranean heartland, is very difficult to assess. Some early Christian writers speak of Christianity in Britain: Tertullian, c. 200 AD, speaks of 'parts of Britain inaccessible to Rome made subject to Christ';[3] while Origen, c. 240, asserted that Christianity was a unifying factor in Britain, bringing it closer to Rome.[4] It has been remarked, however, that these comments 'carry more than a hint of optimistic exaggeration, and the remainder of the [third] century produces no testimony to a highly organised and vigorous church in the island'.[5] Gildas, however, writing c. 540, describes the martyrdom of St Alban, a Roman officer at *Verulamium* (now St Albans) during the persecution of Diocletian (303–312); he also mentions the martyrdom of Aaron and Julius, citizens of Caerleon, and adds that there were many other graves of martyrs in lands which were later occupied by the Anglo-Saxons.[6] Since doubt has been cast on whether there was any persecution in Britain during the period

15

303–312,[7] it has been suggested that the martyrdom of St Alban may belong rather to the reign of Septimius Severus (193–211) or some other time later in the third century.[8]

In the fourth century the picture becomes clearer. In 314, within a year of Constantine's edict of toleration, three British bishops, from London, York, and (probably) Colchester, attended the Council of Arles, accompanied by lesser clergy.[9] Clearly a church hierarchy already existed in Britain, and this must have been in existence before Constantine's victory at the Milvian Bridge and the Edict of Milan. According to Athanasius, British clergy attended the councils of Nicaea (325) and Sardica (342–3).[10] Three British bishops attended the Council of Arminium (Rimini) in 359, and accepted an offer by the emperor to pay their homeward expenses;[11] this may indicate that the British church was still relatively poor despite the wealth of the province.

Archaeology provides some clues which help to confirm and fill out this picture. In Roman villas, mosaics have been found which could bear a Christian interpretation: Orpheus passing into the Underworld in order to rescue a departed soul from death and returning to life, or Poseidon with his dolphins and fishes (the fish was early adopted as a Christian symbol, presumably because the Greek word ιχθυς is an acronym for 'Ιησοῦς Χριστος Θεοῦ Υιος Σωτηρ (Jesus Christ, Son of God, Saviour)).[12] More impressive are the finds from fourth-century Roman villas. A silver hoard of Christian vessels was buried at *Durobrivae* (Water Newton, Cambs) in the Nene valley some time before 350.[13] From the same period come the fine Christian friezes in a villa chapel at Lullingstone in Kent, and the floor mosaics depicting Christ in majesty at Hinton St Mary.[14] The cumulative evidence suggests 'an educated and wealthy Christian society in the Romano-British countryside in the second half of the fourth century'.[15]

It was this society which produced Roman Britain's only noteworthy theologian, Pelagius.[16] Pelagius was born somewhere in Britain c. 360 AD, and died probably in the 420s, having lived most of his life outside his native land. We do not know whether he had a native British name as well as a Latin one; πελαγος in Greek means the sea, and many Celtic names contain a first element with this meaning (in Welsh *Mor-*, in Irish *Muir-*). He travelled to the continent c. 380, and soon became a student and teacher in Rome; he may originally have studied law, but this is uncertain. He was never ordained, although he is sometimes referred to as a monk. He became a teacher and spiritual adviser to a number of well-born Romans, including women (earning him the opprobrium of the misogynist Jerome); his teaching seems to have been based on a moderate, highly moralistic, asceticism. He was opposed both to the immorality of classical paganism and the extreme asceticism of the Manichaeans, who were opposed to sexual relations in any form and even viewed food with suspicion.

His moderate views may have contributed to his popularity among high society in Rome, but led him into conflict with extreme ascetics like Jerome and the church in North Africa. In particular there were disagreements over the questions of human sinfulness, divine grace, and the freedom of the will. Pelagius' believed that man is created with the innate knowledge of the divine will and with the power of free choice whether to follow the divine will or not. Thus between the time of Adam and that of Moses it had been possible for some men to lead holy lives; but the failure of the majority to do so had led to the giving of the Law through Moses. This Law enabled men to know the divine will even if they were not prepared to use their innate knowledge. But failure to follow the Law led to the fuller revelation through Jesus Christ. Although Pelagius does not deny to Christ his redemptive or atoning role, he stresses his exemplary role as a crucially important element in Christ's mission. Christ's example shows us that it is possible for man to deny his sinful desires and to live fully in accordance with God's will.

There is thus little space in Pelagius' scheme for original sin or the need for infant baptism; baptism for him should be a conscious choice on the part of the Christian believer intending to live a good life. Baptism cancels out past sinfulness; but it is not clear why it should be administered to infants, who do not have a baggage of sinfulness to offload. Nonetheless, Pelagius never denied the need for infant baptism.

This was the main thrust of Pelagius' teaching, which is contained in letters, homilies and biblical commentaries. He was attacked by Augustine and (in characteristically intemperate language) by Jerome. An attempt to condemn him before the Council of Diospolis (415; now Lydda) failed, when the council accepted the Christian orthodoxy of his teaching. But the church in Africa continued to attack him, and condemned him at the Council of Carthage (418), persuading the Pope to join in condemning him as a heretic.

Little is known of Pelagius' movements thereafter. He had fled from Rome about the time of the Ostrogothic attack in 410, going first to Africa, where the hostility of his welcome forced him to move to Palestine. He remained there and in the eastern Mediterranean, despite Jerome's hostility, for most of the second decade of the fifth century; after c. 420 he disappears from record, and the Pelagian cause was chiefly upheld by his friend Celestius until it was finally condemned by the Council of Ephesus in 431. By this time Jerome and Augustine were dead, and probably Pelagius as well.

We do not know how far his Celtic origins influenced Pelagius' thinking. He emerges as a thoroughly Mediterranean scholar and thinker, perhaps more heavily influenced by Origen than anyone else. It may be tempting to view his valuing of human nature, in its potential goodness and dignity, as part of a 'Celtic' attitude to man and his world; but there is an element of speculation in this.

What is beyond doubt is the influence of his teaching in the British Isles. Twice during the 420s and 430s Germanus of Auxerre had to come to Britain to root out Pelagianism,[17] which was spreading there; Faustus, abbot of Lerins and bishop of Riez, and the 'Sicilian Briton', a social radical, were Pelagian writers of British origin who were active in the Mediterranean in the fifth century. The Pelagian bishop Fastidius apparently returned to Britain c. 430.[18] Gildas, we shall see, quotes British Pelagian writings with apparent approbation c. 540, and his teaching was influential in Ireland.[19] Even 100 years later the Pope-elect John IV wrote to the Irish bishops and abbots complaining that 'the poison of the Pelagian heresy has of late revived amongst you', implying that it had previously been widespread and had later been contained before breaking out afresh.[20] So whatever their origins, there can be no doubt that Pelagius' ideas had considerable appeal in Britain and Ireland.

It is important to remember, however, that most of the land which we now call Scotland had never been part of the Roman province, and was only remotely affected by Roman civilisation. The Flavian conquests under Agricola, who fought against a Caledonian confederation, were largely abandoned within a few years, and Hadrian commissioned his stone wall along the Tyne-Solway line c. 120. The Antonine decision to recommission Agricola's Forth-Clyde frontier with a permanent wall c. 140 was also short-lived, although the northern Wall may have been reoccupied several times during the second century.[21] By the end of this century we hear of a tribe called the *Maeatae*, dwelling close to this Wall, raiding into Roman Britain with the help of the *Caledonii*, who dwelt beyond them. Septimius Severus (193–211) campaigned more extensively in Scotland than anyone since Agricola, but in the end he decided to recommission the Hadrianic frontier. Thereafter there was peace between Roman Britain and the tribes beyond the Wall for most of the third century.

We know little about the tribes living beyond Hadrian's Wall. Ptolemy's *Geography* locates four tribes in the area between the two walls: the *Novantae* in the south-west (Galloway), the *Selgovae* in the Southern Uplands, the *Damnonii* in Strathclyde, and the *Votadini* in Lothian. Beyond the northern Wall he names a large number of tribal groupings, giving the *Caledonii* a prominent and central place.[22] By the time of Severus the northern tribes were divided into two great confederations, *Maeatae* (Dumyat in Clackmannanshire was presumably one of their strongholds) and *Caledonii* (who have left several place-names in the central Highlands, which is where Ptolemy's map locates them).[23] By the end of the third century we hear for the first time of *Picti* and of the 'Caledonians and other Picts', and in the 360s there is a reference to the northern tribes being divided into two groups, *Dicalydonae* and *Verturiones*, who again attacked Hadrian's Wall.[24] The Romans had apparently recruited native scouts whom they called *areani* ('field-dwellers' or perhaps 'desert-dwellers') 'to penetrate deep into enemy territory and give our commanders warning of the movements of border peoples'; but these 'were convicted of taking bribes to betray our army to the enemy', and had to be disbanded.[25]

About this time archaeology detects changes in the nature of the defence of the Wall, with regular legionary camps giving way to fortified villages held by militiamen and their families.[26] Evidence for Christianity from this more militarised northern zone remains thin. But most of the fourth-century emperors had encouraged Christianity among the army, and the two usurpers from the period who were stationed in Britain, Magnus Maximus (383–388) and Constantine III (407–410), commanded the garrison on the Wall and were strongly Christian themselves. A few Christian symbols have been found at military sites in northern England, but before the fifth century the evidence from the north is very slight.

By c. 400, if not earlier,[27] Hadrian's Wall appears to have been abandoned, and Stilicho's 'Pictish War' of 400–402 was the last attempt to hold the frontier. Soon after came the usurpation of

Constantine III, the great barbarian invasion across the Rhine in 406–7, and the sack of Rome by the Goths in 410. Britain was instructed by the emperor to look to its own defence.[29] There seems to have been a rapid deterioration in British culture, with coinage for trafficking going out of use within about a generation; the province passed into the hands of local 'tyrants' who carved it up and ruled their tribal areas from hill-forts.

The fifth and sixth centuries have been described as 'lost centuries' lying between the end of the Roman occupation (c. 410) and the documented histories of the barbarian kingdoms of Great Britain (c. 550).[30] Written sources for this period are very sparse, being confined mainly to the writings of Constantius, Gildas and Patrick, the late compilation known as 'Nennius', and later British legends and genealogies. These genealogies contain names of late fourth- and fifth-century ancestors which have been interpreted as garbled forms of Latin names (e.g. Patern Pesrut, Coel and Cluim have been connected with Latin Paternus, Coelius and Clemens, and Macsen Wledig with either Maximus or Maxentius), but it is doubtful how much reliance we can place on these; even if the names are truly Latin, the genealogies themselves are inconsistent and possibly largely fictitious.[31]

Constantius' *Life of Germanus* is more reliable. This describes how the heretical teaching on free will of Pelagius became so influential in his native country (which he had left long before) that Germanus of Auxerre had to come to Britain c. 429 to preach against it and restore the Britons to Christian orthodoxy. He was met by a sophis- ticated and romanised aristocracy at Verulamium led by a man 'of tribunician power', and there is suggestion of considerable factious feuding among the Britons. About ten years later he revisited Britain and was again preaching to the British aristocracy against Pelagianism when a report of a raid by Picts and Saxons reached them; Germanus allegedly led the faint-hearted Britons into battle and gave them fresh courage by teaching them the battle-cry 'Alleluia', by which they gained the victory.[32] The contrast between the relative peace of Germanus' first visit in the late 420s and the unsettled conditions of his second are perhaps suggestive of changed times. Also by the time of his second visit (perhaps c. 440) the Saxons seem to be well established and the Picts from the north are raiding deep into formerly Roman Britain. But there is no suggestion that either Saxons or Picts were influenced by Roman civilisation or by Christianity.

The evidence of St Patrick's writings will be considered at length in the next chapter. Suffice it to say that they suggest that some kind of Romanised administration persisted in Britain in Patrick's youth, and that by his old age even barbarian warlords on the periphery of Britain had some attachment to Christianity and Roman citizenship. The difficulty of using the evidence is that the dates of Patrick's life and career are the subject of lively controversy, in which there is no general agreement.[33]

From early in the fifth century, however, comes one very important piece of archaeological evidence from the north: the Traprain Hoard. This is a collection of silver plate weighing over 117 kilogrammes (53 lbs), containing pieces of more than 150 different objects. It also contains four coins, one of the reign of Valens (364–378) and three of the reign of Arcadius and Honorius (395–408). 'The most likely date for the burial of the hoard is around AD 410–425, though it could have been later.'[34] Some of the silver vessels had been cut up and the hoard was tightly packed in a pit in the ground, as if the silver was being prepared to be melted down, and then rapidly buried. The burial of the semi-dismantled hoard in a shallow pit is clearly indicative of unsettled times.

A number of interpretations is possible. The hoard could have been booty brought back by raiders from across the Wall. Or it could have been domestic silver used as bullion to pay native mercenaries or allies of the imperial province. Or it could have been the domestic silver of a powerful and wealthy chief of the *Votadini* (the tribe located in this area by Ptolemy in the second century), reflecting his culture and taste, which had been broken up and buried during troubled times.

The archaeology of the hill itself does not solve this question. There was an iron-age hill fort on the site from pre-Roman times; during the Roman period a British village occupied the western part of this site. In the post-Roman period, perhaps round about the end of the fourth century, a rampart was built around the village, and the treasure itself was buried within the area of the village.[35]

The hoard contains a number of overtly Christian items. One silver flask has biblical scenes, including the fall of man; another has a *Chi-rho* monogram and the letters Alpha and Omega. The *Chi-rho* monogram appears on the bowl of a wine-strainer, with the holes perforated in that shape and forming the name **IESVS XRISTVS** round it. The *Chi-rho* also appears engraved on the bowls of two long-handled spoons; another spoon has a fish engraved on it. These are not necessarily the liturgical plate of a church, although some of them, especially the wine strainer, could be; whether they are or not, they certainly came originally from some sort of Christian household or establishment.

So one possible interpretation, though not the only one and perhaps not the most likely, is that the Votadinian chief of Traprain c. 425 AD was a Christian with a chapel containing liturgical vessels. Of course, these objects are small and easily portable, and the circumstances surrounding the burial of the hoard make it possible, indeed perhaps more likely, that they were booty or bullion payment to a mercenary chief; the Christian symbols do not necessarily reflect the taste and religion of the Votadinian chief of Traprain c. 425 AD. Some of the objects, moreover, have overtly pagan symbolism, such as Ulysses and Penelope, and Pan dancing with nymphs and hermaphrodites. However, they do show that Christianity was within reach of the lands north of the Wall by this time, and within a generation or so we should expect to be finding more concrete signs of Christianity.

In a broad sweep through an area to the west and south-west of Traprain we find a group of some half-dozen funerary monuments spaced south to north from Chesterholm on the Wall to the Catstane at Kirkliston; Professor Thomas is of the opinion that 'these are native memorials' and range from the fifth to the seventh century.[36] At the Wall itself we would associate these with the Brigantes, further north in the valleys of the Tweed and its tributaries with the Selgovae, and in the basin of the Firth of Forth with the Votadini.

The most southerly, at Chesterholm, has an inscription which reads **BRIGOMAGLOS HIC IACIT ...... ECVS** ('Here lies Brigomaglos...').[37] Further north, in Liddesdale, comes the inscription **HIC IACIT CARANTI FILI CVPITIANI** ('Here lies [the grave (or the body)] of Carantus son of Cupitianus').[38] The *Hic iacit* formula marks these out as Christian burials. Lacking this formula, but definitely Christian because of a *Chi-Rho* monogram before the name of the (female) person commemorated, is an inscription at Manor Water, Peeblesshire, reading **XP CONINIE [TV]RTIRIE** ('Of Coninia [daughter of Tu]rtiria').[39]

One of the most famous, and certainly the most problematic, is the Yarrowkirk Stone. It has an inscription in very debased Latin characters which has been interpreted in various ways. Macalister would read it:

HIC MEMORIA P[ERP]ETVA [I]N LOCO INSIGNI PI-
IQUE PRINCIPEI NVdOG[EN]I dIMNOGENI
HIC IACENT IN TVMVLO dVO FILII LIBERALI[40]

Romilly Allen's reading is:

HIC MEMOR IACET I VLO IN I I PRINCIPEI [N]VdI
[DV]MNOCENI
HIC IACENT IN TVMVLO dVO FILII LIBERALI.[41]

The reconstruction of this inscription is uncertain. The second part, 'Here in the tomb lie the two sons of Liberalus' seems to be agreed, and it is possible that the names of two princes, Nudus and Dumnogenus (or similar names), precede this phrase. The word *Memor* can also be used as a personal name, but it is not clear that that is its meaning here.[42] But there is no doubt that this is a Christian funerary inscription.

Another expression which is clearly Christian is the use of the word **LOCVS** to mean an enclosed burial ground. A late medieval chronicler records the discovery in 1261 at Peebles of an ancient stone (now lost) with the inscription **LOCVS SANCTI NICHOLAI EPIS-COPI**;[43] some writers have assumed that Nicholas must be a misreading, but the suggested emendations which they would make are a mixture of speculation and wishful thinking.[44] The word *episcopus*, bishop, is presumably trustworthy. Another stone from the same location is inscribed **NEITANO SACERdOS**;[45] it has been dated to the seventh century, but could be earlier. So Peebles seems to have been an important centre of the bishop of the *Selgovae* at latest by the seventh century, and the Yarrowkirk inscription suggests that the princes of the *Selgovae* were Christian earlier. There were other ancient Christian sites in their lands, such as Stow in Wedale with its supposed Arthurian connections,[46] and Stobo, which later belonged to Glasgow and had a 'wide parochia and large number of dependent chapels at Lyne, Broughton, Drummelzier and Dawick'.[47] We cannot, however, be certain if these go back to the fifth and sixth centuries.

Similar in lettering and inscription is the Catstane at Kirkliston, with its inscription **IN OC TVMVLO IACIT VETTA F[ILIVS] VICTI** ('In this tomb lies Vetta son of Victus'),[48] which stands in a burial ground of orientated long-cists which has yielded radiocarbon dates centring on the fifth century.[49] The cemetery and the Latin formula *In hoc tumulo* are clearly Christian.[50]

The inscriptions of Peebles and Yarrowkirk presumably indicate the presence of Christianity among the people whom Ptolemy calls the *Selgovae*. That at Kirkliston with its cemetery is evidence for Christianity among his *Votadini,* quite possibly in the fifth century; and the ambiguous evidence of the Traprain Hoard may possibly, but does not necessarily, point in the same direction. But the most impressive epigraphic and archaeological, as well as literary, evidence for early Christianity comes from Galloway, the south-west of Scotland, where Ptolemy places the tribe which he calls the *Novantae*.

A number of years ago a memorial stone was found at the small cathedral town of Whithorn in the southern Machars of Galloway. It bears an inscription in Latin in Roman capitals which reads:

TE DOMINVM LAVDAMVS LATINVS ANNORVM XXXV ET FILIA SVA ANN[ORVM] IV [H]IC SI[G]NVM FICERV[N]T NIPV[TE]S BARROVADI.

This can be translated as follows: 'We praise thee, O Lord. Latinus, 35 years of age, and his daughter, 4 years of age. Here the grandson[s] of Barrovadus made [this] monument.'[51] On epigraphic grounds this inscription has been dated as early as the mid- to late-fifth century, although there is no universal agreement about its date.[52]

It is thus possibly even earlier than three kindred monuments which have been found at a similar site at Kirkmadrine in the Rhinns of Galloway, which commemorate Christian clergy. One has **A Et [O]** at the top above an encircled *Chi-Rho* monogram, and below it the inscription: **HIC IACENT S[AN]C[T]I ET PRAECIPVI SACERDOTES IDES[T?] VIVENTIVS Et MAVORIVS** ('Here lie the holy and outstanding priests, Ides (? or namely), Viventius and Mavorius'). Another, very similar, stone has the encircled *Chi-Rho* monogram above the words: **[ ]S Et FLORENTIVS**. A third, probably slightly later, stone from Kirkmadrine has the encircled *Chi-Rho* above the words: **INITIVM Et FINIS** ('The Beginning and the end'). Another stone from the Rhinns, now lost, commemorated a deacon (or possibly a subdeacon) called Ventidius.[53] At Whithorn exists another stone, probably slightly later in date (seventh or even early eighth century), in which the encircled *Chi-Rho* has been adapted to resemble an encircled cross on a pedestal base, with beneath it the words: **LOCI [SANC]TI PETRI APVSTOLI** ('[Cross] of the *locus* of St Peter the Apostle').[54] It is not certain that the inscription is of the same date as the encircled cross.

Archaeological evidence is coming increasingly to suggest that the site of Whithorn began as a greenfield site settled by incomers c. 500

AD. The incomers had access to some of the technology of the Roman Empire; their place of origin is uncertain, but Romanised Britain or northern Gaul seems most likely.[55]

We have seen that the Roman imperial province of Britain effectively came to an end c. 410. Mention has been made of a series of usurpations from c. 383 onwards, during which imperial troops were withdrawn from Britain to support rival candidates for the Empire; troops were also withdrawn in 406–7 to combat the great Barbarian Invasion of that time. The sack of Rome by the Ostrogoths in 410 and instructions to the Britons to look to their own defence effectively ended Britain's position as an imperial province. During the fifth century, however, as attested by Gildas, Patrick and Constantius, some semblance of Roman civilisation continued in parts of Britain. There were towns with a money economy up until c. 440; civic government under the families of Vortigern and Aurelius Ambrosianus, 'whose family had worn the purple', continued. We shall see that St Patrick's family were 'decuriones', civic officials, some time in the first half or middle of the 5th century. Even into the sixth century vestiges of *Romanitas* survived, for example in the inscription in Wales reading **MEMORIA VOTEPORIGIS PROTICTORIS**, the memorial of 'Vortipor the Protector'. A tyrant of this name was denounced by Gildas c. 540, and presumably it was the same man who had his memorial stone carved in Latin characters with a Roman title. Perhaps it is symbolic of the ambiguity of his position that his name was also carved on this stone in ogam script.

But there is evidence of decay as well. The circulation of coinage seems to have ended c. 440. Anglo-Saxon mercenaries were settled in eastern England during the first half of the 5th century, but outstayed their welcome in increasing numbers from mid-century onwards. According to Gildas, it was not until c. 490 that the Romanised Britons started fighting back effectively. A series of campaigns under Aurelius Ambrosianus and possibly a shadowy warlord named *Arturos*, Arthur (whose battles are catalogued by 'Nennius'), gave the remnant of Roman Britain a respite until c. 540, when Gildas wrote. Very little of historical value is known about Arthur, but all later tradition makes him emphatically Christian.

Soon after Gildas wrote, Anglo-Saxon incursions began again, with the establishment of permanent kingdoms throughout much of eastern and southern England. At the same time one or more Pictish kingdoms emerged in central and northern Scotland and a Gaelic kingdom (the Dál Riata) on the west coast. The last was made permanent by the conquests of Aedán mac Gabráin (k. 574–608), friend of St Columba. There were other Irish settlements, in Wales and Galloway.

The origins of Whithorn seem to belong to the respite period c. 490–540, when there was a modest revival of British fortunes and a recollection of the past glories of the imperial province. This perhaps suggests that the settlers at Whithorn possibly were not fleeing from external expansionist pressures, but were themselves expanding confidently from secure bases. It may be that this was a period of Christian missionary work among the peripheral barbarians. Bede denounces the Britons for their failure to convert the Anglo-Saxons, but this may simply reflect his prejudice. Patrick, whose career was unknown to Bede, lived possibly a generation or more before Ninian, but he laid foundations on which others were to build. We know of Vinnio or Vindobarr, venerated in Ireland as St Finnian, a British missionary active in Ireland in the first half of the sixth century, who corresponded with Gildas and who taught St Columba; and we know he was not alone.[56] Gildas denounces the clergy of his own day as lazy and luxurious, while excepting 'a very few good pastors'; but he speaks of widely-travelled, foreign educated presbyters as well. Such clergymen would have been aware of the newly-fashionable cult of St Martin in Gaul, which spread to Rome during the pontificate of Symmachus (498–514), and later to England and Ireland.[57]

Geographically, Whithorn does not look like a base for missionary activity among the Picts; with Kirkmadrine, it points rather towards Ireland. In the seventh century an Irish writer equated Patrick's birthplace with a place known to him called *Ventre*, which could possibly be British *Venn tref*, the 'White House'; but it is doubtful if we can hang much weight on this.

If the detailed excavations at Whithorn allow us to place its origin c. 500 and thus set it in an historical context, it is not certain that we can do the same for the finds in the valleys of the tributaries of the Tweed and in Lothian. The arrival of Christianity in south-east Scotland may have been a gradual, osmotic process, in which the surviving monuments are 'native' rather that 'intrusive' (to use Professor Thomas's classification)[58] as they are in the south-west. The radiocarbon dates around the Catstane may suggest that this process was well advanced before the end of the fifth century, and this is perhaps what we would expect on the evidence of the Traprain

Hoard. But more archaeological evidence will be required to confirm or modify this view.

We have thus reviewed the evidence for Christianity among the *Novantae, Selgovae* and *Votadini* in the pre-literary period. The *Damnonii* of Strathclyde will be considered in the next chapter, since there is good reason to believe that Patrick's correspondent Coroticus may have been a king of Dumbarton. Jocelin of Furness in the twelfth century records a tradition that when Kentigern first came to Glasgow he found there 'a cemetery which had long before been consecrated by St Ninian'; but this is not in itself a weighty piece of evidence.[59]

When we move from the anonymous world of archaeology to that of named Christian missionaries such as Patrick and Ninian, Columba and Kentigern, Serf, Adomnán and Maelrubai, we are moving into the 'Age of Saints' *per se*. In the following chapters we will consider the literary evidence for each of these saints in turn.

NOTES

1. On Alexander Severus, cf. Dio Cassius, *Dio's Roman History* (Loeb, 1914–27), books lxxviii ff.
2. F Cumont, *The Mysteries of Mithra* (1956), esp. 188–205; *ODCC*, s.v. Mithraism.
3. Tertullian, 'Adversos Iudaeos', vii, in *Tertulliani Opera*, ii (Corpus Christianorum, Ser. Lat., ii, 1954).
4. Origen, 'Homilies on Ezekiel', iv, in Migne, *PG*, xiii, col.. 698.
5. M Todd, *Roman Britain: 55 BC-AD 400* (1981), 226.
6. Gildas, *De Excidio Britonum*, in *The Ruin of Britain and other works*, ed M Winterbottom (1978), 10–11.
7. Todd, op. cit., 226.
8. J C Mann and R G Penman, *Literary Sources for Roman Britain* (1978), p. 66; Todd, loc.cit.
9. J D Mansi, *Sacrorum Conciliorum Nova et Amplissima Collectio*, ii (1759), cols. 463ff.
10. Athanasius, 'Historia Arianorum', in Migne, *PG*, xxv, cols. 725–6; 'Apologia contra Arianos', in ibid., cols. 249–50.
11. Sulpicius Severus, *Chronica*, ii, 41, in *CSEL*, i (1866), 94.
12. *ODCC*, s.v. 'fish'.
13. Todd, op. cit., 228; J Campbell et al., *The Anglo-Saxons* (Oxford, 1982), 10–11.
14. Todd, op. cit., 228–9. S Johnson, *Later Roman Britain* (1980), 166–9

15. W H C Frend, 'The Christianising of Roman Britain', in M W Barley and R P C Hanson (eds), *Christianity in Britain, 300–700* (1968), 37–49, at 42.

16. On Pelagius, see B R Rees, *Pelagius: a reluctant heretic* (1988); R F Evans, *Pelagius: Inquiries and reappraisals* (1968); T de Bruyn, *Pelagius's Commentary on St Paul's Epistle to the Romans* (1993); M Forthomme Nicholson, 'Celtic Theology: Pelagius' in J P Mackey (ed.), *Introduction to Celtic Christianity* (1989); H Chadwick, *The Early Church* (1967), 227ff.; his works are scattered through Migne, *PL*, xviii, xx, xxii, xxx, xl, xlv, Supplementum i, and elsewhere; for a list of his works and their editions, see Rees, *Pelagius*, 133–4.

17. See below, p. 20.

18. On Faustus, see *CSEL*, xxi (1891); on Fastidius, Migne, *PL*, Supplementum, i; and the articles in *ODCC*.

19. See below, 26.

20. Bede, *HE*, ii, 19.

21. L Keppie, *Scotland's Roman remains* (1990); D J Breeze, *Roman Scotland: a guide to the visible remains* (1979).

22. See A Macbain, *Etymology of the Principal Gaelic National Names, Personal Names and Surnames, to which is added a Disquisition on Ptolemy's Geography of Scotland* (Stirling, 1911), 29ff.

23. Dio Cassius, lxxvi, 12 (quoted in *LSRB*, 28–9).

24. Ammianus Marcellinus, *Rerum Gestarum Libri* (Loeb, 1935–9), 27, 8 (quoted in *LSRB*, 44).

25. Ibid (quoted in *LSRB*, 46). It has been suggested that *areani* could be a misreading for *arcani*, 'spies'.

26. A A M Duncan, *Scotland: the Making of the Kingdom* (1975), 28.

27. R Bromwich, *Trioedd Ynys Pridein* (2nd edn 1978), 452.

28. Claudian, 'On the Consulship of Stilicho', ed. in *MGH*, x (1892), and by Platmauer (Loeb, 1922); quoted in *LSRB*, 47–8.

29. Zosimus, *Historia Nova*, vi, 10, 2; quoted in *LSRB*, 53.

30. Campbell et al., *The Anglo-Saxons*, 20ff.

31. Cf. J Morris, *The Age of Arthur* (1973), 17–18; see L Alcock, *Arthur's Britain* (1971), 10–11, for a more cautious view. Cf. A Macquarrie, 'The Kings of Strathclyde, c. 400–1018', in *Medieval Scotland: Crown, Lordship and Community: essays presented to G W S Barrow*, ed. A Grant and K J Stringer (1993), 1–19, at 2 and n. 4.

32. Constantius, *Vita Sancti Germani* (Life of St Germanus), *MGH*, vii (1920), 247ff.

33. See below, chapter 2, p 31ff.

34. A O Curle, *The Treasure of Traprain: a Scottish Hoard of Roman Silver Plate* (1923); *The Treasure of Traprain* (National Museums of Scotland Information Sheet, no. 7, 1980).

35. G Jobey, 'Traprain Law: a Summary', in *Hillforts: later prehistoric Earthworks in Britain and Ireland*, ed. D W Harding (1976), 191–204; J Close-Brooks, 'Dr Bersu's Excavations at Traprain Law, 1947', in *From the Stone Age to the 'Forty-Five: Studies presented to R B K Stevenson*, ed. A O'Connor and D V Clarke (1983), 206–223.

36. A C Thomas, *Whithorn's Christian Beginnings* (The Whithorn Lecture, 1992), 2–3. They are recorded in R A S Macalister, *Corpus Inscriptionum Insularum Celticarum* (1945) (hereafter *CIIC*), nos. 510–511, 514–515, and some later discoveries.

37. Macalister, *CIIC*, no. 498, p. 475; *Archaeologia Aeliana*, 2nd ser., xiii (1890), 367.

38. Macalister, *CIIC*, no. 514, p. 491.

39. Macalister, *CIIC*, no. 511, pp. 486–7; illustrated in G and A Ritchie, *Scotland: Archaeology and early History* (1981), 147.

40. Macalister, *CIIC*, no. 515, pp. 491–3.

41. J R Allen and J Anderson, *Early Christian Monuments of Scotland* (1903, reprinted 1993), iii, 432 and fig. 452 (hereafter Allen and Anderson, *ECMS*).

42. *Memor* is a Latin surname; cf. *Lewis and Short's Latin Dictionary*, s.v.

43. *Chron. Fordun*, Annalia, liv; *Chron. Bower* (ed. Watt), Lib. x, cap. 14.

44. A A M Duncan, 'Bede Iona and the Picts', in R H C Davis and J M Wallace-Hadrill (eds), *The Writing of History in the Middle Ages: Essays presented to R W Southern* (1981), 1–42, at 32; Thomas, *Whithorn's Christian Beginnings*, 10.

45. K A Steer, 'Two unrecorded early Christian Stones', *PSAS*, ci (1968–9), 127–9.

46. Cf. G W S Barrow, *The Kingdom of the Scots*, 154.

47. I B Cowan and D E Easson, *Medieval Religious Houses: Scotland* (1976), 53.

48. Allen and Anderson, *ECMS*, iii, 426–7.

49. J Close-Brooks, 'Pictish and other Burials' in J G P Friell and W G Watson (eds), *Pictish Studies* (BAR, 15, 1984) , 87–114, at 94–7.

50. Thomas, *Whithorn's Christian Beginnings*, 5.

51. Allen and Anderson, *ECMS*, iii, 496–7; Macalister, *CIIC*, no. 520 ; Thomas, *Whithorn's Christian Beginnings*, 3–6.

52. Campbell et al., *The Anglo-Saxons*, 21.

53. J Wall, 'Christian Evidences in the Roman period', *Archaeologia Aeliana*, 4th ser. xliii (1965), 208–11; Thomas, *Whithorn's Christian Beginnings*, 7–9.

54. Macalister, *CIIC*, no. 519; Thomas, op. cit., 10–11, 19.

55. P Hill et al., *Whithorn Excavation Reports* (1987-); at the time of writing Peter Hill's final published report is still awaited.

56. D Dumville, 'Gildas and Uinniau', in M Lapidge and D Dumville (eds),

Gildas: new approaches (1984), 207–14; R Sharpe, 'Gildas as a father of the Church', in ibid., 193–205, at 196–201.

57. See below, Chapter 3, p 63f.
58. Thomas, *Whithorn's Christian Beginnings*, 2ff.
59. See C Thomas, 'The Evidence from North Britain', in Barley and Hanson, *Christianity in Britain, 300–700*, 93–121, at 110.

2

St Patrick of Ireland

It might seem to require explanation why an Irish saint finds inclusion in this book at all. But traditionally there are strong links between Patrick and the West of Scotland, which can be traced at least as far back as the end of the ninth century. There was a thriving cult of St Patrick, with a pilgrimage centre based at his reputed birthplace, his holy well and his sacred stone at Kilpatrick, throughout the Middle Ages. And, it will be argued below, the career of St Patrick may cast light on the state of the church and the activities of missionaries in Scotland round about the same time. Given the large number of people of Irish extraction living in the West of Scotland today, it is fitting that Ireland's national saint should also find a place in a book about the saints of Scotland.

Of all the early saints of the British Isles, none has aroused greater controversy or generated a more voluminous literature than has St Patrick. This is perhaps curious, because of all these early church-men he is the person about whom we know most; he is more of a flesh and blood personality even than St Columba. This is because of the survival of two of his own letters, whose authenticity has never been seriously questioned.[1] But these documents are both tantalis-ingly suggestive and infuriatingly vague. They cannot be combined with the accretion of later legend without being selective, because the later legends are in part mutually contradictory. So in the past historians have judiciously selected from the later accretions such evidence as fits their theories, and jettisoned the rest as late and untrustworthy. Some writers, conscious of the problems which this approach involves, have attempted to draw conclusions about Pat-rick's life and mission only from his authentic writings, without reliance on later traditions. Unfortunately, different writers claiming to work under this discipline have still managed to arrive at very different conclusions.

31

It is not my intention here to review the whole of the vast modern literature on this subject.[2] Neither is it intended to put forward a view which is strikingly new or radical. I wish, rather, to review the evidence about St Patrick (primarily the contemporary evidence, but with some regard to the later legend), with particular reference to its relevance and implications for the development of Christianity in North Britain, and to say a little about the cult of St Patrick at Kilpatrick on the Clyde.

The written sources for St Patrick's life and career fall into three categories. First and most important are St Patrick's own writings, the *Confessio* and the *Epistola Militibus Corotici*. The *Confessio* is an affirmation, partly autobiographical and partly deeply personal, of the faith and career of its author. It is written in a halting and stumbling low Latin which clearly caused its author some difficulty and embarrassment. It describes his early life, his captivity in Ireland, and the subsequent success of his mission there, with clear implications that his mission is the subject of criticism and attack from colleagues outside Ireland; but it is so personal that it is more than an official response to official criticism. The *Epistola* is an angry letter to a British king and his war-band, condemning their piratical slave-raid on a group of Patrick's newly baptised converts, some of whom were killed and others carried off into captivity; the king and his men are excommunicated and restitution is demanded. The letter also contains some anguished comments on the disregard with which Patrick was viewed in his own country (i.e., Britain).

The authenticity of these documents appears to be beyond question. They purport to have been written by a man called Patricius, a Briton living as a missionary bishop in Ireland, some time before the conversion of the Franks (496). Linguistic analysis is consistent with this, though there is some debate as to whether their Latin is entirely British or could have some Gaulish influence. The tone of these letters is so halting, diffident and deeply personal that it is impossible to believe that they could have been concocted (or even doctored) at a later date in order to glorify their putative author; indeed, the earliest manuscript of the *Confessio* omits certain passages. Of the MSS of the complete text, none is earlier than the tenth century.

The second source is a body of hagiography emanating mostly from the church of Armagh, no part of which in its present form is earlier than the mid-seventh century – some 150 years or more after St Patrick's lifetime. The purpose of this 'dossier' is clearly to assert and extend the prestige and territorial pretensions of the church of Armagh. The most important parts of it are the *Life of Patrick* by the priest Muirchú maccu Mactheni and the 'Memoir' by bishop Tírechán, both written in the second half of the seventh century.[3] These are partial accounts, both concerned to link Patrick with institutions and political groups. Muirchú's concern is to link Patrick with the Gaulish catholic church, most notably with Germanus and Amator, bishops of Auxerre, with the site of Armagh in northern Ireland, and with the great dynasty of the Uí Néill, who in this period were extending their authority in the north at the expense of the Ulaid (the north-eastern people who have given their name to Ulster). Tírechán's concern is to establish for Patrick's successors at Armagh a vast jurisdiction over churches in northern, central and western Ireland. He makes Patrick a contemporary of many Irishmen who lived long after the time of Germanus of Auxerre, and thus his account is impossible to harmonise with that of Muirchú. The two lives are both incorporated in the *Book of Armagh*, a ninth-century compilation which also contains other Patrician material: the 'Book of the Angel', an account of the territorial and jurisdictional claims of the church of Armagh, whose date is uncertain, but which, it has been argued, could be earlier than either Muirchú or Tírechán;[4] a collection of 'Sayings of Patrick', part or all of which is unlikely to be authentic; some additional material added on to Muirchú's Life, including the chapter headings and an account of Patrick's death and burial; and other additional materials, including a set of highly abbreviated notes ('*notulae*') which seem to be an index or notes towards another *Life*, which is not now extant.[5] Beyond the *Book of Armagh*, the most important document is the *Tripartite Life of St Patrick* of c. 900, a fully developed Hiberno-Latin version of the Patrician legend and the pretensions of the church of Armagh.[6] Beyond it again lie later Latin Lives, including a twelfth-century *Vita* by Jocelin of Furness.[7]

Obviously this material is of much less intrinsic value for Patrick himself than are his own writings; it is of great value for the study of the development of the claims of Armagh from the seventh century onwards. As evidence for events in the fifth century, it must be used with extreme caution, and must be regarded as of greatest value where it does not purport to substantiate the claims of a church, most notably the church of Armagh. Thus identifications in the later material of persons or places mentioned by Patrick but not definitely identified by him can be regarded as honest attempts at elucidation where they do not contribute to the greatness of Armagh or its dependencies. Statements which might seem to be an inconvenience or an embarrassment to the church of Armagh (e.g., that Patrick's first church was founded at Saul and that he was buried at Downpatrick nearby) must be taken very seriously. Armagh would have dearly loved to make such claims for itself; if it was unable to, it can only be because the known facts were otherwise.

The third source of evidence is perhaps the most difficult of all to use. This is the compilations of Irish annals, which appear in a number of redactions surviving now mostly in late medieval or even later MSS. Judgements on their historical value for the relative and absolute dating of fifth-century events have varied widely, from wholehearted acceptance to total rejection.[8] Modern opinion treats them with much greater scepticism than used to be the case, particularly for the fifth century. In their present form the annals seem to offer two sets of dates for Patrick's mission to Ireland: either arriving in Ireland in 432 and dying in 461 (which would harmonise with Muirchú's chronology), or arriving in Ireland c. 457 and dying on 17 March 493 (which would agree with Tírechán's).[9] Even more disturbing, the Annals hint at the existence of a *sen Phátric*, 'Patrick the elder', who lived in the fifth century but who is not identical with the author of the *Confessio* and *Epistola*. From this has arisen the suspicion that the Patrick of later legend is something of a composite figure, assimilating the author of the two letters with the obscure Palladius, who was sent 'to the Irish believing in Christ' in 431 by Pope Celestine, or with some other early and obscure missionary.

Our certain knowledge about St Patrick derives entirely from what he tells us about himself, and limited inference.[10] He is British, with a family living in Britain (C 23, 43); he came from the *vicus* of *Bannavem Taburniae*, where his father Calpornius was a deacon, and his grandfather Potitus a presbyter (C 1); his father was also a *decurio* or civic official (E 10), owner of a *villula* or estate (C 1), and owner also of slaves of both sexes (E 10). When he was nearly sixteen, Patrick was torn away from this prosperous existence by Irish raiders and carried into slavery in Ireland (C 1, 16); there he spent six years herding flocks, some, if not all, of the time at a place called *Silva Vocluti*, the forest of Foclut, 'beside the western sea' (C 16, 23). As a result of a vision, Patrick ran away from his master, travelled on foot some 200 miles to a seaport, where he obtained passage on a ship which took him away from Ireland (C 17, 18). The sea journey lasted three days and brought Patrick and his companions to a land which he does not name, where they walked for twenty-eight days before they came to human habitation (C 19, 22). It may be reasonably inferred that the land was not Britain, since Patrick immediately goes on to say 'A few years later I was in Britain with my family' (C 23); although even this has been questioned. Northern Gaul is most likely, since Patrick hints that he had friends in Gaul (C 43), and was acquainted with the practice of certain communities there in redeeming captives from the heathen Franks (E 14). (This last point incidentally provides the only internal evidence about the date of the letters, since it must antedate the conversion of the Franks in 496.) But the rusticity of Patrick's Latin does not suggest an extended stay in Gaul, and firmly contradicts a long period of education at Auxerre or Lerins.[11]

Once back in Britain, perhaps now in his twenties, Patrick was reunited with his family, who begged him never to leave them again. But in a vision he heard the voices of the Irish 'who were beside the forest of Foclut, which is near the western sea', begging him to come and walk with them, and so he determined to work as a Christian missionary among the people who had once enslaved him (C 23). So he trained for the priesthood, and shortly before being ordained he confessed to a friend (probably his spiritual director) a sin which he had committed when he was about fifteen (C 23–5, 27) – in other words, before his captivity. The nature of his sin is not stated, but it did not disqualify him for the diaconate. Nor, in the eyes of his friend and confessor, did it disqualify him for the episcopate, for the same friend told him that he should be made bishop (C 32). Subsequently he was consecrated bishop and sent to Ireland (C 26, E 1). He must have been at least thirty, the minimum age for consecration, and was not perhaps too much older.

Judging by his description, his missionary years in Ireland were many and successful, though fraught with dangers. He baptised many converts and ordained clergy (C 38, 50; E 3); some of his converts became monks and nuns (C 41–2). He travelled round the country with a retinue of the sons of kings and visited the courts of kings (C 52), making payments to them and to 'those who gave judgement', the *brithem* lawyers (C 53). On at least two occasions he was imprisoned, once for a fortnight and once for a month (C 52, 21), and he states that his life was in danger twelve times (C 35). Clearly he made many friends in Ireland, including powerful men who were able to negotiate his release from captivity on one occasion (C 52), and he mentions converting one lady *genetiva nobilis* (C 42), who subsequently became a nun against her parents' wishes. On one occasion a large group of newly baptised converts was attacked, some killed and some enslaved, by the war-band of a ruler called Coroticus; Patrick exerted himself to have the captives released and their goods restored (E *passim*).

After about thirty years of his ministry in Ireland, however, Patrick was faced by another serious threat. He was attacked (*temptatus*, perhaps 'put on trial') by a group of his *seniores*, presumably bishops (C26). It is clear that his trial and *defensio* took place in Britain (C 32), in Patrick's absence; so his *seniores* were British bishops. Patrick learned from some brethren that his old friend and spiritual adviser ('to whom I had entrusted my very soul') would speak in his defence, but instead the man betrayed him by revealing in public the sin which Patrick had confessed to him thirty years before (C 32, 26–7). As a result his defence was rejected and his name stripped of honour (C 26). The principal accusation against Patrick seems to have been that he accepted bribes for performing baptisms and ordinations, accusations which he indignantly refuted (C 37, 50–4). He refused to leave Ireland and abandon his converts (C 43), asserting that he had not gone there voluntarily but by the will of God (E 10), and that his episcopate was conferred on him by God (E 1). The *Confessio* was written near the end of his life (C 62), after a long and arduous episcopate (C 26). Its tone is defensive, and it reads in part like an explanation of why Patrick has refused a recall by his superiors and has chosen instead to remain in Ireland (C 3, 43, 61–2).

It has usually been assumed that the *Epistola* is earlier in date than the *Confessio*, though the reverse has also been argued. The two documents may in fact be close in date, as the same general circumstances seem to underlie both. The *Epistola* contains an explanation why Patrick cannot leave Ireland (E 10), hinting that he either has been recalled or fears that he might be; he also asserts that he is despised, resented and dishonoured by his own people (E 11–12). Again, his affirmation that he is a bishop and that 'what I have I have received from God' (E 1) clearly hints that his episcopate is under threat.

This is the bulk of our certain knowledge about the historical Patrick; but informed and intelligent guesswork can enable us to establish certain additional probabilities. The concern here is to examine Patrick's relevance to the history of the church in North Britain; and to that end we must seek at least partial answers to a number of questions. Where was the place of his birth and upbringing? Where was the place of his enslavement? Where later was the location of his mission? What is the identity of the Coroticus to whom he wrote? And when, approximately at least, did he carry out his mission? To some of these questions answers can be found with reasonable probability, to others with less certainty; and some of the answers are interconnected.

The first question is that of Patrick's birthplace, which he calls *Bannavem Taburniae* or *Taberniae* (C 1). This looks like an accusative and genitive construction, and should perhaps be read *ad Bannavem tabernae,* 'at Bannavis of the tavern'; but no such place has been identified. An alternative reading of the name could be *Bannaventa Berniae,* on the model of known Roman place-names in Britain, for example a Bannaventa in Northamptonshire and Glannoventa, now Ravenglass in Cumbria; *Berniae* is perhaps unlikely to be a corruption of Bernicia, the name of a large district east of the Pennines, but it may contain the same first element.[12] Almost the only clue we have as to its identity is Muirchú's statement that *Bannavem Taburniae* lay near the Irish sea, and that he had discovered that it was identifiable with the town (*vicus*) known as *Ventre* (M 1). But as well as appearing in this form, in some later MSS Muirchú's name for it also appears as *nemthor, nentria*; we should probably assume an original *✱Ventia* or *✱Ventria*.[13] This name looks close to the second element in Bannaventa, but can be no more readily identified.

Some writers have argued for a location in southern Britain – England or Wales – because that is where they would expect to find a society with *vici, villulae, decuriones, servi* and *ancillae*.[14] This is based on the assumption that Patrick's letter describes the villa-owning society of late Roman or immediately post-Roman Britain of perhaps c. 400 AD. This is, however, a rather large assumption. Authors writing in Latin had to find Latin names for familiar things and institutions, even if these were not identical with Roman provincial institutions of the fourth and early fifth centuries. We have seen that as late as c. 550 Gildas's tyrant Vortipor styled himself *protector,* using a Roman military title.[15] Perhaps the strongest argument in support of this interpretation is the suggestion that Patrick's father and grandfather had taken holy orders in order to gain exemption from military service, which could explain why Patrick claimed that he had grown up in a clerical family without having any deeply personal religious experience.[16] But against this, it would not be unusual for someone experiencing a profound religious conversion of the sort described by Patrick (C 2, 16) to belittle his earlier religious state, even though he may well have come from a clerical family and been conventionally devout.

There is not sufficient internal evidence in Patrick's writing to warrant the assumption that he came from the southern Britain of c. 400 AD. Other writers have argued that he could have come from somewhere further north, and indeed probably did if his mission was in the north of Ireland; but would still locate his homeland south of Hadrian's wall, if only just.[17] But we have noted the late fifth- or early sixth-century inscriptions at Whithorn and Kirkmadrine in Galloway, well beyond Hadrian's Wall, which suggest the existence there of some kind of sub-Roman society.[18] Of course there can be no doubt that the tyrants and aristocrats of this area and of Strathclyde further north, the people referred to in Ptolemy's geography as Novantae and Damnonii, would have had estates, *villulae*, slaves of both sexes, *servi* and *ancillae*, and settlements to which the term *vicus* could have been applied. They had Christian clergy, like Patrick's father and grandfather (C 1); and it is perhaps not difficult to imagine Barrovadus, Latinus and their descendants calling themselves *decuriones* in the same way that a mid-sixth-century British tyrant from Wales styled himself as Vortipor *Protector*, using a Roman military title.[19] When addressing the war-band of the British tyrant Coroticus, Patrick writes that 'I do not call them my fellow-citizens or fellow-citizens of the holy Romans, but fellow-citizens of demons, because of their evil actions' (implying that they would have liked to think of themselves as Roman citizens and Christians), but he still gives them the Latin title *milites*, 'footsoldiers', and speaks of their *regnum* (E 2, 19). There is nothing in the evidence which would be inconsistent with Patrick being a native of north Britain, even of areas like Galloway or Strathclyde north of Hadrian's Wall.

For what it is worth, the *Tripartite Life* and later lives of St Patrick assert that he was a native of the kingdom of Strathclyde, having been born in the vicinity of Dumbarton Rock. Medieval Scottish tradition, which we will examine below, located Patrick's birthplace at Old Kilpatrick on the Clyde. Attempts have been made to locate Muirchú's *Ventre* in this area. One suggestion is that *Ventre* might be identifiable with Fintry in Strathendrick, about twelve miles north-east of Dumbarton.[20] Certainly it is true that both Fintry and *Ventre* can be read as forms of British **venn tref* or **gwenn tref*, 'white house'. Attractive though this sounds, it has to be rejected, because in the twelfth century the name Fintry was spelt *Fintryf*, *Fyntryf*, with a final -f which was still sounded centuries after Muirchú's time.[21]

On the question of why the *Tripartite Life* should have made the identification of Patrick's birthplace with Dumbarton, I think we have to look no further than the place-name Kilpatrick. A name incorporating the Gaelic element *cill* and a dedication to a Gaelic saint cannot have developed before the penetration of Gaelic-speaking settlers into that area; and that penetration is unlikely to have begun too long before c. 870.[22] The evidence of the *Tripartite Life* suggests that the dedication of Kilpatrick was in existence by the time it was written (c. 900), but may not indicate anything else. Kilpatrick became an important pilgrimage centre in the middle ages, with its holy well in which Patrick was allegedly baptised, its sacred stone, and the 'great thatched house' beside the kirkyard which served as a pilgrims' hospital;[23] but there is nothing in the traditions which surround these which is suggestive of fifth- or sixth-century origin.[24] It is hard to believe that an oral tradition linking Patrick with Kilpatrick can have survived for four centuries without being known to the compilers of the *Book of Armagh*.[25]

Still, the possibility that Patrick came from North Britain cannot be ignored. He is likely to have come from somewhere near the west coast of Britain. His one known correspondent, Coroticus, was an ally of the Picts, and, we shall argue below, was probably a north British tyrant; by the time the *Book of Armagh* was written he had become identified as a king of Dumbarton (M chapter headings).[26] The dedication at Kilpatrick probably came later in the ninth century, and was followed by the story in the *Tripartite Life*.

Our next question concerns the location of Patrick's captivity in Ireland. Muirchú locates the site of Patrick's captivity at Mount Slemish in County Down, near Strangford Lough (M 11); but this area can hardly be equated with *silva Vocluti*, the forest of Foclut, since Patrick himself says that this was near the western sea, i.e., the Atlantic (C 23). Indeed, Muirchú does not attempt the equation *silva Vocluti* = Slemish, which he would clearly have found impossible; he does know the former name, but suppresses its proximity to the western sea. Tírechán locates *silva Fochlothi* in the lands of the sons of Amalgaid on the western shore by Mag Domnon (*Tír Amalgada*, now Tirawley), near the River Moy in the north of County Mayo; this has long been identified with a formerly wooded district near Killala.[27] This identification is unlikely to have been invented at Armagh, but Tírechán certainly was connected with the place. It seems to have embarrassed Muirchú, who discreetly omits Patrick's reference to the western sea, and places his captivity in the lands of the Ulaid; Tírechán also locates his captivity at Slemish, and was apparently not concerned that Patrick himself placed it at *silva Vocluti* (C 23). The identification with Killala in County Mayo is possibly to be accepted, but not without caution.

The location of Patrick's mission in Ireland is also difficult to determine. The *Confessio* does not mention any places by name, but indicates that Patrick travelled widely, visiting a number of royal courts and penetrating into areas where no missionaries had gone before (C 51–2)(seemingly implying, incidentally, that there were areas where missionaries *had* penetrated). The place most closely associated with him in later legend is Armagh, and the rulers of the church of Armagh claimed for themselves the title 'successors of Patrick'. It has been seen that most of our early documents about St Patrick come from Armagh, and were intended to enhance the prestige and extend the patronage of the church there. The Lives of Muirchú and Tírechán were written at a time when other great churches, most notably Kildare and Iona, had developed great *paruchiae* of lesser churches and territorial units outside their own immediate *terminus* or surrounding territory. It has been said that Armagh was relatively late as an entrant into the sport of church-bagging, but spectacularly successful.[28] Its pretensions were vast; Tírechán claimed that almost the whole of Ireland should be the *paruchia* of Patrick's successor, and the 'Book of the Angel' placed it in Ulster, Meath and Connacht, allowing St Brigit of Kildare her rights in Leinster. Muirchú was concerned to connect Patrick with the dynasty of the Uí Néill and Tara as well as with Armagh.

Until recently most historians, including the most sceptical, accepted the connection between the historical Patrick and Armagh.[29] But some of them have pointed out that Patrick's connection with Armagh is not as straightforward as at first sight appears. Other early saints, such as the very obscure St Secundinus, are connected with Armagh.[30] The *Book of Armagh* does not claim Armagh as St Patrick's first foundation in Ireland, or, more seriously, as the place of his burial. Indeed, there is more than a hint of a dispute over the possession of Patrick's relics between Downpatrick in the lands of the Ulaid and Armagh in the lands of the Airthir, who were tributaries of the Northern Uí Néill; and, to the considerable embarrassment of Armagh, Downpatrick and the Ulaid seem to have had the better claim.[31] There may be good reason to believe that Patrick was buried at Downpatrick. Other places in the same area with strong Patrician associations are Slemish, identified (possibly wrongly) as the place of his captivity, and Saul (*Saball Phátric*, 'Patrick's Barn'), named by Muirchú and the *Tripartite Life* as the site of Patrick's first church — another embarrassment for Armagh. The Book of Armagh says that Patrick died at Saul. Admissions like this on the part of Armagh, against its own interest, must be taken seriously. It appears virtually certain that the area with which Patrick is most closely associated, the site of his first church and the places of his death and burial, were in the lands of the Ulaid around Strangford Lough in what is now County Down.

The claim of Armagh depends in part on a supposed association with a secular capital at Emain Machae (now Navan Fort) nearby, the royal centre of the Ulaid according to the Ulidian cycle of tales. But recent archaeology has shown that Emain had been abandoned as a centre of population many centuries before the time of the historical Patrick. Thus the whole story of the origins of Armagh as set forth in the Book of Armagh, and its connection with the historical Patrick, begin to look flimsy.[32] His connection with Saul and Downpatrick, although partly obscured by the pretensions of Armagh, looks rather stronger.

This has important implications when considering the place of Patrick's origin and education. If he were a native of south Wales or south-west England, Patrick's mission would most likely have taken him to Leinster; but this is the area of Ireland where his traces are most faint. We should probably look for his origins further north. The shortest sea crossing to Ireland was from Galloway, where there was a Christian community by c. 500 at latest. We are reminded of the later devotion at Whithorn to St Martin of Tours, a great missionary saint, which also appeared at Armagh; and of the apparent 'fact' that it was from there that St Ninian set out on his mission to the Picts.[33] I would not go so far as to suggest that St Patrick came from Galloway or Strathclyde; but I would suggest that this would not be inconsistent with the evidence.

Next we must consider the identity of Patrick's enemy Coroticus. Patrick does not directly call him a king (although he implies it by speaking of his *regnum temporale*, E19) or identify his area of influence, but the *Epistola* does contain certain indications. It is clear that Coroticus was a powerful lord with a war-band which he could send on piratical raids in alliance with Irish and Picts (*socii Scotorum atque Pictorum*, E 2). The mention of Picts as Coroticus's allies immediately points to north Britain. The name itself is British Ceretic (later Ceredig), which first appears as Caesar's Caratacus. It is clear from Patrick's words that Coroticus and his men considered themselves to have some veneer of *Romanitas* and Christianity; otherwise his taunt *Non dico civibus meis, neque civibus sanctorum Romanorum, sed civibus daemoniorum* (E 2) would have had no point. It also seems clear that Coroticus normally had access to Christian clergy, to whom he gave alms, and whom Patrick begs to shun him. (E 7, 13) Although the point has been disputed,[34] it is reasonable to assume that Coroticus was a British tyrant of the type later denounced by Gildas; and his alliance with the Picts indicates that he was a northerner.

In the chapter-headings of Muirchú's *Life*, he is called *Coirthech rex Aloo*.[35] This must represent *alo* or (later) *ala*, genitive of *ail*, 'rock'; so to the *Book of Armagh* he was 'Coroticus, king of the Rock'. The rock in question was almost certainly Dumbarton Rock, fortress of the British kings of Strathclyde; this is *Ail Cluade* in the *Tripartite Life*, *Petra Cloithe* in Adomnán's *Life of Columba*, both meaning 'Rock of the Clyde'.[36] It was only later that it became known to the Gael as *Dùn Bretann*, 'Fort of the Britons'. It is not important here to enter into discussion over the authorship of the chapter-headings to Muirchú's *Life*. What is important is to note that by the early ninth century at latest it was believed that Patrick's Coroticus had been a king of Dumbarton. Whether this resulted from knowledge of the existence of such a king or from guesswork based on other known facts cannot now be determined.

Such a king is named in one Old Welsh genealogy of the kings of Dumbarton. In the Harleian pedigrees he is placed two generations before Dyfnwal Hen, who appears as the ancestor of a number of historical figures. Dyfnwal Hen is placed two generations before Nwython (d. c. 620); three generations before Ywain (fl. 642; d. × 658); and four generations before Elffin (d. 693) and Dyfnwal (d. 694). He is also placed two generations before Rhydderch Hael (fl. c. 580, d. c. 614).[37] Generation counting is a hazardous business, and this does not really allow us to say anything more definite than that Ceredig of Dumbarton was a fifth-century figure. We know also that Patrick's Coroticus was a fifth-century figure. There is a danger, however, of falling into a circular argument, using Coroticus to date Patrick and at the same time using Patrick to date Coroticus. Both can be independently dated to the fifth century, but it is dangerous to try to use either of them to date the other more precisely than that. If Ceredig had a long reign (his by-name *wledig*, 'wealthy', might indicate a long and successful plundering career), then he could be fitted into almost any chronological scheme for Patrick which would place the saint between c. 430 and c. 490.

This of course initiates discussion of another question, the date of St Patrick's mission to the Irish. This question has perhaps aroused greater bitterness than any other; but it is not clear why this should have been so. Almost all writers are agreed that Patrick was active in Ireland for a period of some thirty years somewhere within the limits c. 430 × c. 495; and by dark-age standards, that is not particularly inaccurate. We have one absolute *terminus ante quem*, 496, because Patrick describes the Franks as heathen (E 14).

The dates offered by the annals are so confused and hazardous as to be virtually worthless. The date 432 looks suspiciously close to that of Palladius (431) taken from Prosper of Aquitaine; and the obit in 461 looks like a confusion or assimilation with the obit of Pope Leo the Great (461). The annals also have a later date, 17 March 493, which is both very precise and does not appear to have been confused with anything; so insofar as the Annal dates are of any value at all, this is perhaps the one with the strongest claim. Some scholars doubt, however, whether weight can be placed on any fifth-century annalistic dating at all.[38]

Supporters of the earlier dating for Patrick mostly make a judicious selection from the seventh-century evidence, pointing to his supposed contemporaneity with Amator and Germanus of Auxerre and with Lóegaire mac Néill in Ireland.[39] But linguistic experts doubt that Patrick's Latin is the product of a lengthy education in Gaul.[40] Furthermore, Muirchú's chronology is very shaky: he states (M 6–9) that Patrick was consecrated bishop by Bishop Amathorex (i.e., Amator, who died in 418) a year after Palladius had been sent to Ireland by the pope (431), and after years of study under St Germanus (bishop of Auxerre 418–448). This clearly is totally unreliable. Equally unreliable are the dates and reign-lengths assigned to fifth-

century Irish kings such as Lóegaire mac Néill, which have probably
been adjusted to fit in with Patrician chronology; their evidence is so
suspect that they cannot be used as a foundation for any dating
hypothesis.[41]

If contemporaneity with Lóegaire mac Néill and St Germanus of
Auxerre is suspect, what of the other people mentioned as Patrick's
contemporaries in the *Book of Armagh* (especially in Tírechán's
memoir and the '*notulae*') and *Tripartite Life*? Analysis of these names
has found that for the most part they are given obits in the Annals
within a generation of 493, and so cumulatively appear to support
the later date for St Patrick's death.[42] But again, it has been argued
that these dates could have been adjusted or simply made up to
conform to Armagh chronology. The one exception here appears to
be the date for the death of St Maucteus or Mochta (*AU* 535), who
is described both by himself in a fragment of a letter and by Adomnán
as 'disciple of St Patrick'.[43] It appears that his date is independent of
Armagh tradition, and may be the closest thing we have to external
corroboration of the *floruit* of the historical Patrick; if Mochta was a
younger contemporary of Patrick and his obit is independent of
Armagh tradition, we could have independent evidence that Patrick
died in the late fifth century, perhaps c. 493.[44] On the other hand,
the fact that Mochta styles himself 'disciple of Patrick' may not
necessarily mean that he was a younger contemporary of Patrick, but
indicate discipleship in another sense.

On balance, those sources which support a later date seem to
present a more consistent pattern than do the obvious anachronisms
of Muirchú, whose historical value clearly extends no further than
his use of an incomplete copy of the *Confessio*. If there is no clinching
final certainty about St Patrick's dates, and if the possibility of the
traditional 'early' *floruit* (432–461 or thereabouts) cannot be excluded, still the balance of probabilities seems on the whole to favour
a late-fifth-century date.

This is not the place to ask some other vexed questions about St
Patrick's mission, such as the existence of other missionaries and
Patrick's relationship with them. Who, for example, were the *Scoti in
Christo credentes*, to whom the papally sponsored, and very obscure,
Palladius was sent in 431? Who were Secundinus, Isserninus and the
rest, who are named as Patrick's companions? Is Patrick implying,
when he describes himself as going 'to the remote parts beyond which
there is no-one, and where no-one had gone before to baptise or

ordain clerics or confirm the people' (C 51), that in some parts of Ireland these activities had taken place, or were taking place, independent of his mission? The answers to these and other questions are for others to seek. Our conclusions are that Patrick could have been a north Briton, possibly even from Galloway or Strathclyde, conducting a British-sponsored mission in northern Ireland, some time in the middle, or perhaps more likely in the second half, of the fifth century.

We are able now to turn to some other questions: how extensive was Christianity in post-Roman north Britain? How was the church structured? What influence did it have with kings and aristocrats? And what evidence is there for Christianity among the Picts and the *Scoti* of western Scotland in Patrick's time?

Among the most striking facts shown by Patrick's letters is that Ceredig and his war-band, probably based at Dumbarton, apparently considered themselves to be Christians. Patrick's denunciation of them as 'fellow-citizens of demons' rather than Romans and Christians, would otherwise have no point (E 2). He advises 'every God-fearing man' that these soldiers are alienated from him and from Christ (E 5); and he insists that all 'of holy and humble heart' (i.e., clergy?) must not accept alms from them (E 7), since 'the Most High despises the gifts of the wicked' (E 8, quoting Ecclus. 34.23). This implies that Ceredig and his men were almsgivers, although it is also said that Ceredig 'does not fear God or his priests' (E 6), and that his men 'roared with laughter' at the priest and clerics whom Patrick sent to demand restitution immediately after the raid (E 3). We should perhaps see the Christianity of these aristocrats as being similar to that of the nominally Christian kings of Wales and south-west England in the mid-sixth century whom Gildas denounced as bloodthirsty and impious,[45] or of the Gododdin c. 600, of whom it was said that they would rather go to die in battle than to the altar, but who still sought a place in heaven in union with the Trinity.[46]

As for ecclesiastical structure, Patrick writes of a church with bishops, priests and deacons, clerics, monks and virgins. He mentions a gathering or synod of his *seniores*, senior bishops, who attempted to depose and recall him. We have seen evidence of *praecipui sacerdotes* in sixth-century Galloway, and must presume that there was some kind of episcopate in parts of north Britain. This does not mean that Ceredig will have had his own bishop, nor does

it imply an unbroken episcopal succession between Ceredig's time
and that of Rhydderch Hael and his bishop Kentigern about a
hundred (or so) years later. Jocelin's *Life of Kentigern*, for what it is
worth, makes Kentigern the reviver of Christianity in the kingdom
of Strathclyde after a hiatus.[47]

Patrick belonged also to a missionary church. He himself was
chosen as a missionary bishop among the northern Irish because
his captivity had familiarised him with the language, customs and
terrain of Ireland. His lack of education and youthful sin did not
disqualify him in the eyes of his *seniores*, although many years later
these were brought against him by critics of his methods. But were
the Irish the only targets of north British missionary activity in the
fifth century?

Patrick refers three times in the *Epistola* to the Picts. On two
occasions he links them also with Scoti, i.e., Irish, presumably of the
Dál Riata settled in Argyll (E 2,12). On one occasion he also links
the Picts with *apostatae* (E 2), 'renegades', and on another he calls
them the 'most worthless, evil, and apostate Picts' (E 15). The term
apostatae, applied only once exclusively to the Picts themselves along
with a string of other pejorative adjectives, clearly cannot be taken as
evidence of a previous conversion of the Picts followed by backsliding.[48] Patrick also calls the Picts *gens extera ignorans Deum*, 'a foreign
race which does not know God' (E 14). This is in marked contrast
to the language used of Coroticus and his men, who are *alieni a Christo
Deo meo*, 'alienated from Christ my God' (E5) and *rebellatores Christi*,
'rebels against Christ'.(E 19) It is fairly clear that there had been no
attempt to Christianise the Picts by Patrick's time. He was writing
before the Picts, in Bede's words, 'abandoned the error of idolatry
and received the true faith through the preaching of the word of God
by the holy and reverend Bishop Ninian', a bishop from Whithorn
in Galloway.[49] We shall see in the next chapter that there are good
reasons for believing that Ninian's mission belongs to the early sixth
rather than the fifth century.[50] Certainly what Patrick writes cannot
be used to substantiate the traditional, early fifth-century, date
suggested for Ninian; it seems rather to support the view that the
Picts had not yet been visited by Christian missionaries, but were still
'a foreign race which does not know God'. That having been said, it
seems likely that Ninian came from the same British Christian
background as Patrick: that of a missionary church in north Britain.
The same responsibilities, difficulties and fears which Patrick faced

in fifth-century Ireland faced Ninian in the lands of the Picts; the presence of devotion to St Martin at both Armagh and Whithorn is no coincidence. Patrick's mission provides an insight into Ninian's, and the converse may also be true.

NOTES

1. There are a number of editions of the *Confessio* and *Epistola Militibus Corotici*: most recently *Libri Epistolarum S Patricii Episcopi* ed. L Bieler (1961), and *St Patrick: his Writings and Muirchú's Life*, ed. J Morris and A B E Hood (1978); a good English translation is *The Works of St Patrick*, ed. L Bieler (Early Christian Writers, 1953).
2. Among the most important of the many works are: J B Bury, *The Life of St Patrick* (1905); E MacNeill, *St Patrick* (1934, reprinted 1964); T F O'Rahilly, *The Two Patricks* (1942); J Carney, *The Problem of St Patrick* (1961); C Mohrmann, *The Latin of St Patrick* (1961); D A Binchey, 'St Patrick and his Biographers, ancient and modern', *Studia Hibernica*, ii (1962), 7–173; R P C Hanson, *St Patrick* (1968); A C Thomas, *Christianity in Roman Britain* (1981); R Sharpe, 'St Patrick and the See of Armagh', *Cambridge Medieval Celtic Studies*, iv (1982), 33–59.
3. Edited in *The Patrician Texts in the Book of Armagh*, ed. L Bieler (1979)(hereafter *PT*).
4. Edited in *PT*; also translated with commentary in K Hughes, *The Church in early Irish Society* (1966), 275–81; on its date see R Sharpe, 'Armagh and Rome in the seventh Century', in P Ní Chatháin and M Richter (eds), *Irland und Europa: Die Kirche im Frühmittelalter* (1984), 58–72.
5. All edited by Bieler in *PT*.
6. *The Tripartite Life of St Patrick*, ed. W Stokes (RS, 1887).
7. Edited by Colgan in *Trias Thaumaturga* (1647).
8. In addition to the writers mentioned in n. 2 above, see also K Hughes, *Early Christian Ireland: Introduction to the Sources* (1972), 97ff.; J W M Bannerman, *Studies in the History of Dalriada* (1974), 9ff.; A P Smyth, 'The earliest Irish Annals: their first contemporary entries, and the earliest centres of recording', *Proceedings of the Royal Irish Academy*, lxxii (1972), 1–48.
9. The main editions of the Annals are: *Annals of Ulster*, ed. S Mac Airt and G Mac Níocaill (1983); cf. also the old edition, ed. W M Hennessy and B MacCarthy (Dublin, 1887–1901); *Chronicon Scotorum*, ed. W M Hennessy (RS, 1866); 'Annals of Tigernach', ed. W Stokes, *Revue Celtique* xvi (1895), 374–419, xvii (1896), 6–33, 116–263, 337–420, xviii (1897), 9–59, 150–303, 374–91; *Annals of Innisfallen*, ed. S Mac Airt (1951); *Annals of Clonmacnoise*, ed. D Murphy (1896); *Annals of*

the Four Masters, ed. J O'Donovan (1856)(hereafter *AU, CS, AT, AI, AClon, AFM*).

10. In what follows, C = Confessio, E = Epistola; the modern chapter numbers appear in all modern editions.
11. Mohrmann, *Latin of St Patrick*. She believes that Patrick must have spent at least some time in Gaul.
12. Hanson, *St Patrick*, 113–8; Thomas, *Christianity*, 317–8.
13. Muirchú's *Vita* is hereafter referred to as M with chapter numbers. On these variants, see *PT*, 66 and 66–7nn.
14. Hanson, *St Patrick*, 114–18.
15. See above, Chapter 1, p 25; for other examples, cf. Thomas, *Christianity*, 390, n. 53.
16. Hanson, *St Patrick*, 114–8.
17. Thomas, *Christianity*, 310–14.
18. See above, Chapter 1, pp. 22–5; Thomas, *Christianity*, 275ff.; C A R Radford and G Donaldson, *Whithorn and Kirkmadrine* (1953); J Wall, 'Christian Evidences in the Roman Period', *Archaeologia Aeliana*, 4th ser., xliii (1965), 208–11.
19. J Campbell et al., *The Anglo-Saxons* (1982), 22–2.
20. A Boyle, 'The Birthplace of St Patrick', *SHR*, lx (1981), 156–60.
21. W J Watson, *A History of the Celtic Place-Names of Scotland* (1926) (hereafter Watson, *CPNS*), 364.
22. A Macquarrie, 'Early Christian Govan: the historical Context', *RSCHS*, xxiv (1990), 1–17; idem, 'The Kings of Strathclyde, c. 400–1018', in *Medieval Scotland: Crown, Lordship and Community: Essays presented to G W S Barrow*, ed. A Grant and K Stringer (1993), 1–19. W F H Nicolaisen, *Scottish Place-Names* (1976), at 142–4, argues that the *Kil*-names 'are in general not likely to be much younger than 800'; but this argument has to be modified in view of the fact that the Gaelic 'conquest' of Strathclyde was about a generation later than that of Pictland, and settlement probably correspondingly later. On the *Aberdeen Breviary* evidence, cf. A Macquarrie, 'Lives of Scottish Saints in the *Aberdeen Breviary*: some problems of sources for Strathclyde saints', *RSCHS*, xxvi (1996) (forthcoming).
23. *Aberdeen Breviary*, PH, 17 March; *Paisley Registrum*, 164–5.
24. See above, Introduction, p. 9.
25. A Macquarrie, 'Lives of Scottish Saints in the *Aberdeen Breviary*'.
26. Hereafter M = Muirchú. Cf. *PT*, 66.
27. Tírechán, 14, 15, 42, 43 (*PT*, 134–6 156–8).
28. Hughes, *Church in early Irish Society*, 57ff, and esp. 86ff.
29. Even Binchey, 'St Patrick and his Biographers', accepts it.
30. Carney, *Problem*, devotes much attention to Secundinus and denies Patrick's foundation of Armagh.

31. ii, 13; *PT*, 120.
32. Sharpe, 'St Patrick and the See of Armagh', passim.
33. On Ninian, see Chapter 3 below.
34. E A Thomson, 'St Patrick and Coroticus', *Journal of Theological Studies*, n.s. xxxi (1980), 12–27
35. M preface; *PT*, 66.
36. *Tripartite Life*, 8; *Adomnán's Life of Columba*, ed. A O and M O Anderson (1961; 2nd edn 1991) (hereafter *VC*), 238.
37. E Phillimore, '*Annales Cambriae* and Old Welsh Genealogies from Harleian MS 3859', *Y Cymmrodor*, xi (1888), 141–83, at 172–3. For the dating of Strathclyde kings of this and later periods see Macquarrie, 'Kings of Strathclyde', passim. Most of the sources are collected in A O Anderson, *Early Sources of Scottish History, AD 500–1286* (1922) (hereafter Anderson, *ESSH*).
38. The best discussion is in Binchey, 'St Patrick'; cf. also Hanson, *St Patrick*, Appendix I.
39. The exception is Bishop Hanson (*St Patrick*, 171ff., who argues that the earlier dates can be supported from internal evidence; but Professor Thomas (*Christianity*, 317–8) is not convinced.
40. Mohrmann, *Latin of St Patrick*, passim.
41. Carney, *Problem*, argues that Lóegaire's reign may have been shorter and later than used to be supposed; but he probably overestimated the value of the fifth-century annals.
42. T F O'Rahilly, *The Two Patricks* (1942), 75ff.; Binchey, 'St Patrick', 111–12. But against this, cf. E A Thomson, 'St Patrick and Coroticus', passim.
43. *AU*, s.a. 535; *VC*, 2nd preface.
44. R Sharpe, 'Saint Mauchteus, discipulus Patricii' in A Bammesberger and A Wollmann, *Britain 400–600* (1990), 85–93.
45. *Gildas: the Ruin of Britain (De Excidio Britanniae)*, ed. M Winterbottom (1978), caps. 27–36.
46. *The Gododdin*, ed. K H Jackson (1969), 37, 128–9, 117–8.
47. A Macquarrie, 'The Career of St Kentigern of Glasgow: *Vitae, Lectiones*, and Glimpses of Fact', *Innes Review*, xxxvii (1986), 3–24.
48. This case is argued at greater length in A Macquarrie, 'The Date of St Ninian's Mission: a Reappraisal', *RSCHS*, xxiii (1987), 1–25; cf. Chapter 3 below. The opposite view is taken in Thomas, *Christianity*, 291; and cf. P Grosjean, 'Les Pictes Apostats dans l'Epître de S Patrice', *Analecta Bollandiana*, lxxvi (1958),354–78.
49. *Bede's Ecclesiastical History of the English People*, ed B Colgrave and R A B Mynors (1969) (hereafter Bede, *HE*), lib. iii, cap. 4.
50. Below, Chapter 3, pp 50–73.

3

St Ninian of Whithorn

The importance of St Ninian for the early history of the church in Scotland has never been doubted.[1] He is traditionally regarded as a fifth-century bishop of Whithorn in Galloway who converted the Pictish tribes south of the Mounth to Christianity. There is less agreement about other aspects of his career. There are doubts about whether he ever travelled to Rome, and about the extent of his missionary activity. It was once argued, on the strength of place-names and dedications, that his missionary activity extended as far north as the Shetland Isles, but no modern writer would agree with this.[2] The identity of the 'southern Picts' whom Ninian converted has also been disputed: were they in fact Picts dwelling between Forth and Mounth, or a southern offshoot dwelling south of the Forth?[3] It used to be believed that he was a contemporary and disciple of St Martin of Tours (d. 397), but this is no longer widely accepted.[4]

But even historians who would reject any direct contact with St Martin of Tours are still prepared to accept a traditional early to mid-fifth century *floruit*. For example, A B Scott wrote in 1905 that Ninian appeared 'when the Roman world was fast loosening its hold on Britain,' i.e., c. 400.[5] W D Simpson asserted in 1940 that 'we should consider St Ninian as what he was, namely, a Romano-British provincial.'[6] N K Chadwick agreed with this view, adding that 'Ninian is the most important link that we possess between the Roman and the medieval period, between the Ancient World and the Dark Ages'.[7] A W Wade-Evans opined that 'One would infer... that Candida Casa... dates from the early fifth century.'[8] J MacQueen in 1961 accepted this as the floruit 'generally accepted for Nynia' and did not question it.[9] Sadly, in a more recent (1990) revision of his earlier work on the subject he rejects criticism of this view, and maintains that 'we are left with something like the traditional period in the early fifth century';[10] while at the same time making the seemingly contradictory concession that he is 'happy to accept... that the dedication of Candida Casa to St Martin belongs to the sixth rather than the fifth century.'[11] Another recent writer, A A M Duncan, has written that 'Nynia is generally dated to the first half of the fifth century; that date must rest as the best we have.'[12] A C Thomas has also supported an early date.[13] The late Professor Donaldson also accepted a date 'around the year 400' for Ninian, while commenting, with his usual perception, that this is 'assigned on somewhat slender evidence'.[14] Most recently the Galloway historian Daphne Brooke has suggested 'the latter half of the fifth century'.[15]

Some dissenting voices have been heard in recent years. A P Smyth suggested a *floruit* for Ninian c. 500, but without adducing any supporting argument.[16] The work of the Whithorn Excavation team is coming increasingly to suggest that Christian Whithorn began as a 'greenfield site' colonised by incomers c. 500.[17] The argument which I put forward here has been arrived at independently: it is that there is in fact no good reason for assigning Ninian to the fifth century; there may be grounds for assigning him rather to the first half of the sixth century.

The argument for a traditional 'early' Ninian rests on a number of pieces of evidence. We have seen that there are early Christian stones both at Whithorn and at Kirkmadrine further west, which most authorities would date to the fifth or sixth centuries. If Ninian founded Whithorn, then, he must be a fifth-century figure. Bede states that his mission took place 'a long time before' (*multo ante tempore*) St Columba's preaching to the northern Picts (563 × 597). 'A long time before' is vague enough, but in the context could perhaps be interpreted as up to a century or more. St Patrick (whose dates, as we have seen, are uncertain, but who definitely is a fifth-century personage) describes the Picts as *apostatae* (renegades, apostates). This has been taken to mean that the Picts had been previously converted to Christianity (by St Ninian, presumably) but had subsequently apostasised. Finally, the twelfth-century *Vita Niniani* attributed to Ailred of Rievaulx names Ninian as the founder of Whithorn and as a contemporary of St Martin of Tours. This *Vita*, together with the eighth-century poem *Miracula Nynie Episcopi*, also makes him contemporary with a British king called Tudwal; a person of this name appears in a Welsh genealogy of a later king who ruled in the Isle of Man in the section which covers the fifth century. So (on the doubtful assumption that ninth-century genealogies are reliable evidence for fifth-century ancestors) we have a likely candidate for the historical Tudwal in question.

These are the main props for the argument in favour of a traditional 'early' Ninian. But they leave certain problems. It has been pointed out that it would be anachronistic in the fifth century to dedicate a church to a saint whose relics were not preserved there.[18] There is also an anachronistic element in St Ninian's visit to Rome, where the papacy had not yet reached its later pre-eminence and prestige; so most Ninianists reject it as a hagiographic fiction. Archaeological evidence for a fifth century conversion of Picts to Christianity is so poor that it has led some scholars to look for St Ninian's sphere of activity south of the Forth. Explaining away these difficulties involves judicious selection from the written evidence; what suits the hypothesis is accepted, what does not is dismissed as later hagiographical fiction. But there is an alternative view: that if the evidence is approached without any preconceptions about St Ninian based on the twelfth-century *Vita*, then what Bede says could all be true – in a sixth-century context.

Bede's words about St Ninian have been quoted so often that it should hardly be necessary to repeat them; but it is important to remember what Bede does *not* say about him. His words are: 'In the year 565 ... there came from Ireland a priest and abbot named Columba, a monk by his habit and his way of life, coming to preach the word of God to the provinces of the northern Picts, that is, those who are divided from their southern regions by a range of rough mountains. The Southern Picts, however, who live on this side of these mountains, had received the word of faith a long time before, as it is said, and abandoned the error of idolatry, through the preaching of the word to them by Nynia, a most holy and reverend bishop, a man of the British race, who was regularly instructed at Rome in the faith and mysteries of Truth. His episcopal see is celebrated for its church and the name of St Martin, where his body rests with those of many saints. The English race now [c. 730] holds it. This place, belonging to the province of Bernicia, is commonly called *ad Candidam Casam* ('At the White House'), because he built there a church of stone, of a kind unknown among the Britons.'[19] Bede does not make Ninian the founder or even necessarily the first bishop of a church dedicated to St Martin at Whithorn (Old English *Hwit ærn*, 'White House'), universally and almost certainly rightly identified as the site of Bede's *Candida Casa*, but says only that he built there a church of stone where he was buried; Bede's words cannot be taken to indicate whether the burials of 'many saints' were previous or subsequent to Ninian's own. Indeed, Bede is little concerned to tell us about Whithorn at all in this passage. His concern is the conversion of the Picts; it is for this reason that he introduces Ninian as a missionary independent of Columba, and only mentions *Candida Casa in* passing as the site of Ninian's see. Bede does not make Ninian a contemporary of St Martin of Tours, or give any clue as to when he lived, except that he was active 'a long time before' Columba's activities in the North. Other than this vague statement, Bede offers no grounds for assumptions about Ninian's dates.

The important points of Bede's account are as follows:

1. Ninian was a Briton and a bishop.
2. He conducted a mission to the Southern Picts, i.e., those Picts living south of the Mounth.
3. He had undergone 'regular', i.e., monastic, training at Rome.
4. He was buried, together with 'many saints', at a cathedral church dedicated to St Martin, *ad Candidam Casam*, i.e., at Whithorn.
5. He built there a stone church, of a kind unusual among the Britons.
6. He lived 'a long time before' St Columba (d. 597).

Bede's account is the most important, most reliable, and almost certainly the earliest written evidence about St Ninian. Professor Duncan has demonstrated that the bulk of it came to Bede from an eighth-century Pictish source,[20] although some additional information may have been supplied by Pehthelm, the Anglian bishop of Whithorn, c. 725.

But there are other pieces of evidence as well. The next is a Latin poem called *Miracula Nynie Episcopi*;[21] this was probably written 731 × 804, since it is unlikely to be earlier than Bede and may in part rely on his writings, and it was known to Alcuin, who died in the latter year. It appears to have been composed at Whithorn at the time of the Anglian occupation mentioned by Bede; both Anglian and Celtic elements are evident in its makeup, but it is difficult to establish its *stemma* with certainty.[22] It provides a few circumstantial details which are not in Bede. The saint is called Nynia or Ninia; he travels to Rome, where he is consecrated bishop; he returns to convert the lands of the Picts (called in a chapter heading the *Naturae*); he then comes to his own homeland, where he builds his own church at Candida Casa 'with fired-brick walls and lofty roof', and dedicates it to St Martin; he is exiled by a wicked local king called Thuuahel or Tuduael, and is recalled when the king is struck blind and healed by his prayers. He performs a number of miracles, and more occur posthumously at his tomb.

The similarities to Bede are obvious, and so are the differences. Ninian is made to found Candida Casa, which is given brick walls (*coctilibus muris*)[23] unlike Bede's stone church (*ecclesia de lapide*). The Latin poem mentions two other proper names, which may be added to the slender dossier of Ninianic 'facts':

7. The Pictish tribe which he converted was called the *Naturae*.
8. He was contemporary with a king called Tudwal.

Like Bede, the *Miracula* does not make Ninian a contemporary of St Martin of Tours, and apart from the name of a contemporary king gives no clue as to his dates.

A third written source is the twelfth century *Vita Niniani* attributed to Ailred of Rievaulx.[24] Its author states that it is a translation and improvement of an earlier *Vita,* and proceeds to apply to Ninian all the conventions of medieval hagiography. Ninian is made to visit St Martin at Tours on his return journey from Rome, and to have built his church at *Witerna* before undertaking his missionary journey among the Picts. The site of his stone church is described in some detail: it is said to have stood on a narrow peninsula surrounded by the sea on three sides, a description which better suits the site at Isle of Whithorn than that of the medieval cathedral.[25] The wicked local king whom Ninian heals in body and soul is called Tuduvallus or Tudwaldus. The saint performs a number of miracles and others occur at his tomb; some of these appear in the *Miracula*, but others are found only in the *Vita*.

To this *Vita* we owe the modern form of Ninian's name with final *-n*; this is probably a misreading of *u* in the original, since the saint's name was probably British *Niniaw,* latinised as **Niniauus*; this would account for the forms *Nynia* and *Ninia* found in Bede, Alcuin, the *Miracula,* and the *Hymnus*.[26] The *Vita* also speaks for the first time of St Ninian as a contemporary of St Martin of Tours. Like the *Miracula,* it calls the local king Tudwal, but does not know the name of the Pictish tribe converted by Ninian, and follows Bede in calling them southern Picts.

The prose *Vita* and the *Miracula* poem must ultimately go back to a common source. The *Miracula* as it survives, however, cannot be the direct source of the later *Vita*; there are many divergences of spellings of names, and each contains details and incidents which are not shared by the other. One of the MSS of the *Vita* contains, in addition to the attribution to Ailred, the statement that its source was an English Life, written in a barbaric style and rustic language;[27] this description could not apply to the *Miracula*.

Such are the principal written sources for St Ninian's life. Taken together, they give grounds for believing that Ninian was a Briton, a missionary among the southern Picts, and a bishop of a church dedicated to St Martin at Whithorn. He may possibly have been contemporary with a king in south-west Scotland called Tudwal, but not necessarily with St Martin. The only source which supports the traditional 'early' chronology for Ninian is the *Vita* attributed to Ailred; indeed, many modern assumptions about St Ninian can be traced back to this source and no further.

The archaeological evidence has been used to support the traditional view. Galloway is rich in early Christian stones, including some which could be as early as the mid- to late-fifth century.[28] If these dates are correct, and if one could be certain from the written sources that St Ninian was the founder and first bishop of Whithorn, one would have to accept him as a figure of that period. But, as Professor Duncan pointed out, 'Bede does not make Nynia builder of the first kirk there nor call him the first bishop, and there is a measure of agreement that Nynia came to a church and see already in existence.'[29] Radford's excavations at Whithorn in the 1950s uncovered an early Christian stone church at the east end of the medieval cathedral, which had been daubed on its outer faces with 'a coarse cream mortar of poor quality'; he took this to be Candida Casa, but was sufficiently lacking in confidence about its date to judge that it was 'built by S. Ninian or one of his immediate successors' (presumably because he accepted the traditional dating for St Ninian).[30] Radford seems to have preferred a rather later date for the early Christian church itself. However, much more recent archaeological work in the area is modifying our picture substantially. The latest archaeological findings are coming to suggest, as mentioned above, that Whithorn began as a 'greenfield site' colonised by incomers c. 500, and that the community arrived as a group.[31] If so, they may have had a bishop from the earliest time of their arrival; if this was Ninian, he belongs to the early sixth century.

If the archaeological evidence at Whithorn itself casts increasing doubt on the traditional dating of Ninian, evidence from further afield does not seem to point to a fifth-century conversion of the Picts. We have seen that early Christian inscriptions similar in date to those in Galloway have been found further east in southern Scotland, most notably in the valleys of the tributaries of the Tweed.[32] North of the Forth, however, similar evidence which would corroborate an early conversion of the Picts is singularly lacking. There are a number of oriented long-cist cemeteries north of the Forth, as at Lundin Links, St Andrews, and Dundee; archaeological techniques of dating are not conclusive, but seem to point towards a period later than the fifth century.[33] Although the flowering of Christian art in Pictland does not appear to have come until later, Mrs Henderson has drawn attention to a considerable number of stones bearing a cross but no other ornament which have been found in the Pictish area, some of which at least are likely to be earlier in date.[34] But the absence of any definitely fifth-century archaeological evidence for Christianity north of the Forth has led some scholars to doubt whether St Ninian's activity spread beyond the Forth at all. Professor Duncan has suggested that Ninian's centre of activity could have been Peebles, and that his converts were Britons, not Picts;[35] Professor Thomas likewise locates Ninian's mission in Scotland south of the Forth, but argues a measure of Pictish settlement there on the basis of a very small number of Pictish sculptured stones and place-names.[36]

Place-name evidence, however, does suggest that British missionaries were active north of the Forth during the Pictish period, though more precise dating is very difficult. Professor Barrow has drawn attention to the significant distribution of the element *eccles* in Scottish place-names.[37] The name, from vulgar Latin *eclesia* or British *eglwys*, must indicate an early Christian church founded under British influence; where it is found in Pictish territory, it should belong to a period (of indeterminate date) of British missionary activity among the Picts. Thus *eccles* place-names are found in similar distribution and numbers throughout southern Scotland and in eastern Scotland north of the Forth as far as the Mounth, with a single isolated example north of the Mounth and no examples west of the Great Glen. This pattern seems to fit well what Bede tells us about St Ninian's missionary activity among the Picts as far as the Mounth. It is perhaps significant that among the *eccles* names between Forth and Mounth there are found church dedications to St Peter, St Martin of Tours, and St Ninian himself.[38]

Unfortunately, place-name evidence can only provide a relative framework for dating, and cannot help to date an undated event, the mission of St Ninian. All that can be said is that the *eccles* names belong to the earliest period of Christian penetration north of the Forth, that they show the influence of British missionaries, and that they confirm the area of activity described by Bede, the lands of the Picts dwelling south of the Mounth. They cannot tell us when this activity took place, or indeed whether the name of Ninian can be definitely attached to it.

So what clues, other than archaeological ones, do exist for the dating of St Ninian's mission to the Picts? There are three, one of which is of certain value and provides a *terminus ante quem*, one of which is probably to be accepted and helps to provide a rough *terminus post quem*, and a third which lacks certainty but which if accepted might possibly point towards a closer date. We shall also examine certain other possible indicators.

Our first clue is Bede's statement that Ninian preached to the southern Picts a long time before (*multo ante tempore*) Columba visited the northern Picts.[39] Columba came to Scotland in 563 and died in 597, so his visit (or visits) to the northern Picts with their stronghold beside the River Ness must have taken place within these dates, perhaps most likely in the middle part of that period, say the 570s and 580s.[40] Can Bede's vague phrase *multo ante tempore* be used to support a date for Ninian's mission a century and more before Columba's time? Bede always tries to provide an *annus Domini* date for the events which he describes, or at least to date them as closely as possible; his vagueness about St Ninian is unusual, and seems to indicate that he had no information available.

Because of his usual chronological precision, phrases such as *multo ante tempore* are rare in the *Historia Ecclesiastica*, and this use of the expression has no close parallels. On one occasion, however, Bede uses *multo post haec tempore* to separate events in the boyhood and maturity of one man, and in another place he uses *multo exhinc tempore* between the maturity and old age of another; on another occasion he writes *quod dum multo tempore sedulus exsequeretur* regarding a penitent following a prescribed fast over a prolonged period of time.[41] Thus for Bede *multo tempore* could be within one lifetime, and certainly does not necessitate a gap of centuries or even generations. It might be argued that in the context *multo tempore* should be taken to imply a longer gap; but this is doubtful, since Bede uses the phrase so rarely, and is rarely so imprecise.[42] All that can be taken from this passage is that Bede had no real idea when Ninian was active. The assumption of a fifth-century *floruit* for Ninian cannot rest on Bede's vagueness; but Bede is probably correct in stating that he was active before Columba (witness the *eccles* place-names and long-cist cemeteries). Bede's statement is probably based on an assertion made by King Nechton to Abbot Ceolfrith; but even if is no more than an intelligent deduction on Bede's part, it still provides a *terminus ante quem*, although without necessitating a gap of centuries or generations.

A second, rather less definite, clue concerns allusions to the Picts in one of St Patrick's letters.[43] It has often been assumed, on the basis of these allusions, that the Picts had at one time been Christians but had subsequently apostasised.[44] In fact, as we have seen, a careful reading of Patrick's writings shows that the Picts were not Christians at the time he was writing, and never had been. We have seen that Patrick refers three times in the *Epistola* to the Picts. On two occasions he links them also with *Scoti*, i.e., Irish, presumably of the Dál Riata settled in Argyll (E 2,12). On one occasion he also links the Picts with *apostatae* (E 2), 'renegades', and on another he calls them the 'most worthless, evil, and apostate Picts' (E 15). The term *apostatae*, applied only once exclusively to the Picts themselves along with a string of other pejorative adjectives, cannot be taken as evidence of a previous conversion of the Picts followed by backsliding.[45] Patrick also calls the Picts *gens extera ignorans Deum*, 'a foreign race which does not know God' (E 14).[46] Patrick uses a quite different expression, *rebellatores Christi*, of Coroticus and his warband, true backsliding Christians who enslaved their fellow-believers (E 19).

Thus to Patrick the Picts, far from being a backsliding Christian nation, are foreigners totally ignorant of the Christian God. For them *apostata* can have its Vulgate meaning of 'criminal, evil-doer'; it could have its classical Greek meaning of 'renegade, defector' in the sense of a breaker of oaths or treaties; but 'a foreign race which does not know God' could hardly be religious apostates.[47] Such an interpretation would be difficult to reconcile with Bede's description of the southern Picts, who 'abandoning the error of idolatry received the true faith', and by implication held to it.[48] If Ninian had been an early and ultimately unsuccessful missionary, it is doubtful that Bede would have heard of him, and impossible that he should have described his achievement as he did.

In any case, it would be very dangerous to take a single ambiguous reference by St Patrick as the basis for an elaborate hypothesis about a fifth-century conversion and backsliding of Picts to which the name of St Ninian could be attached; if this is the best evidence that exists for Christianity among fifth-century Picts, then it has to be said that it is not very good. Patrick's Picts are 'evil, worthless renegades', 'a foreign race which does not know God' (i.e., outside the Roman Empire as well as the Christian commonwealth); apparently they have not yet been converted by anybody. There are thus good reasons to believe that missionary activity among the southern Picts came after St Patrick's time. We have seen that there is still no general agreement about St Patrick's dates; but at least this leaves us with rough termini of c. 461/493(?) × 563 for Ninian's activities.

To get any closer, we must turn to the third clue, the local king Tudwal. I have said above that this clue lacks certainty, but might possibly point towards a closer date; it is not central to my argument, and I advance it with caution.[49] Scholars have searched the Welsh genealogies looking for a Tudwal, but they have already made assumptions about St Ninian's dates, and their chosen Tudwal must conform to these assumptions. In the Harleian MS genealogies, the name Tudwal occurs four times, three times in Pedigree IV and once in Pedigree VI.[50] Later members of Pedigree IV had connections with the Isle of Man, a short sea journey from Galloway. Only the earliest Tudwal in this list is a candidate, as the other two are later than Columba. In the Harleian MS he is placed seven generations before Merfyn Mawr (d. 681), and should therefore have lived in the mid-fifth century. But the pedigree makes him a great-grandson of Magnus Maximus (d. 388), and this, inconveniently for Professor MacQueen, should push him well into the second half of the fifth century, besides casting doubt on the historical authenticity of this part of the list.[51]

To make matters more awkward, the Jesus College MS version of this pedigree places Tudwal eight generations before Merfyn Mawr;[52] this would push him back into the early years of the fifth century, but would hardly be consistent with his being a great-grandson of Magnus Maximus.

Selecting judiciously from the evidence, this Tudwal can be juggled backwards and forwards through the fifth century to fit more or less any chronology one wishes. It makes little difference, because the pedigrees are not historical documents for the fifth century anyway; the place of Magnus Maximus in them is no longer accepted, and for a century and more beyond his time they are historically suspect.[53]

Attempts to locate Harleian Pedigree IV as a northern list are not convincing either, since they are based on a circular attempt to connect its Tudwal with St Ninian.[54] It does not claim descent from either Coel Hen or Dyfnwal Hen, prominent in all other northern pedigrees; Man is as close as it can come to Galloway, but it is by no means certain that the ancestors of a dynasty which later claimed descent from Maximus were already ruling in Man in the fifth century. The only reason for introducing this Tudwal from Harleian Pedigree IV is that he can be vaguely assigned a *floruit* which may vaguely correspond to a vague *floruit* generally assumed, for no good reason, for St Ninian. He is not an historical figure or necessarily a northerner, and the mention of a Tudwal as contemporary of St Ninian cannot be used to make him so.

The only other possible Tudwal mentioned in Welsh genealogies (though we must bear in mind the possibility of unrecorded bearers of the name as well)[55] appears in Harleian Pedigree VI.[56] He is named as a grandson of Dyfnwal Hen, and is therefore definitely a northerner. His pedigree is carried only one generation further, but that is to a major historical figure who can be independently dated. This is Rhydderch Hael, king of Dumbarton. He is named in a number of sources, which all point towards a *floruit* in the later sixth century. He is named in the *Historia Brittonum* as one of a group of northern kings led by Urien Rheged who campaigned against the Angles of Bernicia c. 590.[57] A Welsh 'triad' names Rhydderch Hael as a contemporary of Aedán mac Gabráin, king of the Dál Riata (574–c. 608).[58] Adomnán, a very reliable source here, names Roderc f. Tothail (i.e., Rhydderch map Tudwal) as king of Dumbarton (*Petra Cloithe*) during the time that Columba was active in Scotland (563–597),[59] and thus incidentally confirms the historicity of Rhydderch's father Tudwal. Less certainly, the twelfth-century hagiographer Jocelin of Furness names Rederech (i.e., Rhydderch) as king of Strathclyde when Kentigern was bishop of Glasgow, and says that his death took place within a year of the saint's (independently dated to c. 612–13).[60] For what it is worth, Jocelin may have believed that Ninian and Kentigern were not widely separated in date, as he also states that Kentigern performed the first burial in a cemetery formerly (*quondam*) consecrated by St Ninian, but in which no burials had taken place (*in quo nondum quisquam positus fuit*).[61] This would be clearly impossible if one accepts a gap of 150 years between them. The historical reliability and value of Jocelin's *Vita Kentigerni* will be discussed below.[62]

In a sense, all this is inconclusive. We do not really know how much weight we can place on the name of King Tudwal at all. It could be that the name of a known ancestor of Rhydderch Hael of Dumbarton has been introduced simply in order to establish Ninian's antiquity in relation to Rhydderch's contemporary Columba, thus setting him up, in Père Grosjean's words, as '*un contre-Columba*'.[63] It has been suggested that Tudwal could have been introduced to demonstrate Whithorn's authority in relation to a dynasty, perhaps that of Merfyn Mawr.[64] It has even been pointed out that the story of Ninian's encounter with Tudwal (which is however of a very typical hagiographical form) resembles an episode in the *Vita* of St Finnian of Moville concerning Tuathal Maelgarb king of Tara, and may have no original connection with Ninian or with Whithorn.[65] None of this seriously affects the argument, which is simply that if the supposed contemporaneity with a king called Tudwal has any significance, then the mid-sixth-century king of Dumbarton is at least as likely a candidate as any other; he at least has the virtues of being a northerner and a historical personage, which Merfyn Mawr's supposed ancestor does not.

So our three literary clues point to a date for St Ninian somewhere between the late fifth and the mid-sixth century. If Ninian's alleged contemporary Tudwal was the king of Dumbarton of that name, then possibly he belongs towards the end of that period. These clues fit well with the archaeological record, which shows little sign of Christianity among the southern Picts before the sixth century, and is coming increasingly to suggest that Whithorn itself was founded c. 500.

We must turn now to other indicators, such as Ninian's alleged journey to Rome and the dedication to St Martin of Tours. We will see that these point in the same direction.

One difficulty in accepting Bede's and later accounts of St Ninian is the statement that he was regularly trained at Rome. Some writers have doubted the truth of this statement, and have suggested that it was a hagiographical device of the eighth century when it became fashionable to associate patrons with Rome. Mrs Chadwick writes that 'it is ... very doubtful if the authority of Rome – in ecclesiastical matters – was at the time to which Ninian is assigned sufficiently recognised – as it undoubtedly was later – to call for such journeys.'[66] Professor MacQueen agrees that 'there is more than a little doubt as to whether or not Nynia ever received instruction at Rome'.[67] These doubts are based, of course, on the traditionally assumed dates for Ninian in the early fifth century, and the consequent assumption that a spurious career and associations were being developed for him by later generations with a particular purpose in view, as was done for so many other early saints.

The year 407 saw the great barbarian invasion of the Empire, when hordes of Vandals and Alans swept across the frozen Rhine and terrorised the length and breadth of Gaul; Rome fell to Alaric's Visigoths in 410, and from the 430s Italy was prey to regular piratical raids by Vandals from north Africa. The destruction wrought in Gaul and Italy in 451–2 by Attila and his army was appalling, but what the Huns were dissuaded from doing by Pope Leo in 452 was completed three years later by Gaiseric's Vandals, with a destructive sack of Rome itself in 455. Evidence suggests that the population of Rome declined sharply in the early fifth century.[68] The condition of both Gaul and Italy was very disturbed for long stretches of the fifth century, before the stronger rule of Clovis in Gaul (481–511) and of Theodoric in Italy (488–526) restored more stable conditions. To some extent the reign of Theodoric was a time of cultural revival at Rome, the time of Cassiodorus, Boethius, St Benedict, and the assertion of papal pretensions under Pope Symmachus (498–514)(who, as we shall see below, introduced the cult of St Martin at Rome). Justinian's destructive wars of reconquest in Italy from 536 onwards initiated a fresh period of disturbance during which Rome 'was taken and retaken', and left weakened in the face of the Lombard invasion in 568.[69]

It cannot, of course, be categorically stated that Ninian could not have studied at Rome at almost any time between c. 380 and c. 540. The fifth century missions to the British Isles of Palladius and Germanus show contact with Gaul and the papacy. But weighing up the probabilities, the most likely periods for such a visit are either before the great Barbarian invasion of 406–7, or else during the stable period of Theodoric's rule nearly a century later. On balance, the latter is much more likely. The papacy had grown in prestige through its resistance to the Arian and Eutychian heresies (as in Pope Leo I's triumph at the Council of Chalcedon) and to barbarian attacks (as in the same pope's dealings with Attila and Gaiseric); and the schools of Rome and northern Italy were again attracting students from further afield.[70] The passage of Gaul was safer than it had been for much of the fifth century, indeed, almost since the time of St Martin of Tours himself.

Arguments about the likelihood of St Ninian's period of study at Rome are bound to be inconclusive. But the balance of probabilities seems to favour a later rather than an earlier date, with intermediate dates in the middle of the fifth century being even less likely.

There remains, of course, the argument that St Ninian may never have studied at Rome at all. It cannot be denied that at later times hagiographers were anxious to connect saints with Rome, and in later *vitae* a visit to Rome and ordination by the pope became almost an obligatory part of a saint's credibility. But it is not clear that such visits were a feature of hagiography before Bede's time, when the story of Ninian's visit to Rome was already in existence. Of Irish saints' lives, those of Cogitosus and Adomnán make no mention of continental journeys for their heroes, and Muirchú's hero Patrick travels to Gaul, but no further than Auxerre. Of saints' lives from England, the lives of Cuthbert and Wilfrid refer to much more recent figures for whom fabrication would have been impossible. The wide travels of Wilfrid and of Benedict Biscop (who really did visit Rome), as related by Eddius and Bede, may have contributed to the development of this hagiographical fashion; but that cannot have influenced the earliest traditions about St Ninian as recorded by Bede. The story of Ninian's visit to Rome, therefore, is unlikely to have been concocted in order to conform to an existing fashion of hagiography which demanded such visits; it must be one of the earliest stories of this kind. The alternative possibility is that it describes an actual event.

Another consideration is the question of the dedication at Whithorn to St Martin of Tours. It has been pointed out by Père Grosjean that such a dedication, to a saint whose relics were not present at the site, was an anachronism in the fifth century.[71] By the beginning of the sixth century, the cult of St Martin, a missionary bishop who had organised the evangelisation of the countryside around his cathedral city, was spreading. Rome was the first recipient of his cult, with Pope Symmachus founding a church dedicated to

St Martin near St Peter's.[72] Later the cult spread to the British Isles, with Bede associating it with the first Roman missionaries in England,[73] and the Book of Armagh connecting it with the mission of St Patrick.[74] If Bede is in fact associating St Ninian with the dedication of a new building at Whithorn to St Martin (this detail is unlikely to have been invented, but Bede's words are slightly ambiguous), then this too may be taken as an indicator of a late (sixth century) date for St Ninian.[75]

The lack of archaeological evidence for a fifth-century conversion of Picts may be taken as another indicator. Bede is quite unambiguous that Ninian's mission was to the southern Picts, living south of the Mounth. There is positive (but undated) place-name evidence to suggest that British missionaries were active in this area, but the archaeological evidence is rather less impressive, until we come to the apparently sixth-century long-cist cemeteries beside the east coast estuaries.[76] So slender is the archaeological evidence for an earlier period that some scholars, notably Professors Duncan and Thomas, have looked for signs of Ninian's activity south of the Forth;[77] but this is difficult to reconcile with Bede's statement.

The only literary clue which exists as to the identity of these southern Picts is the statement in a chapter heading of the *Miracula* that Ninian's mission was to the lands of the Picts called the *Naturae*.[78] Many scholars have accepted that this should be emended to read *Niduari*, the 'Nith-folk' of Fife mentioned by Bede in his prose *Life of St Cuthbert*; Bede has borrowed this from their mention as *Niuduera* in the earlier anonymous *Life of St Cuthbert*.

Why scholars should be so anxious to make such a drastic emendation is not clear, but it simply cannot be accepted. The Anglian monks of Whithorn would have recognised *Niduari* for what it was, namely a compound of a place-name with OE *were*, 'folk', as for example in *Cantuarii*, 'Kent-folk', or the north German *Boructuari* mentioned by Bede.[79] It is far more likely that *Naturae* owes nothing to Bede, but is a form, possibly a misreading or corruption, of a genuine Pictish place- or tribal name; but this cannot now be identified.[80] So the only literary clue about the location of Ninian's mission (other than Bede's statement) turns out to be of little value.

We have thus examined most of the props for the traditional fifth-century view of Ninian, and found them to be deficient. The one which remains is the reference in Irish sources to Whithorn as a great monastery in Scotland to which Irish saints resorted for study and training. Whithorn, under a Gaelic guise as *Futerna,* appears in some Irish saints' lives and in a preface in the *Liber Hymnorum* as a centre of scholarship in Alba which was visited by Irish saints. The most famous of these was 'St Finnian of Moville' (d. *AU* 579) who was said to have been studying at *Futerna* when Drust was ruler over the Britons.[81] The name Drust does not appear in any Welsh genealogies; it is mostly a Pictish name, which occurs several times in the historical section of the Pictish king-list.[82] It also occurs in the prehistorical section of the list, and there are a number of (unhistorical) kings of this name in the century or so preceding the reign of Bridei f. Mailcon (ob. *AU* 584), with whom the list becomes a historical document.[83] So a king called Drust could have been ruling over the Picts during the 520s and 530s, when Finnian was presumably in his student years; by inference, *Futerna* should then have been an established and renowned foundation attracting Irish scholars, presided over by Mugint, presumably one of Ninian's successors.[84] This might appear to be evidence for Whithorn's existence in the 520s, pushing Ninian himself back into the fifth century.

On examination, the evidence collapses. The source, an Irish preface to a Latin hymn, belongs to the eleventh century, and its curious anecdote about Finnian and Mugint has no historical relevance for fifth- and sixth-century Whithorn;[85] the Drust in question was a British rather than a Pictish king, so it is irrelevant to introduce a Drust from the Pictish king-list; and finally, some Irish saints' lives make their subjects study in Scotland not at *Futerna,* but at *Rosnat,* which cannot be convincingly equated with Whithorn.[86] It has been shown that 'St Finnian of Moville' was probably not a native Irishman who came to Scotland to study, but a Briton who worked as a missionary in Ireland in the middle of the sixth century.[87] As such, he has interesting parallels not only with the earlier St Patrick, but with St Ninian himself, apparently a sixth-century Briton carrying out missionary work in non-Romanised parts of the British Isles. 'Finnian' and Ninian may well have been contemporaries.[88]

If so, Ninian must also have been contemporary with Gildas; but is it possible to reconcile active missionary work among the barbarians with Gildas's picture of the British church? For him, priests are vicious, lazy, schismatic, simoniacal, and have a host of other vices besides. They hardly ever preach the word or conduct the sacraments, being idle and luxurious, frightened of the least danger. They do travel extensively overseas, but only for personal gain, so that on their return they can strut more proudly than they did before.[89] Can such a description of a decadent and lazy church be reconciled with a view of Ninian as a successful and industrious missionary?

For a start, Gildas's denunciations appear to be exaggerated. He does himself admit that all was not totally evil: 'One might say that not all bishops and priests ... are evil, because they are not schismatic, not proud, not stained with worldly infamy; with this we wholeheartedly agree.... We know [some] to be pure and virtuous'; elsewhere Gildas makes one fleeting reference to 'a very few good pastors'.[90] Perhaps Ninian was one of these. In the light of Bede's statement that he travelled to Rome, there is interest in Gildas's mention of those who delight 'to travel across the sea and journey to distant lands'.[91] Continental travel was common in Gildas's time, perhaps more so than at any time since the loss of Britain as a province of the Roman Empire.

So for a number of reasons which may be summarised here, Bede's and other accounts of Ninian and his activity make better sense in a sixth-century context than in an earlier one. A church was not normally dedicated to a saint whose relics were not preserved there; not until a change in fashion c. 500 did it become common to dedicate churches to popular but remote saints. The cult of St Martin was popularised in Rome by Pope Symmachus (498–514). There is little evidence of Christianity in southern Pictland before the sixth century; orientated long-cist burials at Lundin Links, St Andrews and Dundee appear to belong to the sixth century rather than earlier. When St Patrick wrote about the Picts in the 5th century (possibly d. as late as 493, but possibly up to thirty years earlier), they were still pagans, 'a foreign race which does not know God'. The only known historical personage in south-west Scotland called Tudwal was a king of Dumbarton, father of King Rhydderch Hael who was contemporary with Columba. Tudwal presumably flourished c. 550; but our hypothesis of a sixth-century dating of Ninian is not dependent on this suggested possible identification.

The internal evidence of Patrick, Bede, the eighth-century poem, and Pictish archaeology, points to a date for Ninian and his mission within the *termini* c. 461/493(?) × 563. The increasing confidence of archaeologists that Whithorn's earliest settlers arrived c. 500 and not earlier seems to provide independent confirmation of this evidence.

Most of our chronological assumptions about Ninian, however, have been based on the twelfth-century *Life of Ninian* attributed to

Ailred of Rievaulx. It is not clear why this has been so. It is also unfortunate, because this *vita* belongs to a *genre* of myth-making with scant regard for chronological accuracy. But on the basis of this *Life* Ninian has been made the contemporary of St Martin (d. 397) and the founder of the first church at Whithorn. To make sense of this some scholars have been led to distort the historical and archaeological record. The reason for assigning so much weight to the *Life* attributed to Ailred is not clear; if we had no evidence other than this *Life* we would have to conclude that St Ninian probably existed, but without any chronological data. Taken with a careful examination of literary and historical evidence, we are led to the conclusion that Ninian belongs to the first half of the sixth century.[92]

NOTES

1. This essay is based on my article 'The Date of St Ninian's Mission: a Reappraisal', in *RSCHS*, xxiii (1987). I have taken account of criticism in J MacQueen, *St Nynia* (2nd edn. 1990), which, however, has not led me to alter my views. Neither has chapter 1 of Daphne Brooke's rather conservative but well written book *Wild Men and Holy Places* (1994); for her comment on my earlier essay ('a strongly argued case for an opposing view'), cf. ibid., 23, 188. More significant are the latest archaeological reports from the Whithorn dig. At the time of writing Peter Hill's final report is still awaited.
2. A B Scott, 'Nynia in Northern Pictland', *SHR*, ii (1905), 278–88.
3. A C Thomas, *Christianity in Roman Britain* (1981), 285–90.
4. *Lives of SS Ninian and Kentigern*, ed. A P Forbes (Historians of Scotland, v, 1874), Introduction.
5. Scott, 'Nynia in northern Pictland', 278.
6. W D Simpson, *St Ninian and the Origins of the Christian Church in Scotland* (1940), 1.
7. N K Chadwick, 'St Ninian: a preliminary Study of Sources', *TDGNHAS*, 3d ser., xxviii (1951), 9–53, at 9.
8. A W Wade-Evans, 'Who was Ninian?', *TDGNHAS*, 3d ser., xxviii (1951), 79–91, at 79.
9. J MacQueen, *St Nynia* (1st edn, 1961), 8.
10. J MacQueen, *St Nynia* (2nd edn, 1990), 31 and chapter 3 passim.
11. Ibid., 31. See my comments in A Macquarrie, 'The Kings of Strathclyde, c. 400–1018' in A Grant and K J Stringer (eds), *Medieval Scotland: Crown, Lordship and Community: Essays presented to G W S Barrow* (1993), 1–19, at p. 7, n. 5.
12. A A M Duncan, *Scotland: the Making of the Kingdom* (1975), 38.

13. A C Thomas, *Christianity in Roman Britain to AD 500* (1981), 285ff.
14. G Donaldson, *Scottish Church History* (1985), 1, 12.
15. Brooke, *Wild Men and Holy Places*, 23.
16. A P Smyth, *Warlords and Holy Men: Scotland AD 80–1000* (1984), 255. More recently, Dr Smyth has stated that 'Ninian's missionary career is now more plausibly dated to the sixth century rather than the fifth', citing my earlier (1987) version of the present study: A Williams et al., *A Biographical Dictionary of Dark Age Britain* (1991), 184–5.
17. Personal communications from Messrs Peter Hill and Dave Pollock. See the *Whithorn Excavation Reports* (1987-).
18. P Grosjean, 'Les Pictes apostats dans l'Epître de S Patrice', *Analecta Bollandiana*, lxxvi (1958), 354–78, at 357.
19. Bede, *HE*, iii, 4.
20. A A M Duncan, 'Bede, Iona and the Picts', in R H C Davis and J M Wallace-Hadrill (eds), *The Writing of History in the Middle Ages: studies presented to R W Southern* (1981), 1–42.
21. Ed. K Strecker in *Monumenta Germaniae Historica, Poetae Latini Aevi Carolini*, iv (1923), 943–62; ed. and trans. W MacQueen in *TDGNHAS*, 3d ser. xxxvii (1960), 21–57; translation in MacQueen, *St Nynia* (2nd edn), 88–101. The *Miracula* is accompanied in the MS by a shorter abecedarian poem, *Hymnus Sancti Nynie Episcopi*, which is of great literary interest but has little historical information. It is edited by Strecker, loc. cit., and described by MacQueen, op. cit., 10–11. No English translation has been published.
22. MacQueen, *St Nynia* (1st edn), 2–6, arguing that a lost Celtic *vita* underlies all the later sources.
23. This appears to be a borrowing from classical verse; there is no evidence of a brick church at Whithorn. Cf. C A R Radford's excavation reports in *TDGNHAS*, 3d ser., xxxiv (1957), 85–126, and ibid., xxxvii (1960), 131–94.
24. Text, translation and commentary in Forbes, *Lives of SS Ninian and Kentigern* (hereafter *VN*); also translated in MacQueen, *St Nynia* (2nd edn), 102ff. In ibid., 11, Professor MacQueen casts doubt on the attribution to Ailred, though he usually continues his earlier practice of referring to it as Ailred's *Vita*. In my 1987 version of the present paper, I accepted the attribution and referred to it as Ailred's *Vita Niniani*, but I have here preferred to refer to it as 'attributed to Ailred'.
25. *VN*, 143–4.
26. Grosjean, 'Pictes apostats', 378; MacQueen, *St Nynia* (1st edn), 70. The traditional form Ninian has been preferred here as more commonly recognised.
27. Forbes, *VN*, 143–4.
28. C A R Radford and G Donaldson, *Whithorn and Kirkmadrine* (1953); J

Wall, 'Christian Evidences in the Roman Period', *Archaeologia Aeliana*, 4th ser., xliii (1965), 201–25, at 208–11; J Campbell et al., *The Anglo-Saxons* (1982), 21; A C Thomas, *Whithorn's Christian Beginnings: the Whithorn Lecture 1992* (1992), 3–13; above, Chapter 2, pp. 24–5.

29. Duncan, *Scotland: the Making of the Kingdom*, 37.
30. Radford, 'Excavations: first Session', 87–94, 115, 119.
31. Personal communications from Messrs Peter Hill and Dave Pollock. See the *Whithorn Excavation Reports* (1987-). At the time of writing, Peter Hill's final published report is still awaited.
32. K A Steer, 'Two unrecorded early Christian Stones', *PSAS*, ci (1969), 127–9; C Thomas, 'The Evidence from North Britain', in *Christianity in Britain, 300–700*, ed. M W Barley and R P C Hanson (1968), 93–121; above, Chapter 1, pp 22–3.
33. J Close-Brooks, 'Pictish and other Burials', in J G P Friell and W G Watson (eds), *Pictish Studies* (BAR, 125, 1984), 93–121.
34. I Henderson, 'Early Christian Monuments of Scotland bearing Crosses but no other Ornament', in *The Picts: a new Look at old Problems*, ed. A Small (1987), 45–58.
35. Duncan, 'Bede, Iona and the Picts', 32–3.
36. Thomas, *Christianity in Roman Britain*, 285–90.
37. G W S Barrow, *The Kingdom of the Scots* (1973), 60–64; idem, 'The Childhood of Scottish Christianity: a Note on some Place-name Evidence', *Scottish Studies*, xxvii (1983), 1–15.
38. Ibid.
39. Bede, *HE*, iii, 4.
40. The death of Bridei f. Mailcon is *AU* 584. I argue below (chapter 4, pp. 80–1, 110), that Columba's diplomatic activity in the north probably took place after the accession of Aedán mac Gabráin in 574.
41. Bede, *HE*, ii, 20; iii, 23; iv, 25. Cf. P F Jones, *Concordance to the Historia Ecclesiastica of Bede* (1929), s.v. tempus, tempore.
42. Cf. MacQueen, *St Nynia* (2nd edn), 22–3. Professor MacQueen's contention that in the present case 'the context is not a lifetime but the Christian era' is not easy to understand. Certainly Bede provides an incarnational year for Columba's arrival (AD 565); he also provides an imperial year (*quo tempore gubernaculum Romani imperii post Iustinianum Iustinus minor accepit*). Following Professor MacQueen's logic, we would have to choose whether this provides a 'context' going back to the foundation of the City (753 BC) or within the lifetime of Justinian. Professor MacQueen seems to have missed my point, which is simply that Bede had no chronological data available for St Ninian; if he had, he would have given them.
43. On St Patrick and his date, see above, Chapter 2; on the *Epistola*, see pp. 32ff.

44. Grosjean, 'Pictes apostats', passim.
45. See above, Chapter 2, pp. 46–7.
46. Professor MacQueen (*St Nynia* (2nd edn), 24–5) attempts to get round the difficulty that Patrick calls the Picts both *apostatae* and *gens ignorans Deum* by suggesting that 'although they were demonstrably ignorant of God in that they owned and purchased Christian slaves, they still had some nominal claim to be called Christians'. This is certainly an alternative argument to Père Grosjean's view, that '*il s'agit d'autres Pictes, restés paiens*', i.e., that Patrick distinguishes between two groups of Picts, some *apostatae* and others *gens ignorans Deum* ('Pictes apostats', 376), but it is not any more convincing. Neither distortion of Patrick's actual words is necessary. On the Vulgate use of the word, cf. Job, 34, 18: *Qui dicit regi apostata, qui vocat duces impios*; Prov. 6, 12: *Homo apostata vir inutilis, graditur ore perverso*; Sir. 19, 2; *Vinum et mulieres apostatare faciunt sapientes*. The context in these cases makes it clear that *apostatare/apostata* does not have a specifically religious significance, or relate specifically to backsliding.
47. MacQueen's statement (ibid., 25) that 'Jerome knew Greek as well as Hebrew, and would not have used *apostata* in his translation if he had not felt that the Hebrew text provided justification for his choice' is misleading. J N D Kelly, *Jerome: his Life, Writings and Controversies* (1975), in his analysis of the *Liber Interpretationis Hebraicorum Nominum*, points out that many of Jerome's definitions of Hebrew words are fanciful or erroneous (The *Liber Interpretationis Hebraicorum Nominum* is edited in *Corpus Christianorum*, ser. Lat., lxxii (1959)). Further, Professor MacQueen states that my three illustrations 'are drawn from the Old Testament' (see previous footnote); in fact Ecclesiasticus (or Ben Sira) is a deuterocanonical book, where Jerome was definitely translating from the Septuagint. Our concern, however, is why Patrick borrowed the word from his Latin Bible, not why Jerome used it in his translation (whether from Greek or Hebrew).
48. Bede, *HE*, iii, 4.
49. Dauvit Broun, 'The Literary Record of St Nynia: Fact and Fiction', *IR*, xlii (1991), 143–50, states that my alternative dating hypothesis 'depends crucially' on Ninian's contemporaneity with an identifiable King Tudwal; in fact, *pace* Dr Broun, I speak only of 'the possibility that Ninian's contemporary King Tudwal may be identifiable with a mid-sixth-century king of Dumbarton', and state that 'the model does not rest on that identification alone'; *RSCHS*, xxiii (1987), 1–25, at 15, 24.
50. E Phillimore, '*Annales Cambriae* and Old Welsh Genealogies from Harleian MS 3859' *Y Cymmrodor*, ix (1888), 141–83, at 172–3.
51. Ibid., 172. Merfyn Mawr's death is recorded in *AU* 681.

52. Ed. in *Y Cymmrodor*, viii (1886), 83–92, at 87.

53. See M Miller, 'Historicity and the Pedigrees of the Northcountrymen', *Bulletin of the Board of Celtic Studies*, xxvi (1976), 255–80.

54. Radford, 'Excavations at Whithorn: first Session', 89–92; N K Chadwick, 'Early Culture and Learning in North Wales', in N K Chadwick et al., *Studies in the early British Church* (1958), 29–120, at 74–80.

55. It is a common enough aristocratic name, from Celtic *Tudo-ualdos*, 'tribe ruler'. The Irish cognate is Tuathal.

56. '*Annales Cambriae* and Old Welsh Genealogies', 173.

57. *Nennius: British History and the Welsh Annals*, ed J Morris (1980), cap. 63; Anderson, *ESSH*, i, 13.

58. R Bromwich, *Trioedd Ynys Prydein* (1961; 2nd edn 1978), 147.

59. *Adomnán's Life of Columba*, ed. A O and M O Anderson (1961; 2nd edn 1991), i, 15.

60. *Lives of St Ninian and St Kentigern*, 144.

61. Ibid., 178–9.

62. See below, Chapter 5. Professor MacQueen complains that my suggested dating for Rhydderch, 'centring on the period c. 570 - c. 600, and perhaps stretching for a few years on either side' is, in his words, 'not really in accordance with the few dates positively associated with Rhydderch'; but his conclusion, that 'a reign extending from c. 580 to 612 or 613 would fit all the known facts', does not seem all that different from mine. Whether or not Rhydderch's death can be fixed with 'some apparent precision' in 612 or 613 depends on the value one is prepared to attach to Jocelin's account. I would like to be optimistic about this, but I am not sure that I would go so far as to speak of 'apparent precision'. See MacQueen, op. cit., 23. See below, Chapter 4, pp. 81–2, 108–9, and Chapter 5, pp. 136–7.

63. Grosjean, 'Pictes apostats'.

64. Broun, 'Literary Record', 147; presumably this argument could equally be applied to the dynasty of Dumbarton.

65. P A Wilson, 'St Ninian: Irish Evidence further examined', *TDGNHAS*, xlvi (1969), 140–59; Broun, op. cit., 148.

66. Chadwick, 'St Ninian', 33.

67. *St Nynia* (1st edn), 88. In the 2nd edn, p. 26, he assembles, from J N D Kelly's *Oxford Dictionary of Popes* (1986), a rather thin collection of papal pretensions down to Innocent I (401–417). These do not really address Mrs Chadwick's argument, or mine.

68. H St L B Moss, *The Birth of the Middle Ages* (1935), 45–50; L Musset, *The Germanic Invasions* (1975), 26–60 passim, 219–20.

69. Moss, *Birth of the Middle Ages*, 102–5; Musset, *Germanic Invasions*, 47–51.

70. Moss, *Birth of the Middle Ages*, 70–1; Musset, *Germanic Invasions*,

204–6. On the increasing prestige of the papacy, cf. Kelly, *Oxford Dictionary of Popes*, 43–51; and in general, J Richards, *The Popes and the Papacy in the early Middle Ages* (1979), 9–113.

71. Grosjean, 'Pictes apostats', 357.

72. Ibid;, F Prinz, *Frühes Mönchtum in Frankenreich* (1965), 22–46, esp. 29–30.

73. Bede, *HE*, i, 26.

74. Sulpicius' *Life of Martin* was copied into the *Book of Armagh*; see L Bieler, *Patrician Texts in the Book of Armagh*, Introduction.

75. It is curious, then, that Professor MacQueen expresses himself 'happy to accept Dr MacQuarrie's [sic] argument that the dedication of Candida Casa belongs to the sixth rather than the fifth century' (*St Nynia*, 2nd edn, 31). Bede does not specifically attribute to Ninian the dedication to St Martin, but he implies it: 'his episcopal see, notable for the name and church of St Martin the bishop.... he built there a church of stone' (*HE*, iii, 4). The *Miracula* explicitly attributes the dedication to Ninian: 'This shrine... which the father the exalted of Christ and worthy priest consecrated to the Lord, dedicating it in the name of Martin' (Mrs MacQueen's translation in MacQueen, *St Nynia* (2nd edn), 90). If Bede and the *Miracula* are correct in attributing the dedication to Ninian, and if Professor MacQueen and I are correct in dating the dedication to the 6th century, then Ninian must be a 6th-century figure. In fact, the supposed connection with St Martin is Ninian's only link with the early 5th century, and abandoning it is fatal to the whole argument of a 5th-century date. See my comment in *Medieval Scotland: Crown Lordship and Community*, 7, n. 5.

76. Close-Brooks, 'Pictish and other Burials', 94–6.

77. Duncan, 'Bede, Iona and the Picts', 32–3; Thomas, *Christianity in Roman Britain*, 285–90.

78. *Miracula*, Chapter 3.

79. P H Blair, 'The Bernicians and their Northern Frontier', in N K Chadwick, ed., *Studies in early British History* (1954), 137–72, at 165–8; cf. Bede, *HE*, v, 9 and 11.

80. *N*, both in initial and other positions, can sometimes be a misreading of *u* in insular scripts. If we were to speculate that we might have an original **uaturae*, we would be reminded of the many place-names in eastern Scotland in *fetter-*, *fothar-* and *for-*. See Watson, *CPNS*, 509–12. The River Forth was *Boderia* to Ptolemy, and part of its northern shore was *Fothrif* into the Middle Ages; but this does not help much.

81. *The Irish Liber Hymnorum*, ed. J H Bernard and R Atkinson (Henry Bradshaw Society, 1898), i, 22; translation in Anderson, *ESSH*, i, 7–8.

82. M O Anderson, *Kings and Kingship in early Scotland* (1973; 2nd edn 1980) (hereafter Anderson, *KKES*), 262, 266, 280.

83. M Miller, 'The disputed historical Horizon of the Pictish King-Lists', *SHR*, lviii (1979), 7–34.
84. *Irish Liber Hymnorum*, i, 22.
85. K Hughes, *Early Christian Ireland: Introduction to the Sources* (1972), 283; Anderson, *ESSH*, i, 7–8.
86. C Plummer (ed.), *Vitae Sanctorum Hiberniae* (1910), ii, 60, 263; and cf. index s.v. Whithorn.
87. D Dumville, 'Gildas and Uinniau', in *Gildas: new Approaches*, ed. M Lapidge and D Dumville (1984), 207–14; R Sharpe, 'Gildas as a Father of the Church', in ibid., 193–205, at 196–201.
88. Confusion may have arisen between Finnian and Ninian because of the similarity of their names, causing some of Finnian's exploits to appear also in Ninian's dossier (see Wilson, 'St Ninian: Irish Evidence further examined', passim), and perhaps causing Finnian to be associated with Whithorn.
89. *Gildas: the Ruin of Britain (De Excidio Britanniae)*, ed. M Winterbottom (1978), caps. 66–8 and ff.
90. Ibid., caps. 69, 110.
91. Ibid., cap. 67.
92. In the first edition of this paper I thanked Professor A A M Duncan and Mr C P Wormald for their comments and support. I wish to repeat these thanks, and to add my thanks also for their help and advice to Mr Peter Hill, Mr Dave Pollock, and Dr Richard Sharpe.

4

Saint Columba of Iona

The island of Iona off the western tip of Mull is a place of world-wide renown, a magnet for pilgrims for over fourteen centuries. Its fame must be credited to the personality of one remarkable man, who in the year 563 or soon after made the island his permanent home: St Columba.

It is well known that Irish ascetics from the sixth century onwards frequently embarked on pilgrimages and journeys of exploration, leaving home and family and following Christ.[1] Sometimes they sought a desert in the uncharted ocean, like the monks who built their beehive cells on Sgeilig Mhicheil in Kerry or Eileach an Naoimh in the Firth of Lorn; sometimes they went to more populous regions like Gaul, trusting to their innate Celtic tendency for homesickness to provide suitable mortification.[2] This form of ascetic self-denial, the renunciation of home and family by an intensely kin-based and home-loving society, was characterised as 'white martyrdom', to distinguish it from the 'red martyrdom' of those whose blood was actually shed for their faith.[3]

Columba himself is occasionally held up as an example of 'white martyrdom', and so his later cult portrayed him. But it is not certain that he would have viewed himself in that light, and it is worth examining his career in Scotland, especially his relationships with his lay contemporaries, to see how far it conforms to the ideal.

Most of our knowledge about Columba comes from the *Life* written by Adomnán, abbot of Iona, about 700 AD, a century after the saint's death.[4] Additional information is provided by the English historian Bede, writing some thirty years after Adomnán;[5] and by the collections of Irish annals, which seem to embody material compiled at Iona down to the mid-eighth century.[6] Adomnán had access to at least one earlier written source, a book of *The Virtues of St Columba* written by his predecessor Abbot Cumméne (657–669), but the bulk of his narrative is probably based on oral tradition preserved among the monks of Iona from the time of Abbot Ségéne (c. 624–652) onwards.[7] Later hagiography tells us much about how later generations viewed Columba, as a powerful miracle worker and ascetic, but tells us little of historical value.[8]

Little is known about Columba's career in Ireland. He was born probably in 521, and his given name is said to have been *Cremthann* (= fox). His father was Fedlimid son of Fergus, an aristocrat of the family called the Cenél Conaill which ruled over much of County Donegal (the name is still preserved in the barony of Tirconnell, from Irish *Tír Conaill*, 'land of [the family of] Conall').[9] At an early age Columba was fostered to a priest, and in his youth he studied under some of the greatest ecclesiastical teachers in Ireland at the time, including St Finnian.[10] It is uncertain whether he began his career as a founder of monasteries before he came to Scotland. Bede states that the Columban monastery of Durrow (County Offaly) was founded before Columba left Ireland, but Adomnán implies that it was founded, and the buildings were in process of being built, after Columba settled at Iona.[11] It seems that Columba's visit to Clonmacnoise during the abbacy of Ailither (c.586–599) was connected with the foundation of Durrow.[12] Although there was later a Columban monastery at Derry, the date of its foundation is uncertain. Since Iona 'held the pre-eminence' over all other Columban foundations, it seems likely that Iona was in fact the earliest of Columba's houses.

A turning point in Columba's life seems to have come in 561, the year of the battle of Cul Dreimne (or Cul Drebene); this battle was fought between branches of the royal house of the Uí Néill, of which Columba's own Cenél Conaill was part, and Columba was held responsible for instigating the battle and for the bloodshed involved.[13] The details of the battle and its causes are very obscure; but it seems to have resulted in considerable unpopularity for Columba, for in the following year (562) he was excommunicated by a synod of Irish clergy meeting at Tailtiú (now Teltown, County Meath).[14] Adomnán, perhaps not surprisingly, is rather coy about these events. Although Columba's excommunication was not long-lasting, and he was defended at the synod by St Brendan of Birr, it was probably these events which decided Columba to leave Ireland. So in 563, accompanied by twelve companions, he sailed away from Ireland to the court of Conall mac Comgaill, king of the Dál Riata in Scotland.[15]

So here, in what is nearly our first glimpse of the historical (as opposed to the legendary) Columba, he is already found interacting with powerful aristocratic laymen: With Diarmait mac Cerbaill king of the Uí Néill, with the leaders of the Cenél Conaill, and with Conall mac Comgaill, king of the Dál Riata. But from this story Columba emerges as a political exile, as much as, if not more than, a pilgrim saint. And although the Dál Riata were not related to the Uí Néill, they shared a common Gaelic language and culture. Adomnán's comment, *de Scotia peregrinaturus enauigauit*, 'he sailed away from Ireland to be a pilgrim',[16] is expanded in the *Secunda Praefatio* to read *de Scotia ad Brittanniam pro Christo perigrinari uolens enauigauit*, 'he sailed away from Ireland to Britain, wishing to be a pilgrim for Christ.'[17]

Later tradition has it that Columba sailed directly to Iona, and landed at Port na Curaich on the south side of the island. But this appears to be contradicted by Adomnán's statement that on his first arrival in Britain Columba resided with King Conall (*coram Conallo rege filio Comgill in Brittannia conversatus*),[18] and the Irish annals state that it was Conall who gave him Iona for the foundation of his monastery.[19] Bede's date for the foundation of Iona (565) and his statement that it was granted to Columba by Bridei king of the Picts, are less likely to be accurate than the evidence of Adomnán and the Annals.[20] Iona was probably established as Columba's home and monastic centre soon after his arrival in Scotland, perhaps c. 564.

Adomnán has little to say about Columba's relationship with Conall after his initial (probably brief) residence at court. Perhaps these early years in Scotland were spent in work at Iona and on the foundation of other island monasteries in the southern Hebrides.

It was while staying at one of these, the island of Hinba,[21] that Columba learned of the death of Conall in 574; according to Adomnán, an angel in a dream instructed him to consecrate Conall's cousin, Aedán mac Gabráin, as his successor; Columba was reluctant to do so, because he favoured Aedán's brother Eoganán mac Gabráin. But the angel insisted, going so far as to strike Columba with a scourge, and Columba complied shortly afterwards at a service of laying on of hands at Iona.[22]

This ceremony is, I believe, one of the earliest recorded instances of a barbarian king being inaugurated in a Christian ritual, and as such the story deserves special attention. Not surprisingly, Adomnán's account has led to some incredulity.[23] It is indeed doubtful that

Columba's prestige and influence can have been so high, less than ten years after his arrival among the Dál Riata, without any kinship-base among them, and living on the periphery of their kingdom, that he should have been sought out to take part in a royal election and inauguration.

There is no suggestion in Adomnán's account, however, that Columba took part in Aedán's election. Adomnán merely states that Aedán came to Iona at the same time that Columba returned from Hinba; Columba accepted his kingship as a *fait accompli*, and 'laying his hand upon his head he ordained and blessed him.' Nor does Adomnán offer any explanation of why Columba had allegedly earlier favoured Eoganán mac Gabráin in preference to Aedán. Part of the explanation may lie in the obscure power struggle which followed Conall's death, during which 'Dúnchad mac Conaill meic Comgaill, and many other allies of the sons of Gabrán' fell in a battle somewhere in Kintyre.[24] Presumably Aedán emerged as the victor, and other eligible candidates, including Eoganán, were forced to accept a subordinate role.[25] If Adomnán is right in stating that Columba favoured another candidate, Eoganán, then his influence was not sufficient to ensure his success. Later on, Eoganán was not considered as a possible successor to his brother.[26]

There is no suggestion, either, that Aedán did not undergo the normal secular inauguration of a Gaelic king, which probably would have involved oath-taking and acclamation, the recitation of the king's genealogy and the setting of his foot in a sacred carved footprint (possibly the one still visible at Dunadd in Knapdale; a similar footprint, fancifully associated with St Columba, is extant near Southend in Kintyre). It cannot be determined whether his 'ordination' by Columba preceded or followed such a ceremony. The point is, however, that Columba does not emerge as a kingmaker; the allegation that Adomnán promotes 'an inflated interpretation of the rights and powers of Iona abbots with regard to kings' overstates the claims that Adomnán is in fact making.[27]

There may, however, be a different possible interpretation of Adomnán's story. There are indications that Aedán may himself have been a political exile, in the east of Scotland or possibly on the upper Forth, before his accession as king.[28] It is uncertain how far Christianity had penetrated into this area by the mid-sixth century. If Aedán had been dwelling among pagan Picts he might not have been baptised, and his visit to Columba on Iona might have been to secure baptism rather than inauguration. The very similar account of Columba's encounter with Domnall mac Aeda at Druim Cett, considered below,[29] looks like a baptismal ceremony.

Another point worth making is that this 'political' version of Columba's vision on Hinba may not be the only version of this episode incorporated in Adomnán's narrative. In another place Adomnán describes how a vision granted by the Holy Spirit came to Columba on Hinba, over the space of three days and nights, which revealed to him many secrets and made plain many obscure passages of Scripture. He regretted that Baithéne was not with him at the time, having been detained on Eigg (Egea) by contrary winds; because if he had been present he could have passed on to others the communications which Columba received, both regarding the mysteries of the past and future, and the explanation of obscurities in Scripture.[30] Although Adomnán does not link this vision with the one previously mentioned, it is possible that he is here recording a different version of the same event; there are other possible examples in *Vita Columbae* of duplication of events or personages under different guises.[31] The two narratives have a number of features in common: location (Hinba), duration (three nights), context (angelic vision), and one point of detail (mysteries of the future, unknown to other men). This second narrative is linked with the name of Baithéne, and may be a 'non-political' recollection of his version of the same story.

Subsequently, Columba and Aedán seem to have co-operated closely on a number of occasions. At some point in his reign, Aedán took Columba with him to a meeting with Aed mac Ainmirech, king of the northern Uí Néill (and thus Columba's kinsman), at Druim Cett (or Druim Ceate) near Limavady in northern Ireland, at which Columba acted as Aedán's adviser in matters concerning the relationship of the two kings.[32] Dr Bannerman has shown that much of the later legend which surrounds the Convention obscures the fact that it was a secular gathering, a meeting of kings to discuss matters of taxation and military service.[33] In fact the main purpose of the meeting may well have been to conclude a military alliance between the Northern Uí Néill and the Dál Riata against the Ulaid, one of the most powerful Ulster peoples. At some point early in his reign (574 × 581), Aedán is said to have made a submission to the king of the Ulaid, Baetán mac Cairill, in Seimne (Island Magee).[34] If this preceded the Convention of Druim Cett, then that meeting may have been intended to restore Aedán's position in north-east Ireland.

Columba's role will have been to act as a mediator between King Aedán and Aed mac Ainmirech, who was his cousin.[35]

While he was at Druim Cett, Columba had two other important meetings with secular figures. In one of these, he met the youthful Domnall, son of his cousin Aed mac Ainmirech, who was brought to him by his foster-parents; in language which echoes that used in his description of Columba's meeting with Aedán, Adomnán describes how he blessed Domnall and prophesied for him a long and successful future as king.[36] Here again Adomnán does not say so, but it would be natural to read Columba's blessing of the boy as part of a baptismal ceremony.

In the other encounter, Adomnán describes how Columba visited and comforted a prisoner, Scandlán mac Colmáin. He prophesied that Scandlán would outlive King Aed, who was holding him, would return to his own people and become their king for thirty years, would then spend a second short period in exile before being recalled and dying as king after three months.[37] It is possible that this person is identifiable as Scandlán Mór son of Cennfaelad, king of the Osraige, who died c. 643.[38] Adomnán does not say that Columba requested or obtained the prisoner's release; a later legend makes this claim, but it has been shown to be unhistorical.[39] Indeed, if Columba did treat for Scandlán's release, he appears to have been unsuccessful. As in his involvement in King Aedán's inauguration, we can see that Columba's influence on secular figures was limited. On the whole, Adomnán's treatment of events at the convention of Druim Cett does not support the view that he is making inflated claims of political influence for Columba.

Adomnán describes how later, before Aedán embarked on a campaign against the *Miathi*, a Pictish tribe located at the head of the Firth of Forth, Columba spoke with him about the succession to the kingdom in the event of the king's premature death.[40] According to Adomnán, it was Columba who initiated the discussion, asking Aedán who would be his successor. Aedán named three of his sons as possibilities, but said that he did not know which one would succeed him. Interestingly, Columba's alleged favourite Eoganán was not even mentioned, even though succession by a brother or cousin would have been equally, if not more, common in Gaelic succession custom; Aedán spoke only about one of his sons succeeding him. According to Adomnán, Columba then prophesied that the three sons named by King Aedán would all predecease him, and that a younger son, Eochaid Buide, would in fact reign after him.

The significance of this is difficult to determine, and the story has again been treated with incredulity. A biblical model has been suggested in the anointing of David by Samuel (1 Sam., 16, 1–13; *Vulg.* 1 Reg., 16, 1–14),[41] but what Adomnán describes is in fact very different: Columba does not nominate or anoint a favoured candidate, but rather makes a prophecy about the future, as he had done when at Aedán's ordination 'he prophesied the future concerning his sons and grandsons and great-grandsons'.[42] The parallels with the story of Samuel and David are slight, and certainly do not warrant the suggestion that Adomnán is modelling Columba as a second Samuel in the way that Armagh proclaimed Patrick as a second Moses.[43] Adomnán's concern is to emphasise Columba's supernatural power, his ability to prophesy the future, rather than to show his influence over kings.

Columba, as well as questioning Aedán about who should succeed him, lent him the aid of his and his monks' prayers in the battle, so that the Miathi were defeated; Columba saw the outcome of the battle by the second sight, and told the exact number of the slain in King Aedán's army.[44]

Aedán's aggression may have affected Columba's relationships with other kings in Scotland at the time. On at least one occasion he visited Bridei, king of the northern Picts, who had a royal fortress near the River Ness; the hilltop of Craig Phatric beside Inverness has been suggested as the most likely location.[45] Adomnán records a number of miracles which occurred at King Bridei's court and elsewhere in Pictish lands.[46]

At Columba's first meeting with King Bridei, the king would not open the gates of his fortress to him. Columba struck them with his staff so that they flew open, and the king and his counsellors hurried from the hall to meet him.[47]

Probably it was during the same visit that Columba asked for safe-conduct for the pilgrim monk Cormac, seeking a hermitage in the northern ocean; he asked Bridei to instruct the sub-king of the Orkneys, who was at his court and of whom Bridei held hostages, not to molest Cormac should he come into his territories.[48]

The reference to the Orkneys is of interest, because we know that one of King Aedán's most ambitious recorded military exploits was a raid on these islands c. 580.[49] It is tempting to see Columba's visit to Bridei's court as a diplomatic mission in connection with that event. The narratives of this visit are best known for their account of an aquatic monster dwelling in the River Ness (perhaps not the ancestor of the Loch Ness Monster – both in character and location Adomnán's monster is quite different),[50] and of contests between Columba and the powerful druid Broichan, King Bridei's foster-father.[51] Embedded within this narrative is mention of another purpose, the release of at least one Gaelic female captive. Adomnán himself engaged in redemptive activity of this kind,[52] so it is disappointing that he does not say more about Columba engaging in such work. There are hints in Adomnán's narrative about unsettled conditions in Glen More which might have involved slave-raiding,[53] and it is easy to conceive Aedán's attack on the Orkneys as retaliation for such a raid. The evidence would be consistent with Columba making a diplomatic visit to Bridei's court near Inverness, perhaps c. 580, in connection with raiding and counter-raiding and the redemption of captives. Although Adomnán does mention a small number of Pictish converts made by Columba (for example stating that he converted and baptised a Pictish household in the region of Urquhart when he was travelling beside Loch Ness),[54] he does not speak of a large-scale conversion of Picts such as is described by Bede; most crucially, he does not mention the conversion and baptism of Bridei himself. So it must be doubted if the conversion of the Picts took place on any large scale until after Columba's death, or if his visit or visits into Pictish territory were intended as missionary journeys.[55] If this was in fact, as appears more likely, a diplomatic visit, it follows that King Aedán was able to call on Columba's services for work of this kind, and this tells us something about the relationship between king and abbot.

On another occasion, Adomnán describes how Columba received a secret message from Rhydderch Hael, king of the Britons of Dumbarton, described as a friend of the saint, through one of his own monks.[56] Rhydderch sought to know whether he would die by the hand of his enemies, and Columba assured him that he would die in peace in his own house. The Britons of Strathclyde were Christians by this time, which may explain why Rhydderch is called Columba's friend. But there are known instances of hostility between Aedán and Rhydderch in this period, as when, according to a Welsh 'triad', Aedán by an 'unrestrained ravaging ... came to the court of Rhydderch Hael at Dumbarton; he left neither food nor drink nor beast alive.'[57] Two interpretations are possible: either Columba was assuring Rhydderch that Aedán would not repeat an earlier raid against him; or else Aedán raided into Strathclyde in spite of Columba's assurances to the contrary. If the latter view is the correct one, it would go some way towards explaining Aedán's Welsh nickname, *bradawc*, 'wily, treacherous';[58] it would also remind us again of the limitations of Columba's influence over kings.

There is a likelihood that Aedán's plundering was remembered in Irish folk-tales. The lost tale *Orgain Sratha Cluada* ('The Slaughter of Strathclyde'), which appears in learned lists of Irish tales, is usually assumed to refer to the Viking siege of Dumbarton in 870.[59] But if so it is slightly unusual, since most tales with historical or pseudo-historical subject matter refer to an earlier time.[60] It may be more likely that this tale referred to the same incident as that described in the Welsh 'triad', which combined slaughter with plunder. The lost tale *Orgain Sratha Cluada* may refer to events that actually took place.[61]

In Ireland too Columba's influence over secular figures may have been limited. We have already mentioned the obscure circumstances under which he left Ireland in 563. On a later visit to Ireland Adomnán describes how he was visited by Aed Sláne mac Diarmata, whom he tried to dissuade from an attack on his own kin. If Aed Sláne did attack his own kinsfolk, warned Columba, his reign as king would be short and he would have to share the kingship; and so it happened.[62] Aed Sláne had a brief joint reign as Uí Néill overking a few years after Columba's death.[63] If Columba did try to make peace between different branches of the Uí Néill during a visit to Ireland towards the end of his life, it appears that he was unsuccessful; there was considerable fratricidal bloodletting among the Uí Néill during the years following his death.[64]

Many of Adomnán's stories about his dealings with laymen of lesser rank concern acts of kindness rewarded or slights punished. An example concerns one Tarain, a Pictish prince living in exile among the Dál Riata, whom Columba committed to the care of Feradach, a nobleman in Islay. Feradach received him, but a few days after had the exile put to death. According to Adomnán, Columba prophesied Feradach's untimely death, which duly occurred.[65] It is noteworthy that Columba's recommendation should have been so slighted.

Columba was slighted by others as well. Ioan mac Conaill meic

Domnaill, 'sprung from the royal tribe of Gabrán', repeatedly attacked the house of Colmán, a layman of Ardnamurchan, a friend with whom Columba had stayed. On one occasion Columba tried to prevent the aggressor setting sail with his booty, and when this failed, predicted his imminent destruction; Ioan's ship duly sank in stormy weather between Mull and Coll.[66]

On another occasion an associate of the same family, nicknamed Lam Dess or 'Right-hand', tried to murder Columba on Hinba, because the saint was excommunicating them as persecutors of his churches; Lam Dess failed, and Columba predicted his own death a year later in a battle on another island.[67] These men cannot now be identified with certainty, though the family of Conall mac Domnaill was presumably descended from Domnall mac Gabráin. If they were unsuccessful contenders for the kingship in the succession dispute which brought Aedán mac Gabráin to power in 574, they may have attempted to carve out a lordship for themselves in Mull, Coll, Tiree, and Ardnamurchan, partly at the expense of Columba's churches and his lay friends. A layman called Erc mocu Druidi from Coll poached seals belonging to the monks of Iona on small islands off the Ross of Mull,[68] so there are indications of territorial disputes or friction between Columba and some of his neighbours.

In addition to describing Columba's dealings with the aristocracy of his day, Adomnán also speaks of the monastic life on Iona, its buildings, its monks, and its many visitors. These visitors included kings and their messengers, ecclesiastical pilgrims (including a bishop who humbly tried to conceal his status from Columba),[69] penitents, and sick persons seeking medical and spiritual cures. Adomnán gives the impression that at times the island was a very busy place, with a regular stream of visitors coming and going amidst the constant activity of the abbot and his monks.

The longest and most moving chapter of Adomnán's *Life of Columba* is his description of the saint's death. As well as its touching description of Columba's last days and hours, this chapter also sheds light on monastic life at Iona, so it is worth considering in some detail. Adomnán describes how, in the month of May, some weeks after Easter, Columba was taken in a cart to visit the monks who were at work in the western parts of the island. He told them that his end was drawing near, and blessed them and the island; then his cart was brought back to the monastic enclosure. On the following Sunday, he saw a vision of angels while celebrating the Eucharist in the monastic chapel. On the Saturday after that, he and his personal attendant Diarmait went out for a short walk, but Columba's age (he was in fact about 76) prevented him going further than the nearest farm-buildings. These he blessed, while he told the sorrowing Diarmait that he expected to die that same night. On the way back to the monastery he sat down to rest at a point which was later commemorated by the placing of a wooden cross set in a mill-stone, which still stood in Adomnán's time. While he sat resting, he was approached by one of the monastery's horses, 'an obedient servant who was accustomed to carry the milk-vessels between the cow-pasture and the monastery'. The horse placed its head in the saint's bosom and seemed to weep, as if it knew that its master would soon be taken from it. Diarmait wanted to drive the beast away, but Columba would not allow this; rather he allowed it to nuzzle against him, before 'he blessed his servant the horse, as it turned sadly away from him'. Then he climbed a small hill overlooking the monastery (possibly Sgurr an Fhithich, just west of the Abbey), and gave his monastery his last blessing: 'On this place, small and mean though it be, not only the kings of the *Scoti* with their peoples (i.e., the Gaels of Scotland and Ireland), but also the rulers of barbarous and foreign nations with their subjects, will bestow great and especial honour.'[70]

Then he returned to his writing-hut to continue the copying of a psalter on which he had been working. He continued this activity up to the time of Vespers, the office which initiated the Lord's Day; and after attending Vespers in the chapel he retired to his own lodgings to sleep. Adomnán tells us that right up to his death Columba slept on the bare ground, using a stone for a pillow. When the bell rang for the midnight office, Columba hurried to the chapel ahead of the monks; and they, coming in carrying lamps to light the dark chapel, found him dying in front of the altar. He raised his hand feebly in a last benediction, and expired. The date of his death was Sunday, 9 June 597.[71]

An assessment of Columba's life and career is not easy. Adomnán is more concerned to demonstrate Columba's power and God's favour towards him than to set out the events of his life in chronological order or assess his secular influence and importance. There can be no doubt that Columba did have secular influence, as a high-born aristocrat who moved easily in the company of kings and princes. But it would be misguided and cynical to view him only as a clerical manipulator of secular politics. He was concerned equally with the spiritual well-being of his monks and with the pilgrims and penitents who visited him. It is hinted by Adomnán that sick people came to Iona seeking remedies for physical ailments, and that these were supplied by Columba's monks;[72] and there are constant references to the copying of books, especially the Bible, at Iona. Columba had a reputation as a poet, musician, and computist.[73] The monastic life at Iona also consisted of manual labour, in the fields and on building projects. Columba, however, seems not to have insisted on too rigorous a programme of labour; he once expressed disapproval of the way his monks at Durrow were being overburdened with work.[74] Finally, there are references to the regular monastic offices, including vespers (the evening office) and the midnight office, and the celebration of the Eucharist on Sundays and holy days. Wednesday was normally observed as a fast day at Columba's monasteries, but this could be relaxed if there were important visitors.[75]

It is not certain how far Columba practiced personal austerities. Adomnán does state that he slept on the bare rock with a stone for a pillow; but on the other hand he was constantly attended by his personal servant Diarmait, and Adomnán also describes how after the Convention of Druim Cett Columba and St Comgall of Bangor dined together while their monks waited on them.[76] This must reflect Columba's social status.

It is perhaps impossible to get any closer to Columba. Subsequent tradition and hagiography have obscured him as much as they have revealed him, and tell us as much about the later reputation of Iona as they do about Columba himself. This process had already started long before Adomnán wrote a century after his founder's death, and it is a credit to Adomnán's honesty and singleness of purpose that we know as much about Columba as we do.

Columba's career contrasts strikingly with that of his younger contemporary, St Donnan of Eigg. Donnan appears to have carried out missionary work among the Picts of the west coast and Western Isles north of Ardnamurchan Point before he was martyred with 150 monks in 617. His death was brought about, according to later traditions, because he objected to a local Pictish queen grazing her sheep on his island. One tradition (certainly apocryphal) has it that Donnan sought out Columba to make him his soul-friend (*anm chara*), but Columba refused on the grounds that he did not want to be confessor to a community of martyrs.[77]

Columba was not a 'red martyr' like St Donnan of Eigg. But it is questionable whether he really sought to be a 'white martyr' either. He supported the monk Cormac, when he was travelling to seek a desert in the Northern Isles, and by his recommendation saved him from the fate which befell Donnan;[78] but Columba himself was no hermit. He was an active and vigorous churchman who travelled widely and worked hard among his contemporaries, both lay and clerical. The reasons for his departure from Ireland are now obscure, but it is not certain that they constituted a voluntary withdrawal from home and family; certainly he revisited both later. On the other hand, he was not a clerical kingmaker; the extent of his influence over his aristocratic contemporaries has probably been exaggerated. This is not, however, Adomnán's doing. For Adomnán, Columba's temporal influence and possessions were relatively minor considerations; he was concerned above all to set out his great predecessor's spiritual power and sanctity.

NOTES

1. See, among many other essays, K Hughes, *The Church in Early Irish Society* (1966), 91–102; T O Fíaich, 'Irish Monks on the Continent', in *An Introduction to Celtic Christianity*, ed. J P Mackey (Edinburgh, 1989), 101–39.
2. Ó Fíaich, 'Irish Monks on the Continent', passim.
3. A P Smyth, *Warlords and Holy Men: Scotland AD 80–1000* (1984), 109; D Bray, 'Some Aspects of Hagiography in the Celtic Church', *RSCHS*, xxi (1982), 111–26, at 118.
4. J M Picard, 'The Purpose of Adomnán's Vita Columbae', *Peritia*, i (1982), 160–77, at 167ff.
5. *Bede's Ecclesiastical History of the English People*, ed. B Colgrave and R A B Mynors (1969) (hereafter Bede, *HE*); also *Venerabilis Baedae Opera Historica*, ed. C Plummer (1896).
6. J Bannerman, *Studies in the History of Dalriada* (1974), 9–26. The main collections of annals are: *Annals of Ulster*, ed. S Mac Airt and G Mac Níocaill (1983) (hereafter *AU*); previously ed. W M Hennessy and B MacCarthy (1887–1901); *Annals of Tigernach*, ed. W Stokes, in *Revue Celtique*, xvii (1896), 6–33, 119–263, 337–420(hereafter *AT*); these are the most important. Also noteworthy are: *Chronicon Scotorum*, (an abbreviation of 'Tigernach') ed. W M Hennessy (RS, 1866); *Annals of Innisfallen*, ed. S Mac Airt (1951); *Annals of Clonmacnoise*, (an English translation of a set of annals related to 'Tigernach' and *Chronicon Scotorum*) ed. D Murphy (1896); *Annals of the Four Masters*, ed. J

O'Donovan (1856). In citing *AU* entries, I have followed the usual practice of adding 1 to the later *anno Domini* dates in the MS for this period.

7. *Adomnán's Life of Columba*, ed. A O and M O Anderson (2nd edn 1991)(hereafter *VC*; all refs are to this edn unless otherwise stated), iii, 5; cf. also i, 1; i, 2; i, 3; ii, 4; iii, 19. The 1st edn (1961) has a valuable introduction which has been shortened in the 2nd edn. On Adomnán's use of oral tradition, see P O Riain, 'Towards a Methodology in early Irish Hagiography', *Peritia*, i (1982), 146–59. Since this chapter was written, an important new translation of Adomnán, with extensive introduction, commentary and notes, has appeared: Adomnán of Iona, *Life of St Columba*, trans. R Sharpe (1995); regrettably too late for Dr Sharpe's work to be fully taken into account in this chapter.

8. For the Irish Life of Columba and the development of Columban hagiography, see M Herbert, *Iona, Kells and Derry* (1988), 211–88 and passim.

9. Second Preface; cf. ibid, pp. xxviiiff.

10. Ibid., i, 1; ii, 1; iii, 4. See also D Dumville, 'Gildas and Uinniau', in *Gildas: New Approaches*, ed. M Lapidge and D Dumville (1984), 207–14. On the multiplication of saints of the same name, see O Riain, 'Towards a Methodology in early Irish Hagiography', 147–55.

11. Bede, *HE*, iii, 4; *VC*, i, 3; iii, 15.

12. Ibid., i, 3; N Edwards, 'The South Cross, Clonmacnois', in J Higgitt (ed.), *Early Medieval Sculpture in Britain and Ireland* (BAR, British Series 152, 1986), 23–48, at 31.

13. *AU*, s.a. 561.

14. *VC*, iii, 3.

15. Ibid., iii, 3; i, 7; cf. Bannerman, *Dalriada*, 128.

16. *VC*, i, 7.

17. Ibid., 2nd Preface.

18. Ibid., i, 7.

19. *AU*, s.a. 574: *Conall mac Comgaill... obtulit insolam Iae Columbe Cille*; Iona's own record of its foundation.

20. *HE*, iii, 4. Cf. A A M Duncan, 'Bede, Iona and the Picts', in R H C Davis and J M Wallace-Hadrill (eds) *The Writing of History in the Middle Ages: Studies Presented to R W Southern* (1981), 1–42, at 10.

21. For the identification Hinba, see Appendix 1 to this chapter, below, pp 91–102.

22. *VC*, iii, 5.

23. M J Enright, 'Royal Succession and abbatial Prerogative in Adomnán's *Vita Columbae*', *Peritia*, iv (1985), 83–103, at 86–7. Cf. Also M Meckler, 'Colum Cille's ordination of Aedán mac Gabráin', *IR*, xli (1990), 139–50.

24. *AU*, s.a. 576, 577; *AT*, p. 151. The accounts seem to be very confused. *AT*'s *Cath Delgon* appears to be an *n*-stem, nom. **Delgú*; *AU*'s *Bellum Telocho* looks like a *u*-stem, nom. **Teloch*. *AT* enters the battle immediately after its account of the death of Conall mac Comgaill; *AU* enters the convention of Druim Cett in between. *Teloch* or *Delgú* may have been unidentified at a very early date, and cannot be identified now.

25. It has been suggested, however, that Adomnán mentions the favour shown to Eoganán because at the time that he was writing *VC* Eoganán's descendants were laying claim to the kingship of the Dál Riata: Enright, 'Royal Succession and abbatial Prerogative', 86–9.

26. *VC*, i, 9.

27. Enright, 'Royal Succession and abbatial Prerogative', 84.

28. A A M Duncan, *Scotland: the Making of the Kingdom* (1975), 43; Bannerman, *Dalriada*, 85.

29. Below, p. 79.

30. *VC*, iii, 18.

31. O Riain, 'Towards a Methodology in early Irish Hagiography', 147

32. *VC*, i, 10–11; i, 49; Bannerman, *Dalriada*, 157–70; F J Byrne, *Irish Kings and High-Kings* (London, 1973), 110–111. See Appendix II below, pp 103–16.

33. Bannerman, *Dalriada*, 157–70.

34. Ibid., 2.

35. Byrne, *Irish Kings and High-Kings*, 111.

36. *VC*, i, 10.

37. Ibid., i, 11.

38. *AT*, p. 187 (s.a. c. 643).

39. Bannerman, *Dalriada*, 158–9; *VC*, p. 231, n. 10.

40. *VC*, i, 8–9. Dio Cassius speaks of a tribe called the *Maeatae* dwelling just north of the Antonine Wall; see above, Chapter 1, pp 18–19; translated in J C Mann and R G Penman, *Literary Sources for Roman Britain* (1978), 28–30. Presumably they are identical with Adomnán's *Miathi*. The hill-fort of Dumyat (= *Dun Miat*, 'fort of the Miathi') near Menstrie, dominating the Carse of Forth, must have been one of their strongholds. See *VC*, pp. xix-xx.

41. Enright, 'Royal Succession and abbatial Prerogative', 88–9.

42. *VC*, iii, 5.

43. Enright, 'Royal Succession and abbatial Prerogative', 93–4

44. *VC*, i, 8.

45. Craig Phatric was the site of an Iron-age hill-fort, with traces of secondary occupation during the Pictish period; A Ritchie, *Picts* (1989), 44; L Alcock, 'A Survey of Pictish Settlement Archaeology', in J G P Friell and W G Watson (eds), *Pictish Studies* (BAR, British Series, cxxv, 1984), 7–41, at 23; L Alcock, 'Pictish Studies: present and future', in

The Picts: a new Look at old Problems, ed. A Small (1987), 80–92, at 82f. Bridei's fort was 'not far from the River Ness, though far enough for an urgent message to have been carried on horseback'; so the site of Inverness Castle is probably ruled out. Cf. *VC*, p. xxxiv.

46. *VC*, ii, 36. It has been pointed out that some of these stories are said to have taken place *trans Dorsum Britanniae* (i.e., across Drumalban) and others are located *in Provincia Pictorum*. Adomnán may have been working from two narratives which recorded visits to the Inverness area, but that does not in itself require more than one visit. The editors of *VC* (ibid., 1st edn, pp. 81–2) doubt that Columba made more than one visit to Bridei's territories; and see also L Bieler in *Irish Historical Studies*, xiii (1963), 175–84, at 184. On the other hand, the words *in prima fatigatione itineris* could be taken to imply subsequent journeys; and Bridei is said to have honoured Columba *ex ea in posterum die... suae omnibus vitae reliquis diebus*, which might imply that they met subsequently. The evidence is not conclusive either way. See my review of *VC* (2nd edn) in *SHR*, lxxii (1993),213–5.

47. *VC*, ii, 36.

48. Ibid., ii, 43.

49. *AU*, s.a. 580, 581. The entry, however, is in Irish (*Fecht Orc la hAedhán mac Gabráin*), so it may be doubtful if it belongs to the earliest stratum of the Annals, which seem to have been in Latin.

50. ii, 28; G W S Barrow, 'The Sources for the History of the Highlands in the Middle Ages,' in *The Middle Ages in the Highlands*, ed. L Maclean (1981), 11–22, at 14.

51. *VC*, ii, 34, 35; the possibility that Broichan is a mythological figure is discussed in ibid., pp. xxxiii-xxxiv.

52. *AU*, s.a. 687.

53. *VC*, i, 28.

54. Ibid., ii, 32; iii, 14.

55. Bede, *HE*, iii, 4.

56. *VC*, i, 8.

57. R Bromwich, *Trioedd Ynys Prydein* (2nd edn 1978), 147–8; cf. ibid., 264–5. Bannerman, *Dalriada*, 86–90; Duncan, 'Bede, Iona and the Picts', 16–19.

58. Bromwich, *TYP*, 264. See also my review of *VC* (2nd edn) in *SHR*, lxxii (1993), 213–15.

59. The assumption is made, for example, in Anderson, *ESSH*, i, 301, n. 2.

60. P Mac Cana, *The Learned Tales of Medieval Ireland* (1980), 47, 61, 100.

61. See below, Appendix ii, pp 109–10.

62. *VC*, i, 14.

63. *AU*, s. a. 598, 604.
64. Byrne, *Irish Kings and High-Kings*, 87–116.
65. *VC*, ii, 24.
66. Ibid., ii, 33.
67. Ibid., ii, 24. It may be possible to identify the slayer of *Lam Dess* as a member of the Cenél Loairn; *VC*, p. xxxii.
68. Ibid., i, 41.
69. Ibid., i, 44.
70. Ibid., iii, 23. Adomnán, of course, was writing with hindsight.
71. Ibid., iii, 23; cf. Anderson, *ESSH*, i, 103.
72. *VC*, i, 27.
73. T O Clancy and G Márkus, *Iona: the earlierst Poetry of a Celtic Monastery* (1995), esp. 39ff., 121, and n. on p 244.
74. *VC*, i, 29.
75. Ibid., i, 26.
76. Ibid., i, 35.
77. Cf. Smyth, *Warlords and Holy Men*, 107–10.
78. *VC*, ii, 43.

Appendix I

Hinba

One of the most vexed questions concerning the *Life of Columba* is the identification of Hinba. The question is important, because this island figures largely in a number of significant episodes in Adomnán's *Life*; its importance as a Columban monastery may have been second only to that of Iona itself.

A number of passages in Adomnán's *Life* mention this island, and they are summarised below.

[A] *VC*, iii, 5. It was here that Columba had on three successive nights a divine vision instructing him to ordain Aedán mac Gabráin as king, despite his own unwillingness; he proceeded from Hinba to Iona, whither Aedán had come to meet him, and carried out the divine command.

[B] *VC*, iii, 18. A vision granted by the Holy Spirit came to him on Hinba, over the space of three days and nights, which revealed to him many secrets and made plain many obscure passages of Scripture. He regretted that Baithéne was not with him at the time, having been detained on Eigg (Egea) by contrary winds; because if he had been present he could have passed on to others the communications which Columba received, both regarding the mysteries of the past and future, and the explanation of obscurities in Scripture. Although Adomnán does not link this vision with the one previously mentioned, it is possible that he is here recording a different version of the same event.[1]

[C] *VC*, ii, 24. At one time, while Columba was dwelling on Hinba, he excommunicated the sons of Conall mac Domnaill of the Cenél nGabráin. One of them, a man nicknamed Lam Dess or 'Right-hand', tried unsuccessfully to kill him. A year later, 'Right-hand' was himself killed in a battle 'on the island which may in Latin be called *Longa*'; Columba, now on Iona, saw his death by the second sight.

[D] *VC*, iii, 17. On another occasion, four saints from Ireland,

91

founders of monasteries, came to visit Columba in Scotland, and found him on Hinba. Columba celebrated mass for them in the chapel there.

[E] *VC*, i, 21. On another occasion Columba was visiting the monks and penitents on Hinba, and he and Baithéne ordered a food-indulgence to be allowed even to the penitents. This was declined by one Nemán mac Cathair, whose refusal did not please Columba: the saint predicted that Nemán would return to the world and be found eating mare's flesh with robbers concealed in a wood.

[F] *VC*, i, 45. At one time Columba, described as 'venerable', sent his aged uncle Ernán to be prior of Hinba 'which he had founded many years before'. He predicted that he would not see the old man again in life. And so it proved: for when Ernán sensed the approach of death soon after, he returned to Iona; and Columba set out for the harbour to greet him. But as the two men approached one another, Ernán fell dead, so that Columba's prophecy should not be in vain.

[G] *VC*, iii, 23. After Columba's death, an Irish monk called Fergna/Virgno came from Ireland to Scotland and recounted a vision which he had been told by an ancient saint at the time of Columba's death: the old man had in a vision seen the island of Iona, which he had never visited, brightly lit at midnight by angels bearing Columba's soul to heaven. Fergno set out for Scotland and came to Hinba, where he spent the rest of his life, first living obediently among the brethren, then for the last twelve years of his life he lived the life of an anchorite in the hermitage of *Muirbolc Már*, the great sea-bay.

It may be possible to draw some conclusions about the location of Hinba from the above. First of all, it is possible to eliminate those islands to which Adomnán gives other names: thus Hinba cannot be Skye (*Scia*),[2] Eigg (*Egea*),[3] Coll (*Colosus*),[4] Tiree (*Ethica Terra*),[5] Mull (*Malea*),[6] Iona (*Ioua*), Islay (*Ilea*),[7] Rathlin (*Rechrú*),[8] etc.[9]

It is worthwhile to review the known facts which can be deduced from Adomnán's account. From [A] above it is clear that when Columba came to Iona from Hinba and met there with Aedán mac Gabráin, the two were converging on Iona. We have a pretty clear idea where Aedán was coming from: he had just come to power after a struggle culminating in 'the battle of Delgú in Kintyre, in which Dúnchad mac Conaill meic Comgaill fell, and many allies of the sons of Gabrán also fell.' So Aedán was travelling either directly from

Kintyre, or perhaps from Dunadd in Knapdale. He was coming from the mainland, south of Lorn.

Aedán's meeting with Columba on Iona (dateable to c. 574) was not by chance; Columba already dwelt on Iona, which had been given to him by Conall mac Comgaill (father of the pretender who had newly been killed, presumably by Aedán). So it follows that Aedán was actively seeking him out. If Hinba lay between Aedán's starting point, either in Kintyre or Knapdale, and Iona, Aedán would surely have found him there. So it follows that Hinba cannot be an island on the direct sea route between Aedán's starting point and Iona. Eileach an Naoimh therefore is eliminated if we assume that Aedán was coming from Dunadd, and Jura becomes most unlikely if we assume that Aedán was coming directly from Kintyre. Jura remains a possibility if Aedán was coming from Dunadd, especially if we assume that he would have avoided the dangerous waters of the Strait of Corryvreckan.[10]

We have seen that when Aedán came to Iona he was coming from the mainland, either from Kintyre or Knapdale. That does not necessitate, however, that Hinba lay in the opposite direction. It cannot be shown that in coming from Hinba to Iona Columba was moving towards Knapdale or Kintyre, since Iona already belonged to him. He appears simply to have been returning home after a period on Hinba.

If it was known where Aedán's starting point was, any intervening islands could certainly be eliminated; but what remains is an 'either/or' situation. If it was certain that Aedán was coming from Dunadd, then one could eliminate the islands of the Firth of Lorn from Scarba northwards, including the Garbh Eileach group, and possibly Jura; if, on the other hand, he was coming from Kintyre, then one could eliminate Gigha, Islay, and probably Jura.

In [B], Eigg is mentioned as well as Hinba. Baithéne could not be with his master because he was detained on Eigg by contrary winds. It is well known that the south-wester is the prevailing wind of the Hebrides, and on several occasions Adomnán speaks of voyages being prevented or delayed by it. The south-wester (*Favonius* or *Zephyrus*) delayed the sailing of Adomnán's curachs from the mouth of the River *Salea*, probably the River Sheil between Ardnamurchan and Moidart (*VC*, ii, 45);[11] presumably it was the same south-wester which drove Adomnán and his companions onto the island of *Sainea* among the people of *Loern* while they were striving to get to Iona in time to celebrate Columba's feast-day (9 June) in the summer following the great Irish synod (the Synod of Birr, 697) (*VC*, ii, 45).[12] Again, it was the south-wester which Broichan the druid predicted would delay Columba's voyage up Loch Ness. (*VC*, ii, 34)

If it was the south-wester which prevented Baithéne sailing from Eigg to Hinba in order to be with Columba, then Hinba must be south or south-east of Eigg. This is perhaps not very helpful. But Adomnán does not say that it was the south-wester (*Zephyrus*) which delayed Baithéne on Eigg. All we can safely conclude from this story is that Hinba was some distance from Eigg, separated by a voyage across open sea which could have been held up by contrary winds. Hinba is therefore unlikely to have been Muck, Rum or Canna, or any of the smaller islands of their group. Perhaps unlikely also, though not impossible on these grounds, are the offshore islands of Morar and Moidart, which would not have been made inaccessible by the south-wester; reaching them would only have been prevented by the east wind or the south-easter (the wind which Adomnán calls *Auster* or *Notus*, ii, 46). On the whole, this passage does not support the possibility that Hinba could have been north of Ardnamurchan.[13]

In the passage listed as [C] above, Adomnán introduces the family of Conall mac Domnaill of the Cenél nGabráin. In this episode a certain Lam Dess, 'Right-hand' (modern Gaelic *Lamh Dheas*), is on Hinba with his companions, perpetrating some wicked act, possibly a raid, which led Columba to excommunicate them. A year later, Lam Dess was killed in battle on the island 'which may in Latin be called *Longa*'.[14]

Even if we could be confident that we can identify the island 'which may in Latin be called *Longa*', this cannot be interpreted to mean that Hinba lay nearby. The same family, under its leader Ioan mac Conaill, was also active in Ardnamurchan, where they plundered a friend of Columba's named Colmán. Having done this, in spite of Columba's threats and entreaties, they set sail with their booty from *Aithchambas Artmuirchol*, and were duly drowned by a storm in the waters between Mull (*Malea*) and Coll (*Colosus*). (*VC*, ii, 22) Aithchambas is traditionally identified with Kilchoan Bay, and must certainly have been in western Ardnamurchan, at a point from which Mull and Coll are both visible. The implication is that they were heading for an island to the south, possibly in the Coll/Tiree group or one of the Treshnish Isles, or possibly they were sailing through the Sound of Coll for a destination further south. The story, however, has no connection with Hinba (except the remote one that members of the family of Conall mac Domnaill also visited Hinba at another time), and certainly does not imply, as Lamont thought, that Hinba is Gunna; on his reasoning it might equally be one of the Treshnish Isles.[15]

Senchus fer nAlban records that Gabrán had a son Domnall, though his progeny is not recorded.[16] Conall presumably was his son, and Ioan his grandson. The place of Lam Dess cannot be ascertained; Adomnán calls him an associate rather than a member of the family. The fact that the battle in which he was killed stopped immediately upon his death implies that he was an important personage. Adomnán names his slayer as Cronán mac Baitáin, who has been tentatively identified as a member of the Cenél Loairn.[17]

The family of Conall mac Domnaill is therefore associated with western Ardnamurchan, with the Coll/Tiree group or the Treshnish Isles, with the island of *Longa,* and with Hinba. (Dr Lamont also connects with them a thief called Erc mocu Druidi from Coll, who poached seal calves from the small islands off the Ross of Mull, *VC,* i, 33; for this association there seems to be no warranty in Adomnán.)[18] The best that can be said from all this is that the family of Conall mac Domnaill, under the leadership of Ioan and Lam Dess, was a highly mobile seafaring war-band; to strike at Ardnamurchan, Coll and other islands in the same area, suggests a centre of activity somewhere on or near Mull. Presumably then Hinba must have been within reach of Mull as well; certainly it was within easy reach of Iona, for Columba visited it frequently, and an old man was able to sail from Hinba to Iona when *in extremis.*

In another episode (listed as [D] above), Columba was sought out by four Irish saints, who found him on Hinba. There is a natural temptation to interpret this as meaning, although Adomnán does not say so, that Hinba lay on the direct sea route from Ireland to Iona. The saints in question were Brendan of Clonfert, Comgall of Bangor, Cormac úa Liatháin (who is associated with Durrow), and Cainneach of Aghaboe. If they were sailing from Bangor, their route would have brought them past the Mull of Kintyre, on past Gigha, through the Sound of Islay, past Oronsay and Colonsay probably on their leeward (eastern) side, and on towards Iona. If, on the other hand, they were sailing from Derry, their journey would have taken them from the mouth of Lough Foyle past the windward (western) shores of Islay, Oronsay and Colonsay and on to Iona. Derry is mentioned several times in the *Life of Columba* as a place of embarkation for Iona. (e.g., *VC*, i, 2; ii, 40) Unfortunately Adomnán says nothing more about this synod of Irish monastic founders, all of whom except Comgall were from the south Midlands (Clonfert is in Co. Galway, some 3 km. west of the Shannon; Aghaboe is in Co. Laois; Durrow is in Co. Offaly, just south of the Co. Westmeath boundary). Although it is a natural interpretation of the story that the saints found Columba on Hinba while travelling towards Iona, and that therefore Hinba lay on the direct sea-route between Ireland and Iona, this is not explicitly stated.

The same natural interpretation applies to the last mention of Hinba in Adomnán's *Life* ([G] above), the story of the voyage of Fergna/Virgno. Having learned of the vision of the aged saint concerning Columba's death on Iona, he 'sailed from Ireland and spent the rest of his life in the island of Hinba.' It might seem reasonable to presume that he was heading for Iona, but found 'St Columba's monks' on Hinba and told them the vision that had been recounted to him; perhaps if he had come to Iona first one would expect that Adomnán would have said so. But again this is not stated explicitly.

This story also gives us our only information about the topography of Hinba: namely, that it had a 'great sea-bay', *muirbolc már*, on it, beside which was a hermitage. Size, of course, is relative, and the *muirbolc már* may not in absolute terms have been very big, merely bigger than any smaller sea-bays on the same island. But it may be reasonable to look for a bay which was a dominant feature on the island on which it is found. Some suggested identifications have to be ruled out in that case: Gunna is certainly eliminated, and so is Eileach an Naoimh. Eilean Mór at the mouth of Loch Sween is unlikely for the same reason. Nave Island, off the north-west tip of Islay, falls out of consideration for the same reason; Loch Gruinart nearby, with its ancient cross at Kilnave, is certainly a 'great sea-bay', but Adomnán is explicit that the 'place of the anchorites at *Muirbolc Már*' was on Hinba itself. Jura, on the other hand, has the tidal bay of Inner Loch Tarbert, with the ruined chapel of Tarbert nearby.

We learn only a little of the geography and history of Hinba from the story listed as [F] above. When Columba sends his uncle Ernán to Hinba, he is himself 'venerable', Ernán is an old man, and the monastery on Hinba has been in existence for many years. This implies that Hinba was one of Columba's first foundations in

Scotland, perhaps second in age only to Iona itself. This story again seems to indicate that Hinba was within easy reach of Iona: Columba's uncle Ernán travelled from Hinba to Iona in a state of extreme age and infirmity. This makes a remote island like Eilean Shona highly unlikely.

That leaves only one episode to be considered, that listed as [E] above. This concerns the false penitent Nemán, who refused the indulgence which Columba offered. It is stated that the indulgence was offered by Columba and by Baithéne; but this does not imply that Baithéne was prior of Hinba, only that he was associated with Columba in offering the indulgence – which as Columba's deputy and close companion he naturally would have been. The fact that at some stage in their long association Baithéne was prior of the monastery of Mag Luing on Tiree does not imply that Hinba was subordinate to Mag Luing and therefore in the Coll/Tiree group. It appears more likely that Baithéne was Columba's travelling companion. This episode, then, tells us nothing about the location of Hinba; it does tell us, however, that it was a place where penitents were sent to live a life of great strictness.

It is necessary to make a distinction, not always remembered, between the 'great sea-bay' on Hinba, *Muirbolc Már*, and another place named by Adomnán, *Muirbolc Paradisi*. The latter appears to have been in Ardnamurchan. (*VC*, i, 12) It is totally irrelevant to discussion of the location of Hinba, because *Muirbolc Paradisi* is not associated with an island, while Hinba is called an island by Adomnán on every occasion when he names the place. The fact that *Muirbolc Paradisi* was in Ardnamurchan is no help in locating Hinba.[19]

Before drawing conclusions, it is worthwhile reviewing some identifications which have been proposed in the past. Skene attempted to link Hinba with Eileach an Naoimh in the Garbh Eileach group, probably arising from a desire to give an ancient name to an ancient site; but it has been shown that Eileach an Naoimh is more likely to be identifiable with *Ailech* where St Brendan founded a monastery.[20]

Watson favoured Jura, or possibly Colonsay. This is based on much better arguments; but one is still left with the uncomfortable impression that the identification with Jura is favoured partly because Jura is the largest of the Hebrides whose pre-Viking name is nowhere recorded.[21]

More recently, W D Lamont has suggested Gunna in the Coll-

Tiree group; but his arguments have been shown to be unsatisfactory. Unfortunately, W R MacKay's counter-arguments, that Hinba lay north of Iona, involve important mistakes.[22] Another recent suggestion is Eilean Shona in Loch Moidart, but this presents even greater difficulties.[23]

Any possible contender for the identification has to satisfy the following conditions.

1. The island appears probably, though Adomnán is not explicit about this, to have been on the direct sea route from Ireland to Iona; it was not, however, on the direct sea route which Aedán mac Gabráin took from the mainland to Iona in 574, when he was coming from either Kintyre or Knapdale.
2. It is not an island elsewhere named by Adomnán: so Islay, Mull, Coll, Tiree, etc., are eliminated.
3. It is an island within fairly easy reach of Mull, if we assume that the family of Ioan mac Conaill meic Domnaill were based on Mull; certainly their activities seem to have radiated around Mull. It goes without saying that it was also readily accessible from Iona, because of Columba's frequent visits and Ernán's journey when *in extremis*; and this rules out Eilean Shona in Loch Moidart.
4. It is an island which no longer has its original Gaelic name; almost certainly it now has a Norse name. This alone rules out Eileach an Naoimh.[24]
5. It is an island of which a large sea-bay is a feature. So some small islands with early Christian settlements, e.g. Eileach an Naoimh, Eilean Mór, and Nave Island off Islay, cannot be contenders.
6. We might expect to find early Christian remains there, or at least evidence of an early Christian settlement. A dedication to Colum Cille would not in itself be decisive, but might have significance.
7. If, as Watson argued, Hinba is derived from OI *inbe*, incision, then the island should have some topographical feature suggesting the name; most likely it is cut by the sea to make the great sea-bay.[25]

There are only two possible contenders which fulfil all these qualifications. One is Jura. There is an early Christian chapel at Tarbert dedicated to Colum Cille.[26] The suggestion that Kilernadail represents a dedication to Columba's uncle Ernán is of less weight; Adomnán (*VC*, i, 35) states that Ernán died on Iona, so he was presumably buried there.[27] The deep incision of Loch Tarbert could certainly lead to Jura being called 'Island of the Incision', if that is what Hinba means.

Against the identification of Jura are a number of points, none of them conclusive. It is questionable how far we can speak of Jura, and in particular Tarbert, as being on the direct sea-route from Ireland to Iona. Ships from north-east Ireland, say from Bangor, would be expected to sail through the Sound of Islay, then hold to the lee of Oronsay and Colonsay before crossing the open water towards Iona. To sail up Loch Tarbert would represent a considerable deviation off route. Tarbert would be more directly reached through the Sound of Jura; but sailors from the south would probably not have used the Sound of Jura in preference to the Sound of Islay if they were making for Iona, since this would have involved them in travelling through the Strait of Corryvreckan.[28]

Further, wherever on the mainland Aedán was coming from when he went to Iona in 574, whether from Knapdale or Kintyre, he would have had to pass close to Jura.

The other island which may possibly be identifiable with Hinba is Colonsay/Oronsay. This is admitted as an alternative possibility by Watson and the Andersons.[29] It is on the direct sea-route from Ireland to Iona from wherever in Ireland one might set out: from Bangor or the east coast *via* the Sound of Islay, from Derry or elsewhere in the north and west *via* the Rinns of Islay. It is not on the sea-route from Dunadd or elsewhere in Knapdale or the northern half of Kintyre to Iona. Admittedly ships coming from the Mull of Kintyre to Iona might choose to sail near to Colonsay; but from further north they would not, and we do not know that Aedán was coming directly from the southern end of Kintyre.

Colonsay and Oronsay are not elsewhere clearly named by Adom-nán; they now have Norse names, and their original Gaelic name is lost.[30] They are within easy reach of Mull and Iona. They have a large sea-bay in the tidal strand which separates them at high tide; this feature could well give rise to the name 'Island of the Incision', if that is what Hinba means.

No early Christian remains have yet been found at Oronsay Priory, but, as Steer and Bannerman point out, 'The site is traditionally supposed to have been occupied at an earlier period by a Celtic monastery, and ... the curvilinear wall that encloses the substantial remains of the medieval buildings ... may perpetuate the boundary of an original cashel.'[31] This boundary is absent in eighteenth-century

drawings, but is very suggestive nonetheless.[32] The tradition that
there was an early Christian monastery on Oronsay which had been
founded by St Columba is recorded by Bower.[33] The late fifteenth-
century MacDuffie Cross could have been erected to replace an early
Christian cross; it is traditionally assumed that MacLean's Cross on
Iona did so.[34] The dedication is to St Columba.

Oronsay satisfies all the criteria outlined above. It lacks, however,
any concrete early Christian remains to accompany the shape of its
enclosure, its dedication, and the tradition linking it with the early
Christian period. If the site receives the attention it deserves from
archaeologists, these may yet come to light.[35]

NOTES

1. Cf. *SHR*, lxxii (1993), 213–5.
2. *VC*, i, 33; ii, 26.
3. Ibid., iii, 18.
4. Ibid., i, 41; ii, 22.
5. Ibid., i, 19; ii, 15 (also *Ethetica Terra*); ii, 39; iii, 8.
6. Ibid., i, 22; i, 41; ii, 22.
7. *Ilea* in *VC*, ii, 23; and possibly also the *Elena Insula* of ii, 18. For an
   adjectival formation in -*n*, cf. *Hinbina Insula* in i, 21, elsewhere usually
   Hinba Insula.
8. Ibid., i, 5; ii, 41.
9. Adomnán also names some islands which are difficult to identify:
   Airthrago (possibly an Irish genitive, nom. *Airthraig*), is possibly Eilean
   Shona near the mouth of the Shiel in Loch Moidart (*VC*, ii, 45); *Oidech*,
   gen. *Aithche*, is probably identifiable with *Odeich* or *Oidech*, a 'twenty-
   house land' in Islay (Watson, *CPNS*, 91–2; Bannerman, *Dalriada*, 42,
   46, 48,107), and may be Adomnán's name for the Oa. *Ommon*, i, 36,
   is probably beyond recovery.
10. *Carubdis Brecani* in *VC*, i, 5 is probably in Rathlin Sound rather than
    present-day Corryvreckan. Adomnán's *Rechrú*, *Rechre*, is almost cer-
    tainly Rathlin Island; Watson, *CPNS*, 63, 94.
11. Watson, *CPNS*, 75–7. After prayers to Columba, the wind *Zephyrus*
    was changed round to the *Vulturnus*, which would usually mean the
    south-easter. Anderson (*VC* p. 176 n.) points out that in *De Locis
    Sanctis* Adomnán equates *Vulturnus* with *Caecias*, properly a north-east
    wind. *Vulturnus* must mean a more easterly wind than *Notus*, the south
    or south-east wind which brought Adomnán from Sainea in Loern to
    Iona (see following).

12. Adomnán states that he left Sainea at dawn on 9 June and arrived on Iona at 'the third hour' (i.e., mid-morning), in good time to attend Mass at 'the sixth hour' (i.e. midday), aided by *Auster* or *Notus*. Elsewhere (ii, 15) he speaks of *Auster* (the south wind) aiding a voyage from Iona to Tiree, which lies to the north-west. Dr Bannerman suggests that Sainea is Colonsay (*Dalriada*, 112). Certainly with a south or south-easterly wind the journey from Colonsay to Iona would have been fairly straightforward. But the identification is not certain. It appears that Adomnán was coming from Ireland to Iona 'in the summer after the meeting of the Irish synod' when he was delayed (or driven off course?) by contrary winds 'among the people of the tribe of Loern' (*in plebe generis Loerni*, perhaps should be compared with *de regio Gabrani ortus genere*, 'sprung from the royal tribe of Gabrán' in ii, 23), whence he came to the island of Sainea. Sainea could equally be Jura, or one of the smaller islands of the Firth of Lorn (though probably not Shuna; cf. Watson, *CPNS*, 91).

13. A P Smyth is responsible for the suggestion of Shona in Loch Moidart; see the map in M E Falkus and J B Gillingham (eds), *Historical Atlas of Britain* (1981), 46. But we have seen that Shona is probably Adomnán's *Airthrago* of ii, 45.

14. Despite the similarity of the names, this is perhaps unlikely to be Luing in the Firth of Lorn; this name means 'isle of the ship', and could hardly be latinised as *Insula Longa*. The Latin name means 'long island', perhaps from Gaelic *inis fota*, but is unlikely to refer to the Outer Hebrides which are known by that name today. A possible suggestion, though a remote one, would be the long peninsula at the south-west of Mull, formed by Loch Buie, Loch Uisge, and Loch Spelve, dominated by the 'long ridge' of *Druim Fada*. Adomnán appears elsewhere to name the Oa of Islay as *Insula Oidech*.

15. W D Lamont, 'Where is Adomnán's Hinba?', *Notes and Queries of the Society of West Highland and Island Historical Research*, vii (1978), 3–6; W R MacKay, 'Hinba again', ibid., ix (1979), 8–17; W D Lamont, 'Hinba once more', ibid., xii (1980), 10–15.

16. Bannerman, *Dalriada*, 41, 45, 69.

17. *VC*, p. xxxii.

18. Lamont, opp. cit.

19. But cf. Falkus and Gillingham, *Historical Atlas of Britain*, 46. Watson, *CPNS*, 79, suggests Kentra Bay on the north-east of Ardnamurchan as *Muirbolc Paradisi*. Another argument is that Hinba should be sought near Eigg because Baithéne was prevented from reaching Hinba from Eigg by contrary winds; but if anything, this indicates the contrary. Clearly Eigg and Hinba were separated by a journey across open sea.

20. p. lxxiii; Skene's version of Reeves's edition of *Adomnán's Life of*

Columba (Bannatyne Club, 1874), 318–24; *RCAHMS, Argyll*, v, 182 and nn. on p. 344; see n. 24 below.

21. Watson, *CPNS*, 81–4.

22. Lamont and MacKay, opp.cit.

23. Map in Falkus and Gillingham, *Historical Atlas of Britain*, 46.

24. *RCAHMS, Argyll*, v, 182 and nn. on p. 344. For the likelihood that Eileach an Naoimh is Ailech Brenainn, see Watson, *CPNS*, 81–4; C Plummer, *Vitae Sanctorum Hiberniae* (1910), i, 143; Anderson, *ESSH*, i, 17–18.

25. Watson, *CPNS*, 81–4.

26. *RCAHMS, Argyll*, v, 162.

27. The chapel and burial ground are described in ibid., 163–5.

28. It has already been mentioned that *Carubdis Brecani* in *VC*, i, 5 is probably in Rathlin Sound, not the modern Strait of Corryvreckan north of Jura.

29. Watson, *CPNS*, 81–4; *VC*, p. lxxiii.

30. For Dr Bannerman's suggestion, that Sainea is Colonsay (*Dalriada*, 112), see n. 12 above.

31. K Steer and J W M Bannerman, *Late Medieval Monumental Sculpture in the West Highlands and Islands* (1977), 65.

32. *RCAHMS, Argyll*, v, 230.

33. *Chron. Bower*, i, 6.

34. Marsden, *Columcille*, 47.

35. Both Watson, *CPNS*, 81–4, and the Andersons, *VC*, 1st edn, pp. 153–4, admit Colonsay as an alternative possibility to Jura. Presumably they include Oronsay as part of Colonsay, to which it is joined at low tide. The Andersons suggest that the monastery could perhaps have been elsewhere on Colonsay; they suggest Kiloran Bay, 'where there is land suitable for a monastery'. Since this was written I note that Dr Sharpe, on pp. 306–8 of his translation, has independently reached the suggestion of Oronsay Priory.

Appendix II

The Battles of Aedán mac Gabráin (574-c. 608)

Aedán mac Gabráin was one of the most famous and successful kings of the Gael in Scotland. As well as accounts by Adomnán and in the Irish Annals,[1] he is also remembered in other collections of Irish lore, in Welsh literature, and in the *Historia Ecclesiastica* of the Northumbrian Bede.[2] Clearly he was a hero with a wide reputation.

His reputation probably rests mainly on the number of successful battles which he fought. But the accounts of his battles in Adomnán, the Annals, and other sources are confused and difficult to reconcile. The objective here will be to examine the historical accounts of Aedán's battles, and other events of his life, and to try to reconstruct a chronology for them.

The Annals record the following five battles:

1. *AU* 580. Fecht Orc la hAedán mac Gabráin. (Duplicated under 581. Other Annals, *deest*.)
2. *AU* 582. Bellum Manonn in quo victor erat Aedán mac Gabráin mic Domangairt. (Duplicated under 583)
   AT [582]. Cath Manonn in quo victor erat Aedán mac Gabrán.
3. *AU* 590. Bellum Leithreid la Aedán mac Gabráin.
   AT [590]. Cath Leithrigh la hAedán mac Gabráin.
4. *AU* 596. Iugulatio filiorum Aedáin .i. Brain 7 Domangairt.
   AT [596]. Iugulacio filiorum Aedán .i. Bran 7 Domungort 7 Eochaid Find 7 Artúr i Cath Chirchind in quo victus est Aedán.
5. *AU* 600. Bellum Saxonum in quo victus est Aedán.
   AT [600]. Cath Saxonum la hAedán ubi cecidit Eanfraith frater Etalfraich la Maeluma mac Baedán in quo victus erat.
   AClon. The battle between King Aedan and the Saxons was fought, where Aedan had the victory, and Canfrith [*lege* Eanfrith]

brother of King Æthelfrith was slain by the hand of Moyleawa mac Boylan.

The following points may be noted. The dates of the Battle of Circhenn and the Battle of the Saxons can be checked from other sources, and appear to be dated two or three years too early. The Battle of Circhenn (named as such only in *AT*) is placed in the year following the death of St Columba, which is known to have taken place in 597; so this battle should belong to 598. The Battle of the Saxons is identifiable with Bede's Battle of Degsastan, which he dates to 603.

Secondly, the Annals disagree about the outcome of the Battle of the Saxons. *AU* records a defeat for Aedán; the late translation *AClon* gives him a victory. *AT* has an ambiguous account, which in its present form appears to make Aedán the loser, but by a curious phrase (*in quo victus erat*) which makes little sense in the context, and which is not found elsewhere in *AT*. The usual phrase for a victory is *in quo victor erat*, for a defeat *in quo victus est*. The fourteenth- century MS of *AT* has *in quo vict₃ erat*, using the abbreviation for -us (*₃*) which this MS always uses.[3] The result is a pluperfect, 'is which he had been defeated', implying that after Aedán had been defeated his ally Maeluma slew the (presumably victorious) Eanfrith brother of Æthelfrith. A further problem is that the preposition *la* ('with', 'by', usually translating Latin *apud)* is usually followed by the name of the victor; *la hAedán* should mean '[won] by Aedán'. In the case of a defeat, the name of the loser is normally prefixed by *fri*, 'against', or *for*, 'over'. The entry as it stands reads something like: 'The Battle of the Saxons [was won] by Aedán, in which Eanfrith brother of Æthelfrith was slain by Maeluma mac Baetáin, in which he [i.e., Aedán] had been defeated'.

Of course this does not make any sense. If we were to emend the last phrase to read the more common and intelligible *in quo victor erat*, 'in which he [i.e., Aedán] was the victor', the entry makes sense and is accurately translated by *AClon*. There can be little doubt that this was the intended reading of *AT*. This reconciles *AT* and *AClon*, but leaves them at variance with *AU*. Perhaps *AU*'s text has been emended to accord with Bede's account of the battle of Degsastan.

Adomnán, by contrast, makes specific mention of only two battles involving Aedán and his sons. The first of these was the *Bellum Miathorum*, 'Battle against the Miathi', in which Aedán's sons Eochaid Finn and Artúr were killed; it was fought after Aedán's accession and within the lifetime of St Columba, and can therefore be dated 574 × 597. The second was 'a warlike carnage in Saxonia' in which Domangart was killed (*bellica in strage in Saxonia*), within Aedán's lifetime, but not necessarily within that of Columba (therefore 574 × 608, but subsequent to the Battle against the Miathi).[4]

Clearly Adomnán's version cannot be reconciled easily with the Annals. Although at first sight it might appear that *AT*'s account is a conflation of accounts of two or possibly even three battles, it is not certain which battles these were. The Battle against the Miathi cannot have been the same as the Battle of Circhenn, for three reasons: first, Circhenn = Angus and Mearns, whereas the Miathi must be the *Maeatae* of Dio Cassius, living just north of the Antonine Wall;[5] if the place-name Dumyat (in Logie, Clackmannan) represents one of their hill-forts, they must have extended as far as the Ochil Hills. Second, the Battle of the Miathi took place while Columba was still alive, whereas the Battle of Circhenn happened in the year following his death. Finally, the Battle of the Miathi was a victory for Aedán, but the Battle of Circhenn appears to have been a defeat.

Neither Adomnán nor the Annals are contemporary accounts of sixth-century events, so it is not certain which is to be believed. The Annals show clear signs of confusion, however; one suspects that Adomnán's account may be less complete (in that he mentions only two battles), but otherwise more accurate. It must be remembered that Adomnán's main purpose was to depict Columba's character and special powers, and he only mentions these battles incidentally as part of that depiction. Where Adomnán makes Columba predict an event or witness it by second sight, his description of that event is likely to be reasonably accurate; Adomnán would not have made his hero describe something that was not known, or at least generally believed, to have actually happened.

So assuming that Adomnán's account of these battles is accurate as far as it goes, it remains to try to identify his two battles with two of those described in the Annals. The possibility that the Annals have omitted some engagements of Aedán's exists (they fail to mention his alleged submission to the king of the Ulaid early in his reign, for example), but it is unlikely that they have failed to mention his most important campaigns, of which the Battle of the Miathi was clearly one.

The lands of the Miathi or Maeatae must have approximated very closely to the land of Manaw Gododdin, round the head of the Firth of Forth; the place-names Clackmannan and Slamannon seem to incorporate its oblique form. Some scholars, however, have been unhappy with the equation *bellum Miathorum = bellum Manonn*. Mano (gen Manonn) is also the Irish name for the Isle of Man, so the phrase in the Annals could equally be translated 'the Battle of [the Isle of] Man'. We have no certain evidence that Aedán mac Gabráin ever fought campaigns in Man, but we know that his close and hostile neighbours in Ireland, the Ulaid or Dál Fiatach, did so: they campaigned there in 577 (*AU*), evacuating the island in the following year. It has been argued that they may have fought a second campaign there and again evacuated the island c. 582–3.[6] It has been suggested that if Aedán's bellum Manonn was fought in Man, it may have been connected with the second Ulidian withdrawal.

There are objections, however, to the connection of *bellum Manonn* with Man. The Annals elsewhere call Man Eumania, Eufania, [E]umania (*AU* 577, 578; *AT*, 577, 578), as well as Mano (gen. Manonn, Manann, Manand); Muirchú calls it Euonia, the Welsh Annals have Eubonia (*ACam* 584, 'Bellum contra Euboniam', and 684), and the same form appears in the *Historia Brittonum* (caps. 8, 14). Even if we accept O'Rahilly's argument that 'the first expedition of the Ulaid implies that there was a second', we do not need to accept that it took place in 581 or 582; since the Ulaid were in Man in 577 and were turned back (*reversio Uloth*) from Man in 578, we should assume that the first expedition (*periculum*) was followed by a second in the following year, unless we wish to believe that the Ulidian army overwintered in Man in 577–8. Dark Age warfare consisted usually of short seasonal campaigns, and did not normally involve overwintering; it was an occasion for comment when the Vikings began this practice. Anderson has pointed out that the Annalists believed that Aedán's victory at Mano took place some five years after the withdrawal of the Ulaid from Man.[7]

Furthermore, it is not clear whether Aedán is claimed to have been acting in Man as an opponent or an ally of the Ulaid. An Irish antiquarian tract later claimed that Aedán mac Gabráin submitted (*giallais*, lit. 'became hostage') to Baetán mac Cairill, king of the Ulaid, at Ros na Ríg in Seimne (= Island Magee) sometime early in his reign (Baetán died in *AU* 581);[8] it is not clear how this incident is related to the Convention of Druim Cett (dated in the Annals to 575; but on its date, see below), which forged an alliance between

Aedán and Aed mac Ainmirech, king of Cenél Conaill and Northern Uí Néill overking.[9] We would not expect to find Aedán acting as a client or ally of the Ulaid in the late 570s, and certainly not as late as 582, after Baetán's death. On the other hand, the tract does not support the alternative view, that Aedán drove the Ulaid out of Man after Baetán's death (*AU* 581); for it says 'in the second year after his death the Gaidil abandoned Man'. This would be c. 582 or 583, round about the time of bellum Manonn; but if bellum Manonn was a victory for Aedán in Man, we would not expect to find him abandoning his conquest straight afterwards. There is, in fact, no concrete evidence to connect Aedán mac Gabráin with the Isle of Man.

There is, on the other hand, plenty of evidence to connect him with east central Scotland. Adomnán mentions the Miathi, occupying the same area; a later battle took place in Circhenn, Mearns; Aedán's son Eochaid Buide was called 'king of the Picts' at his death; another Pictish king, Gartnait, appears to have been his son; his grandson Domnall Brecc died fighting in Strathcarron; late medieval Scottish chronicles record a tradition that Aedán fought against the Picts;[10] finally, the ninth-century *Tripartite Life of St Patrick* makes Patrick predict greatness for the descendants of Fergus Mór in Fortrenn – a prophecy which was reportedly fulfilled when Aedán mac Gabráin 'seized Alba by Force'.[11] Of course this *Life* is not evidence for St Patrick or his relations with Fergus Mór, but it tells us what ninth-century writers believed about Aedán mac Gabráin's career: namely, that Aedán had 'seized Alba by force' and 'ruled in Fortrenn'.

We cannot be certain that this dramatic expansion of the Dál Riata was the result of a single decisive victory; it is perhaps more likely to have been the result of a series of campaigns. What we can say with confidence is that the Battle of the Miathi was an important episode in it, of such importance that an Iona annalist would have been unlikely to omit it. It could not have been the *fecht Orc* (580), *cath Chirchinn* (598), or *bellum Saxonum* (603). By elimination that leaves a choice between *bellum Manonn* (582) and *bellum Leithreid/Leithrigh* (590).

Another objection to the equation Miathi = Mano rests in the fact that Adomnán describes the Miathi as 'barbarians,' whereas Bede states that the southern Picts had previously been converted to Christianity by Ninian, long before Columba's time. To this it can be replied first of all that it is not certain that by *barbari* Adomnán meant pagans; his barbarians seem to be Pictish tribes dwelling across Drumalban, who are sometimes pagans (like the laymen beside the River Ness), but not necessarily always so. On one occasion Adomnán makes Columba speak of 'barbarous and foreign nations', in apposition to the nations of the *Scoti*, as people who would bestow honour upon Iona; presumably if they were honouring Iona, they could hardly be pagans as well.[12] And secondly, the traces of Ninian's mission, whenever it took place, are slight; there is no evidence for universal Christianity south of the Mounth by Columba's time, and Ninian is otherwise so obscure that it would not be surprising if Adomnán had not heard of him or his mission.[13] So this argument does not seriously weaken the possibility of the equation.

Two Welsh 'triads' allude cryptically to military exploits of Aedán mac Gabráin. One refers to the 'faithful warband' of 'Gafran map Aeddan' (for which read Aeddan map Gafran) 'who went to sea for their lord', or, in a different version of the triad, 'at the time of his complete disappearance'.[14] The implication of the triad, in which examples are enumerated of faithful warbands which were destroyed because of their fidelity to their lord, is that this expedition ended in disaster. Of the battles mentioned in the Annals, this cannot refer to the Battle of Man or Manaw, which was a victory, or to either the Battle of Circhenn or the Battle of the Saxons, which were land battles. The Battle of the Orkneys appears also to have been a success for Aedán. It is possible that the triad is alluding to some incident which is not recorded in the Annals: possibly to Aedán's submission to the king of the Ulaid, which definitely involved going to sea and was a setback for Aedán. The circumstances which caused his warband to be singled out as exceptionally faithful to their lord are unknown.

The other mention in a Welsh 'triad' of a military expedition by Aedán describes an 'unrestrained ravaging' whereby 'Aedán the Wily (*bradawc*) came to Dumbarton, to the court of Rhydderch Hael; he left neither food nor drink nor beast alive.'[15] Rhydderch Hael map Tudwal was a contemporary king of Dumbarton, who died c. 614. This description of hostility between him and Aedán seems to run counter to the account of relations between Rhydderch and the Dál Riata given by Adomnán. Adomnán states that Rhydderch was a friend of Columba's who sent a secret message to the saint desiring to know whether he would die by the hand of an enemy. Columba in reply predicted that he would never fall into the hands of his enemies, but would die peacefully in his own bed.[16] King Rhydderch's *occulta legatio* to Columba may have been to Adomnán another opportunity to display Columba's marvellous powers of prophecy, but to us it gives a rare and fascinating insight into secret diplomacy in the sixth century. Although Adomnán does not say so, we can be in no doubt that Rhydderch was secretly seeking an assurance from Columba that Aedán would not attack him; and apparently, Columba gave such an assurance. What we do not know is whether this was before or after Aedán's 'unrestrained ravaging' of Dumbarton. If it was before, then Aedán may have broken a promise made through Columba, and perhaps thus earned his uncomplimentary Welsh nickname, *bradawc*, 'wily'.[17] If it was after, then Rhydderch was perhaps trying to make peace following Aedán's plundering, seeking and receiving an assurance from Columba that it would not be repeated. Either interpretation would fit Adomnán's story.

Of the five battles mentioned in the Annals, the only one which could have been fought in Strathclyde is *bellum Leithreid/Leithrigh* (590). *Fecht Orc, Cath Chirchinn* and *bellum Saxonum* can all be identified with different places; *bellum Manonn*, as we have seen, is more problematic, but neither of its possible locations is in Strathclyde. So (by process of elimination) if Aedán's 'unrestrained ravaging' against Dumbarton was remembered at all in the Irish Annals, it must have been as *bellum Leithreid*. The place cannot now be identified; but there are a number of places in Lennox incorporating the first element *leth-* or *leitir*: e.g. Letter near Killearn, or Leddriegreen beside Kirkton of Strathblane.

There is a likelihood that Aedán's plundering was remembered in Irish folk-tales. The lost tale *Orgain Sratha Cluada* ('The Slaughter of Strathclyde'), which appears in learned lists of Irish tales, is usually assumed to refer to the Viking siege of Dumbarton in 870. But if so it is slightly unusual, since most tales with historical subjects refer to an earlier time.[18] It may be more likely that this tale referred to the same incident as that described in the Welsh 'triad', which combined slaughter with plunder. Aedán appears as a hero in a number of surviving tales, such as *Scela Cano meic Gartnáin*,[19] *Gein Brandub maic Echach ocus Aedáin maic Gabráin*,[20] and *Compert Mongain*;[21] he was also the hero of a lost tale, *Echtra Aedáin maic Gabráin*.[22] Aedán is also a stock-character in hagiography, as in the *Life of St Berach* and the *Acta Sancti Lasriani*.[23] But the lost tale *Orgain Sratha Cluada* may refer to events that actually took place.

If, as I am suggesting, Columba was trying to make peace between Aedán mac Gabráin and Rhydderch Hael round about the time of Aedán's 'ravaging', perhaps we should view his visit to the court of Bridei son of Mailcon beside the River Ness as serving a similar diplomatic purpose, perhaps in relation to the *fecht Orc* (580). Adomnán states that Bridei held sway over the Orkneys and held hostages of its king.[24] Aedán could not have attacked the Northern Isles without incurring his displeasure; so perhaps Columba was dispatched to make peace between them. Adomnán's account implies disturbed conditions in the Great Glen, with raids and the destruction of villages, and he speaks of Columba's efforts to secure the release of a Gaelic woman who was being held as a slave by Broichan, King Bridei's chief druid and foster-father.[25] So there are hints here of slave-raiding, and it may be that Aedán's attack on the Orkneys was a counter-raid or retaliation. If so, we could place Columba's visit (or one of his visits) to King Bridei c. 580, as an attempt to make peace and redeem captives.

A caveat has to be entered here that the entry in *AU* is in the Irish vernacular. There is good reason to believe that the earliest stratum in *AU* relating to Iona was a collection of Latin Annals, which are preserved in Latin in *AU* and partially translated into Irish in *AT*. The entry mentioning the *fecht Orc* is unique to *AU*, where it is duplicated under the following year; so it cannot be checked against any other source. There is a suspicion that it is a late entry, and not part of the earliest stratum of Iona material in *AU*.[26]

Accounts of the battle which took place in the year following St Columba's death (*AU* 596, but correctly c. 598) are confused:

AU 596. Iugulatio filiorum Aedáin .i. Brain ⁊ Domangairt.

AT [596]. Iugulacio filiorum Aedán .i. Bran ⁊ Domungort ⁊ Eochaid Find ⁊ Artúr i Cath Chirchind in quo victus est Aedán.

AT cannot be correct in adding the names of Eochaid Finn and Artúr, who died at the Battle against the Miathi during Columba's lifetime; but it may be correct in naming the engagement as *Cath Chirchinn*, the 'Battle of Mearns'. We have seen that Adomnán states that Domangart mac Aedáin was killed 'in a warlike carnage in Saxonia', some time after the battle against the Miathi. That must be a reference to the Battle of the Saxons in *AU* 600 (correctly c. 602/3), Bede's Battle of Degsastan. If a son of Aedán's was killed in Circhenn, it was perhaps Bran. But it must be noted that the sons of Aedán named by Adomnán and in the Annals are at variance with the genealogies in *Senchus fer nAlban*, which give Aedán seven sons (Eochaid Finn, Eochaid Buide, Tuathal, Bran, Baithine, Conaing and Gartnait), and number Domangart and Artúr among the sons of Conaing mac Aedáin. Dr Bannerman has shown good reasons for believing that Gartnait king of the Picts (died *AT* [599], probably correctly two or three years later) was a son of Aedán mac Gabráin,[27] even though he is given a different patronymic in the Pictish king-list. Aedán may have had other sons as well. Adomnán tells an anecdote about a 'very powerful' layman of the *Corcu Reti* whom he calls *Goreus filius Aidani*, i.e. Guaire mac Aedáin of the Dál Reti or Dál Riata.[28] The name Aedán was common, but not particularly so, and the Andersons may well be right in their suggestion that this man was a son of the king. If so, he is not otherwise known. Certainty regarding Aedán's offspring, their careers and deaths, seems to be impossible.

We must turn finally to the account given by Bede of Aedán's last recorded battle, against the Angles of Northumbria at Degsastan.[29] This describes how Aedán, aroused by reports of growing Northumbrian power, gathered a mighty army and marched against Æthelfrith; but at a place called Degsastan most of his army was destroyed, and he fled with few survivors. In the same battle Æthelfrith's brother Theobald was slain with almost the whole army which he led. Bede supplies the date 603, whereas the date seemingly implied by the Annals is c. 602. Thereafter, says Bede, no king of the Scots in Britain has dared to make war against the English until his own time.

This account is rather puzzling. It comes at the end of Book I of the *HE*, but bears little relation to the material that precedes and follows it. It appears to have been interpolated, rather clumsily, after the bulk of the *HE* had been drafted. It is not certain where Bede got the story from; some of his northern information came from Pictish sources, but this account cannot have reached him through that channel. The name of the battle and its date (which Bede gives by *annus Domini*, by the imperial year, and by Æthelfrith's regnal year) cannot have come from a Pictish or Gaelic source, and cannot have been calculated in relation to the death of St Columba. Even more confusing is his account of the outcome of the battle itself: Aedán was defeated and fled with few survivors while his army was destroyed, but at the same time Æthelfrith's brother Theobald was killed with almost all his army. The only circumstances under which both these statements can be true would be in a battle with very heavy casualties on both sides, including the death of one of the English leaders. We have seen that *AClon*, and probably the exemplar of *AT*, awarded Aedán the victory, and mention the death of Eanfrith brother of Æthelfrith. Possibly *AU*'s abbreviated account has been influenced by Bede. Adomnán knew of 'a warlike carnage in Saxonia' fought within Aedán's lifetime, in which his son Domangart was killed. On the whole, the evidence suggests a battle with very heavy casualties on both sides, in which both could claim a Pyrrhic victory. It could well be true that after such an encounter neither Aedán nor his successors would venture to attack Northumbria again; but the battle was probably not the resounding victory for Æthelfrith which Bede claims.

Bede may be correct, however, in naming the king's brother as Theobald; he is more likely to have had access to accurate Northumbrian genealogical information, and the Annals may have erred in naming him as Eanfrith because Æthelfrith had a son of that name.[30] The site of the battle has not been identified. Skene's suggestion, Dawston Burn in upper Liddesdale, has not been widely accepted, but neither have any of the suggested alternatives.

Together with these battles, we must consider two other events: Aedán's submission to Baetán mac Cairill, king of the Ulaid, in Island Magee, and the Convention of Druim Cett. The latter is dated to 575 in *AU*, and until recently this date has not been questioned. But Richard Sharpe has pointed out that a date so early in Aedán's reign leaves certain problems.[31] Aed mac Ainmirech, the Uí Néill king with whom Aedán was negotiating, appears not yet to have been king in that year, or for some years thereafter; he may have become king of Cenél Conaill in 586.[32] Furthermore, two royal personages named as present at the Convention, Domnall mac Aedo (later king of Cenél Conaill and overking of the Uí Néill) and Scandlán mac Colmáin (later king of the Osraige), died very much later (Domnall in *AU* 642, Scandlán in *AT* 644). Domnall is described as a child at the time; Scandlán is not, though it may be taken as implied that he was a child or a young man (Columba addresses him as 'son' and prophesies a career for him stretching over more than thirty years). If the meeting took place as early as 575, then both Domnall and Scandlán must have lived well into their seventies or even eighties. As Dr Sharpe points out, Adomnán's account of these meetings would be more credible if the Convention took place some years later than 575.

Another point against so early a date, which has not been otherwise noted, is that it makes the first year of Aedán's reign curiously crowded. I wholeheartedly accept Dr Byrne's interpretation of the Convention as 'an alliance between Aedán mac Gabráin and Aed mac Ainmirech' against the Ulaid;[33] this must have been related in some way to Aedán's supposed submission. So if the Convention met in 575, it follows that Aedán must have come to power by his victory in Kintyre in 574, then hurried to Iona to meet with Columba in the same year, then gone to Antrim and made a submission (probably not voluntarily, and perhaps involving a disaster to his warband) to Baetán mac Cairill, been back in Scotland in the spring or early summer of 575 in time to persuade Columba to intercede for him with Aed mac Ainmirech, and returned to Ireland the same summer with Columba to meet with Aed near Limavady. Even for a very active king like Aedán mac Gabráin, such frequent and rapid movement is well nigh incredible. By removing the Convention from the first year of Aedán's reign, his diary of engagements for this period becomes less crowded.

So when are these events to be entered? Aedán's submission to Baetán mac Cairill (d. *AU* 581) in Island Magee must belong 574 × 581. The Convention of Druim Cett must belong, if we reject *AU*'s 575, to 586 × 597. We know that Columba was in the Irish Midlands some time in the late 580s, when Durrow was founded and he met with Ailither of Clonmacnoise; possibly his meeting with Aed Sláne king of Brega took place during the same visit. Perhaps the meeting at Druim Cett occurred during a different visit, since Adomnán makes it clear that Columba went north to Coleraine straight afterwards, presumably to return to Iona. It is unlikely to have taken place in 590, the year of Aedán's campaign resulting in his victory of Lethreid. It is also unlikely to have taken place during the last three or four years of Columba's life, when he sensed impending death and became increasingly infirm.[34] The latest likely date, then, would be c. 594 or 595; if the event has been misplaced by one nineteen-year cycle in an Easter table, it could belong to 594. It is perhaps unlikely to have been too many years earlier.

We could tentatively reconstruct the list of Aedán's battles and related events as follows.

c. 574. The battle of Teloch/Delgú in Kintyre, by which Aedán came to power. Defeat and death of Dúnchad mac Conaill. It is not clear whether the 'many allies of the sons of Gabrán' who also fell were fighting on Aedán's side or against him.[35]

574 × 581. Aedán's submission to the king of the Ulaid at Island Magee in Co. Antrim. Possibly alluded to in a Welsh 'triad' which hints at a disaster for Aedán's 'faithful war-band' after they had gone to sea.

580. A raid against the Orkneys(?). Possibly part of a series of hostilities between Aedán and Bridei f. Mailcon, king of the Northern Picts. Columba's mission to Bridei's court on the River Ness may have been connected with these raids, and seemingly involved negotiations for the release of at least one prisoner. The fact that the sole account of this battle is in *AU* and is in Gaelic casts doubt on its earliness and accuracy.

582. The battle of Mano, probably Adomnán's battle against the Miathi. A great victory for Aedán, despite the deaths of his sons Eochaid Finn and Artúr. Aedán is left as master in central Scotland, and his son Gartnait becomes king of the Picts at this time or soon after.[36]

590. The battle of Leithreid, probably in Strathclyde. This may be the 'unrestrained ravaging' alluded to in a Welsh 'triad', and also the subject of a lost Irish tale, *Orgain Sratha Cluada*, 'The Slaughter of Strathclyde'.

586 × 597; possibly c. 594. The Convention of Druim Cett. Probably in essence an offensive and defensive alliance between Aedán and Aed mac Ainmirech against the Ulaid, negotiated by Aed's cousin St Columba.

598. The battle of Circhenn (= Mearns). A rare defeat for Aedán, possibly involving the death of his son Bran.

c. 603. The battle of Degsastan against Æthelfrith of Northumbria. An indecisive carnage, involving the deaths of Æthelfrith's brother (called either Eanfrith or more likely Theobald), and of Aedán's son Domangart. As a result, no king of the Dál Riata dared to attack Northumbria for more than a century.

This is not the only possible interpretation of the evidence. But it seems to me to be the most likely. The overall impression is that Aedán recovered from setbacks early in his reign to become very aggressive and successful in the 580s and 590s. In the last decade of his reign, perhaps as a result of over-expansion, he again suffered reverses, including an indecisive but very costly battle against

Northumbria. But for the most part, Aedán was as successful as he was ambitious.

NOTES

1. *VC*, i, 8, 9, 49; iii, 5; *AU*, s.a. 580, 582, 590, 596, 600, 606; also in *AT*, *AClon*, *CS*, and *AFM* for the same period.
2. R Bromwich, *Trioedd Ynys Prydein* (2nd edn, 1978) (hereafter *TYP*), nos. 29, 54; *Bede's Ecclesiastical History of the English People*, ed. B Colgrave and R A B Mynors (Oxford, 1969) (hereafter Bede, *HE*), i, 34. For Irish references, see below, nn. 19–23.
3. Oxford, Bodleian Library, MS Rawlinson B. 488, fo. 9r.
4. *VC*, i, 8, 9.
5. Translated in J C Mann and R G Penman, *Literary Sources for Roman Britain* (LACTOR, 11, 1978) (hereafter *LSRB*), 28–30.
6. Cf. J W M Bannerman, *Studies in the History of Dalriada* (1974), 83–4; T F O'Rahilly, *Early Irish History and Mythology* (1946), 503–5.
7. VC, (1st edn), p. 44.
8. W F Skene, *Chronicles of the Picts, Chronicles of the Scots, and other early Memorials of Scottish History* (1867) (hereafter *Chron. Picts-Scots*), 127–9; A O Anderson, *Early Sources of Scottish History* (1922) (hereafter Anderson, *ESSH*), i, 87–8.
9. Bannerman, *Dalriada*, 157–70; F J Byrne, *Irish Kings and High-Kings* (1973), 110–11.
10. *Chron. Fordun*, lib. iii, cap. 27.
11. *AU*, s.a. 629, 642; Anderson, *ESSH*, i, 121–3; Bannerman, *Dalriada*, 92–4; *Tripartite Life of St Patrick of c. 900*: ed. W Stokes (2 vols, RS, 1887), i, 162.
12. Adomnán mentions *barbari* in i, 8, 46; ii, 27; iii, 23.
13. On Ninian, see chapter 3 above, and A Macquarrie, 'The Date of St Ninian's Mission: a Reappraisal', *RSCHS*, xxiii (1987), 1–25, and works there cited.
14. Bromwich, *TYP*, no. 29.
15. Ibid., no. 54.
16. *VC*, i, 15.
17. Bromwich, *TYP*, no. 54 (p. 147), pp. 239, 264; Bannerman, *Dalriada*, 88–9.
18. P Mac Cana, *The Learned Tales of Medieval Ireland* (1980), 47, 61, 100. The assumption is made, e.g., in Anderson, *ESSH*, i, 301, n. 2.
19. *Scela Cano meic Gartnáin*, ed. D A Binchy (Dublin Institute for Advanced Studies, Medieval and Modern Irish Series, vol. 18, 1963); English summary by M Dillon in *The Cycle of the Kings* (1946), 79–83.
20. Summarised in Watson, *CPNS*, 53 and n; Bannerman, *Dalriada*, 89.

21. K Meyer and A T Nutt (eds), *The Voyage of Bran* (1895), i, 42–5; Bannerman, *Dalriada*, 88; Anderson, *KKES*, 149.

22. Mac Cana, *Learned Tales*, 45. 'Echtrai' were journeys or adventures (cf. OI *echtar*, outside or beneath) often to the Otherworld; ibid., 75–6.

23. C Plummer, *Vitae Sanctorum Hiberniae* (1910), i, 34–5; Watson, *CPNS*, 225; Bannerman, *Dalriada*, 85, 87.

24. *VC*, ii, 42.

25. Ibid., ii, 33.

26. Cf. Anderson in *VC* (1st edn), p. 44.

27. Bannerman, *Dalriada*, 92–4.

28. *VC*, i, 47.

29. Bede, *HE*, i, 34.

30. Ibid., iii, 1.

31. Adomnán of Iona, *Life of St Columba*, ed. R Sharpe (1995), 312–14.

32. Byrne, *Kings*, 110–11.

33. Byrne, *Kings*, 111; if Baetán was in fact dead, the Dál Riata and Uí Néill would have had more freedom of action. Cf. Anderson, *KKES*, 148–9.

34. *VC*, iii, 22, 23.

35. *Telocho* in *AU*, apparently the gen. of a *u*-stem, nom. **Teloch*; *Delgon* in *AT*, apparently the gen. of an *n*-stem, nom. **Delgú*. This place has not been identified.

36. Gartnait f. Domelch (Domech, Domnach, etc.) is assigned a reign of *xx* (or in two MSS *xi*) years following Bridei f. Mailcon in the Pictish regnal lists; he died c. 599 (*AT*). Cf. Anderson, *KKES* (2nd edn), 248, 262, 266, 272, 280, 287, 292. If *xi* is correct, his accession must have been c. 587; but *AU* places the death of Bridei in 584, and *AT* places it in the year following the Battle of Mano, i.e., c. 583. If Gartnait reigned for about 15 (*xv*) years, this was perhaps c. 584–599; or he may have been recognised as king in southern Pictland while Bridei was still living.

5

St Kentigern of Glasgow

The founder and patron saint of the church of Glasgow has always, and rightly, been regarded as a very obscure figure.[1] We possess no authentic writings by him, as we do for St Patrick; there is no early and reliable *Life* comparable to Adomnán's *Vita Columbae*; unlike St Ninian, he is unknown to Bede. What we do appear to possess for St Kentigern is a date for his death which may be reasonably reliable. Apart from this, we must fall back on a hagiographic *corpus* which in its present form does not antedate the mid-twelfth century.

The obit of a Kentigern, possibly a bishop, is recorded in the *Annales Cambriae* appended to a MS of the *Historia Brittonum* in BL MS Harl. 3859, s.a. [612].[2] The entry reads: *Conthigirni obitus et Dibric episcopi*. Since no other Kentigern is known, and the name *Conthigirnus*, meaning 'hound-lord', could give later Welsh *Cyndeyrn*,[3] whence modern Kentigern (presumably through an intermediate Gaelic *Ceanntigearn*),[4] it is very likely that this is the obit of St Kentigern of Glasgow. The Harleian annals are continuous down to the mid-tenth century, which is probably the time at which they reached their present form. For the sixth and early seventh centuries they contain a number of northern entries (with Phillimore's bracketed dates):

[521] Sanctus Columcille nascitur.
[558] Gabran filius Dungart moritur.
[562] Columcille in Britannia exiit.
[595] Columcille moritur.
[607] Aidan map Gabran moritur.
[612] Conthigirni obitus...
[627] Belin moritur.

Most of these bracketed dates seem in fact to be one or two years too early; Columba came to Scotland in 563 and died in 597, and of the kings of the Dál Riata Gabrán may have died as late as 560 and his son Aedán in 608 or 609.[5] Thus there may be grounds for believing that the death of Kentigern occurred a year or two later than the bracketed date assigned in Phillimore's edition, perhaps c. 614.[6] The fact that Kentigern's obit does not contain the *moritur* formula common to the others can be easily explained, since it has been combined with the otherwise unconnected notice of the death of Bishop Dibric.

As far as Kentigern's hagiography is concerned, several scholars have pointed out that there are a number of different strata detectable within the twelfth-century *Lives*, and attempts have been made to analyse and separate these.[7] However, some points made in earlier examinations remain open to question, and so it is worthwhile examining the problem afresh, attempting to isolate the material which is of historical value from that which is not, and attempting to offer a hypothetical reconstruction of the main points of the historical life of St Kentigern.

The starting point must be the two twelfth-century *Lives*, the earlier of them fragmentary and anonymous, the later complete and the acknowledged work of a well-known and experienced hagiographer, Jocelin of Furness. The anonymous *Life* (hereafter cited as H) was composed for Bishop Herbert of Glasgow (1147–1164) by a 'clerk of St Kentigern' who was not himself a Scot but who had settled at Glasgow Cathedral. He was familiar with Symeon of Durham's *Life of St Cuthbert*, and announced his intention to treat St Kentigern's life in the same way. His *Life*, he claimed, was drawn together 'from the material found in the little book of his virtues, and oral traditions told to me by reliable people' (*de materia in virtutum eius codicello reperta, et viva voce fidelium michi relata*).[8] H is fragmentary in that it consists only of a prologue and eight chapters, which describe the conception of St Kentigern, the tribulations and deliverance of his mother, called Thaney, and the saint's birth. It breaks off immediately after St Kentigern's birth, although the author has promised to 'describe his life and miracles' (*vitam et miracula descripturus*). What has survived, then, is only a fragment of a much longer work, whose original size can only be guessed.

The second *Life* (hereafter cited as J) was composed by Jocelin of Furness during the episcopate of Bishop Jocelin of Glasgow (1175–1199). Professor Jackson has suggested that it must have been composed before 1185, when Jocelin of Furness left that Cistercian monastery and settled at Downpatrick in Northern Ireland; if so, it seems that Bishop Jocelin was planning well in advance by commissioning a new *Life* for his founder saint at least twelve years before the dedication of his new church (1197).[9] The monk of Furness states that he has wandered about through the broad and narrow streets of the city of Glasgow, seeking for a *Life* which would be of greater authority and accuracy and in a better style than that which was in regular use in the cathedral (*quam vestra frequentat ecclesia*); this *Life*, he says, is in an unkempt style, and at the very beginning is marred by a narration which is contrary to sound doctrine and Catholic teaching. During his search he found 'another little volume, dictated in a Gaelic style' (*codiculum alium, stilo Scottico dictatum*), full of solecisms, but containing the life and acts of the saint. This he has taken from its barbarous wrappings, and has set himself the task 'to stitch together the material collected from both books' (*ex utroque libello materiam collectam redintegrando sarcire*).[10]

At first sight it must appear that when Jocelin refers to the *Life* 'which is regularly used in your church' he is referring to the *Life* commissioned by Bishop Herbert, and so it has been taken by Professor Jackson and some other scholars; but a close examination of both reveals that this is not so. Professor Jackson's comments, that 'it has always been assumed previously that it was' and that 'it would require very strong arguments indeed to make one believe that another *Life* had superseded the Herbertian one in this short interval' of some thirty years, are unconvincing.[11] H itself was written to supplant an earlier *Life*, 'the little book of his virtues', and it could equally be the case that this is the *Life* mentioned by Jocelin 'which is regularly used in your church', which H in fact had failed to supplant. On a close examination of both it becomes apparent that J is independent of H. The *Life* which Jocelin criticised for containing a narration contrary to sound doctrine and Catholic teaching must have stated that Kentigern was born of a virgin. His mother, out of devotion to the Blessed Virgin, often prayed for a virginal conception, and was eventually found to be with child, though she could not name the father. Jocelin suggested that Kentigern was perhaps conceived while his mother was anaesthetised, so that she had no sinful knowledge; he was thus able to maintain her spiritual purity while denying to her a virginal conception, such as was asserted by the foolish people of the area.[12]

The story in H is quite different. The author knows the tradition that Kentigern was virginally conceived, but he asserts that his mother was violently raped by a man dressed as a woman; thus he too preserves her innocence, but Kentigern is given a natural father, 'because without the male sex the petition of this virgin could not have been fulfilled' (*quoniam absque sexu virili virginis huius nequibat explicari petitio*).[13] There is nothing here which could be called contrary to sound doctrine or Catholic teaching, which is the accusation in J.

There are other differences as well. In H, Kentigern's mother is called Thaney; in J, she is nameless until St Serf christens her Taneu. H knows the name of Kentigern's natural father, Ewen f. Erwegende (i.e., Ywain map Urien); J does not, and regards it as irrelevant to investigate the identity of the father (*sane absurdum et ab re arbitramur, diutius indagare quis quomodo sator terram araverit vel severit*).[14] H abounds in proper names: Thaney's father is *Leudonus*, king of *Leudonia* (i.e., Lothian); when her pregnancy is discovered, Thaney is placed in a wagon on the precipitous hill of *Kepduf*, three miles from the sea, and driven over the edge; when this does not have the desired effect, she is placed in a boat at *Aberlessic* and cast adrift; the boat carries her out as far as *Insula May*, then back up the Firth [of Forth] to deposit her at *Colenros*; meanwhile Leudonus is murdered at another hill, called *Dumpelder*, near which his monument still stands. This displays considerable local knowledge, down to the existence of a standing stone at the foot of Traprain Law (= Dumpelder).[15] Kepduf and Aberlessic are unidentified, though the *Aberdeen Breviary* identified the latter with Aberlady.[16] J does not know Ewen, Leudonus, Kepduf, Aberlessic, or the Isle of May; he does know Dunpelder (spelt with *n*), but names it as the hill from which Kentigern's mother is thrown (without, in this case, the assistance of a wagon). Both *Lives* introduce St Serf (*Servanus*) and give him a short speech in Gaelic; but H makes him say *A Dia, cur fir sin!* (O God, may this be true!), while J makes him exclaim *Mochohe, mochohe!* (My dear one, my dear one!). This may find a faint echo in H's Latin speech for St Serf, *Deo gratias, hic enim erit carus meus!* (Thanks be to God, for he shall be my dear one!), but the correspondence is remote and indirect. In short, H cannot be the source of J, although they both tell broadly the same story: namely, that an East Lothian princess believed herself to have conceived a child in virginity, was punished by her pagan father by being first cast from a hilltop and then set adrift in the sea, and finally landed at Culross where she and her child were cared for by St Serf. H's account is full of personal and place-names, J's is not. Both consider the virginal conception to be a problem, but each explains it in a different way so as not to compromise Teneu's virtue.

Professor MacQueen has pointed out that there are certain parallels between H's story of Kentigern's conception and a Welsh romance concerning Owain map Urien (H's Ewen f. Erwegende). He has also pointed out that the *Aberdeen Breviary lectiones* for the Life of St Baldred of Tynninghame assert that he was the first to commit to memory the facts of the life of St Kentigern. Baldred is stated in the *Historia Dunelmensis Ecclesiae* attributed to Symeon of Durham to have died in 756.[17] Professor MacQueen argues that the connection with Baldred could account for the East Lothian material in the two *Lives*, with Baldred's account incorporating some Glasgow material which could be even earlier, say c. 650–700. He concludes that J is based on Baldred and on the *Life* 'dictated in a Gaelic style', which he would date c. 800, while H 'has no demonstrable connection with Baldred, but seems to be based, at least partially, on the Scottish work'.[18]

These arguments are somewhat puzzling. The curious statement that Baldred of Tynninghame committed to memory the facts of the life of St Kentigern (*Beatissimum Kentigernum preceptorem suum sueque vite sanctitatem iugi meditacione contemplando commendabat memorie*) cannot be dismissed lightly, as Professor Jackson would dismiss it;[19] but if he is the source of the East Lothian material, then his work must underlie H, with its wealth of circumstantial detail, as well as J. Ultimately they do seem to have a common source, probably the lost *Life* in regular use in Glasgow Cathedral, which may have incorporated material attributed to Baldred, said to have been Kentigern's disciple. This presumably had the story of the virginal conception, which H glossed over by recourse to the romance of Owain map Urien. The historical Ywain, son of Urien Rheged (d. c. 590), appears to have been a younger contemporary of St Kentigern, and cannot have been his father.[20] But H is full of topographical detail about East Lothian and Bretonnic proper names, and shows no sign of any connection with a *Life* 'dictated in a Gaelic style'; up until the point where it introduces St Serf just before it fails us, H seems to belong to a British cultural *milieu*.[21]

It appears, then, that from the outset we are dealing with four sources which were all in existence in the twelfth century. Of these J alone survives in its entirety; H exists as a fragment; and two others, the *Life* which was regularly used in the cathedral (*quam frequentat vestra ecclesia*, hereafter cited as F) and the *codiculum* 'dictated in a Gaelic style' (*stilo Scottico*, hereafter referred to as S), are mentioned in J but are now completely lost. The conception and birth story in H and J must ultimately have a common original, probably F. It is probable that H was written to supplant F, which was considered unsuitable because of its unsound story of a virginal conception; if so, it failed to dislodge F from its position in use in the cathedral, and a new *Life*, J was commissioned, which glossed over the virginal conception much more discreetly. The author of H claimed that he made use of oral tradition, and it is possibly from this that he took the name of Owain ap Urien and his role in Kentigern's conception.

These sources allow us to posit the following preliminary *stemma*:

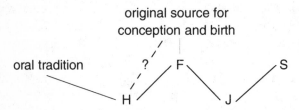

Such are the twelfth-century sources for the life of St Kentigern and their probable inter-relationship. But we must also consider a number of late medieval sources. These are the *lectiones* and canticles for the office of St Kentigern in the Sprouston and Aberdeen Breviaries (of the thirteenth and sixteenth centuries respectively) and for the office of St Teneu in the latter work. The *Aberdeen Breviary* also associates several other saints with St Kentigern: St Teneu, St Serf and St Baldred, whom we have encountered, and St Conval of Inchinnan, who is called a contemporary of St Kentigern and his disciple.[22] The fourteenth-century *Chronica Gentis Scottorum* of John of Fordun also mentions a *Historia Beati Kentigerni*, from which he quotes, and mentions St Conval of Inchinnan as a disciple of Kentigern's.

Turning first of all to Fordun, it is clear that the *Historia Beati Kentigerni* from which he quotes is H. Fordun's passage reads:

Ex historia beati Kentigerni: Iste vero Servanus in primitiva pene Scottorum ecclesia discipulus venerandi pontificis Palladii fuit. Hunc Palladium anno post incarnacionem Dominicam ut supra [430], sanctus papa Celestinus, longe credentibus ante Scottis, primum misit episcopum. Ille vero Scocie adveniens sanctum ibidem invenit Servanum, et eum, ut in vineam Domini Sabaoth operaretur invitans, doctrina postmodum ecclesiastica sufficienter imbutum, in omne Scottorum gente suum constituit suffraganeum.[23]

This appears in H as follows:

Iste quoque Servanus in primitiva Scottorum ecclesia fuit discipulus vener-andi Palladii primi Scottorum episcopi, qui etenim anno Dominice incar-nacionis CCCC.XXX. a Celestino papa primus Scottis credentibus mittebatur episcopus. Hic invenit beatum Servanum in Albania ante illum, virum Christianum; quem ab ipso postmodum ecclesiastica doctrina suffi-cienter imbutum, eum fecit suffraganeum, quod non posset ad docendum.[24]

Since Fordun was a chaplain in Aberdeen Cathedral, it is possible that there was a copy of H (fragmentary or complete) in the cathedral library there. Fordun's other reference to Kentigern is as follows:

Contemporaneus vero cum sancto Columba beatissimus floruit Kentig-ernus Glascuensis episcopus, vir mirande sanctitatis, et multorum opera-tor miraculorum, cuius ibidem ossa veneranda, multis ad laudem Dei clarificata miraculis, tumulata requiescunt. Eius versus austrum episco-patus tunc temporis ultimus finis fuerat, ut esse modo de iure debeat, ad crucem regiam infra Stanemore. Unus vero discipulorum eius precipuus erat sanctus Convallus, miraculis clarus et virtutibus, cuius itaque ossa sepulta quiescunt apud Inchenane iuxta Glascu.[25]

This assertion of the power of St Kentigern and the territorial pretensions of the church of Glasgow as far as the Rere Cross on Stainmoor looks as if it comes from a *Life* of the saint, though there is nothing equivalent to this in J; J states that Kentigern's diocese stretched from sea to sea like the Antonine (?) Wall (*sicut vallum quondam a Severo principe a mari usque ad mare... construebatur*), without mention of its southward extent.[26] So it is possible that here Fordun is quoting a lost part of H which included this information and also some mention of Kentigern's disciple St Conval of Inchinnan.

Whether or not the Aberdeen copy of H was more complete than the MS that has survived, we can be sure of its existence and that Fordun knew it as a *Historia beati Kentigerni*. This is important when we consider the *lectiones* for St Teneu in the *Aberdeen Breviary* (hereafter cited as AT); these are closely connected with the story of St Teneu in H, though very much abbreviated. The saint is called

Thaneuu, her father's kingdom is *Laudonia;* when she rejects her aspirant lover *Euuen,* son of the king of Cumbria, she is banished to the care of a swineherd; her lover, dressed as a woman, rapes her in a solitary place; she is cast from a high hill in a cart, whose wheelmarks dent the hard stone, then cast adrift in a boat from a port called *Aberledy;* the boat carries her out to *Maya Insula,* then back to *Culros,* where Kentigern is born; he subsequently founds the church of Glasgow, and now reigns on high with his mother, who is honourably buried in the city of Glasgow.[27]

All of these points, with the exception of the name of Aberlady (for H's *Aberlessic*), and the fact that Teneu is buried in Glasgow, appear in the surviving fragment of H. The first is a late medieval attempt to identify the lost *Aberlessic* with a roughly similar East Lothian place-name which would fit the story, although the identification might not satisfy modern place-name scholars. The second point is presumably based on tradition current in Glasgow, where in later times St Teneu's (now St Enoch's) church and square stood at the west end of the Trongate, a street in medieval times known as the *vicus Sancte Tenew.*[28] The Breviary spelling of her name, *Theneuu,* also differs from H's *Thaney,* and was presumably similarly derived from current Glasgow tradition.

Professor MacQueen has suggested that the *Breviary* office of Teneu is not derived from H as we know it, but from an intermediate, and he suggests a lost Glasgow *Life of Teneu* drawn entirely from H.[29] This argument does not take into account the existence at Aberdeen of a *Historia beati Kentigerni* which was a MS of H, possibly more complete than the surviving fragment. Professor MacQueen may be right, but we do not actually need to posit a lost Glasgow *Life of Teneu* based on the surviving fragment of H as the source of the *Aberdeen Breviary lectiones* for St Teneu, since it is likely that Aberdeen Cathedral had, or had access to, a copy of H.

It is worth mentioning in passing that there is more than a hint of the pagan supernatural in the story of Teneu. One characteristic of semidivine or euhemeristic figures in Irish heroic literature is that they were very difficult to kill, often requiring multiple deaths before they were finished;[30] and Teneu's resistance to being cast off a cliff and thrown into the sea suggests that she shared this characteristic. The area needs to be explored by an expert on Celtic mythology, but I suspect that this is the direction in which we should be looking for the origin of these details in the story of St Teneu.

Consideration of the 'Sprouston' or Edinburgh Breviary leads us on to examine the succeeding episode in J, Kentigern's childhood with St Serf at Culross. H breaks off with the finding of Teneu and the baby Kentigern by St Serf, while J continues with a series of miraculous anecdotes about Kentigern's upbringing at Serf's monastic school. These are: how Serf's pet robin was killed by some boys while playing and restored to life by Kentigern, who thus averted his master's wrath; how Kentigern's envious companions extinguished all the lights in the church which Kentigern had been charged to tend, and how he summoned down fire from heaven to re-ignite them; how Serf's cook died in old age and was restored by Kentigern's prayers; and how, at his parting from St Serf, Kentigern crossed the Forth (*Frisicum litus*) dryshod at low tide, then brought a flood-tide up the Firth so that Serf could not follow him. The 'Sprouston' or Edinburgh Breviary *lectiones* (hereafter cited as E) have much of this material, but with significant differences. They describe first of all how Kentigern was born in the province of *Leudonia* called after his father *Leudonus*, and given into the care of St Serf at *Colenros*. Here he performed many miracles: he restored the pet robin to life; he re-ignited the extinguished lights; he revived the aged cook; the cook thereafter lived for seven years, and after his death it was written upon his tomb how he had been revived by Kentigern, and the inscription could still be seen, although covered by stones, at *Lokencheinoch*; but immediately after this resuscitation Kentigern left Serf, crossing the river which divides Scotia from the kingdom of the Britons, and causing the tide to rise so that Serf could not follow him.[31]

Although the Sprouston *lectiones* are interspersed with canticles which seem to derive from J (with very interesting musical notation)[32] it is not clear that the *lectiones* themselves are so directly derived. They do not know the name of Kentigern's mother, and contain the interesting reference to a stone monument at *Lokencheinoch* which is not in J; and there are other differences of detail in some of the miracle stories. These *lectiones* seem to incorporate an account of Kentigern's boyhood under St Serf's tutelage, related to J's account, but independent of it. It is uncertain how much of this material was originally in H, which seems to be about to embark on a Serf/Fife episode at the point where it breaks off.[33]

As well as its office for St Teneu (AT), the *Aberdeen Breviary* also has a series of *lectiones* for St Kentigern.[34] Most of these describe

incidents which are also found in J, but there are enough differences
to make it certain that their source is not J as we now know it. The
lectiones (hereafter called AK) begin with a very brief summary of
Kentigern's parentage, making him son of *Eugenius Eufuren'* king of
Cumbria and *Teneuu* daughter of *Loth* king of *Laudonia*; she comes
by sea to *Culros* and is baptised by Servanus. There is no mention of
a virginal conception, nor is reason given why Teneuu was cast into
the sea. There follow anecdotes familiar from J and E, concerning St
Serf's pet robin, the fire, and the dead cook (though, like J, there is
no mention of his monument). Kentigern's passage of the Forth is
followed by his meeting with Fregus (to be examined below), though
there is no mention of the foundation of the church of Glasgow at
this point. The next incident is the loss and recovery of the queen's
ring; this differs significantly from J's version in that J calls her
Languoreth, whereas AK calls her simply *regina de Cadyhouu*, queen
of Cadzow (now Hamilton). AK goes on to describe Kentigern's
recall from Wales, without explaining or previously mentioning his
exile, his meetings with *Redrath* king of *Glasgu* (*Rederech* in J) and
with St Columba *ad torrentem vocatur Malyndinor* (J has *Mellingdenor*,
but does not call it a burn), and his old age and death, with a summary
of other points: how he would recite the entire Psalter while sitting
on stones in freezing water, and how while saying mass his body
would levitate off the ground at the words *sursum corda* (*Et cum
'sursum corda' decanteret, corpus eius in aere a terra elevabatur*). This
last fantastic detail is not in J, who says simply that when Kentigern
lifted his hands when he said *sursum corda* he held up his own [heart]
to the Lord while exhorting others to do the same (*Dum enim elevatis
in modum crucis manibus, 'sursum corda' diceret, ad quod ceteros ammonuit, suum habebat ad Dominum*). The two passages are clearly
related, but J is more restrained and indeed remarkably tame by his
usual standard; he may have toned down or misunderstood an
original which was more fantastic.[35] If so, it appears that AK may in
places be truer to their common original than is J.

    Thus the source of AK is clearly related to, but not identical with,
J. AK draws freely on material which is also in J, but differs in some
significant details, e.g., spellings of names, the name of the queen of
Cadzow and the Molendinar (J knows a *locus nomine Mellingdenor ubi
sanctus tunc degere solebat*, but does not know that it is a burn). AK
does not appear to have had the story of Kentigern's conception and
Teneu's tribulations which is found in J, nor does he have detailed

information about Kentigern's exile in Wales or his death, although these are alluded to. All the material which is detailed in AK seems to come from a Gaelic cultural background: the Fife material, the meetings with Serf, Fergus and Columba, the queen's ring, Kentigern's miraculous masses, asceticism and longevity. AK, indeed, appears to be an abbreviation of a Gaelic-orientated *Life* of Kentigern which was also used by Jocelin of Furness in the composition of J; in other words, AK appears to be an abbreviation of S, Jocelin's source 'dictated in a Gaelic style', with some additional information provided, not in any detail, from another source, possibly generalised Glasgow tradition. Some of his information certainly did not come from J.

The conclusion that AK is an abbreviation of S and largely independent of J, is of the utmost importance for several reasons. Since J only acknowledges two sources, F and S, it follows that what J did not derive from S he found in F (the *Life* normally used in the cathedral before Jocelin's time); it is an assumption, but not an unreasonable one, that most of S is abbreviated in AK, and that AK gives a fair indication of the contents and general nature of S. Similarly, material in J which has no parallel in AK comes probably from F, and gives an indication of what were its contents and general nature. To test the likelihood of this view, we must divide J into its constituent episodes and examine each one in turn.

The following episodes can be distinguished in J.

I. Chapters 1–3; the conception of St Kentigern and punishment and deliverance of his mother. This material is also in H and AT, where it appears with differences and much more circumstantial detail. J, we have argued, is not derived from H, but both have a common original. For this episode, this was probably F, which H padded out with oral tradition, giving such details as the name of Kentigern's father, the Welsh romance element, and the topographical details about East Lothian. The whole seems to come from a Lothian source largely free from Gaelic influence, and so could hardly be dated too long after c. 950. It is not impossible that it could be as early as the time of St Baldred of Tynninghame (d. 756), but it cannot be safely attributed to him.

II. Chapters 4–8; Kentigern's upbringing at Culross with St Serf. This material may not be as Gaelic-orientated as I once argued, but it remains true that it shows efforts to forge links between Strathclyde and the kingdom of Scotia, and as such could not be any earlier than the late ninth century. There is no mention of a connection between St Serf and St Kentigern in the *Vita Sancti Servani*; the Dublin MS mentions it in its title heading, and Wyntoun's verse translation alludes to the relationship very briefly in an interpolation.[36] *Vita Sancti Servani* seems more anxious to establish a relationship between Serf's *parochia* around Culross and the community of Iona, and indeed tells two stories about meetings between Serf and Adomnán.[37] Since St Serf's *vita* appears to be very much a Culross document, we must conclude that this episode, although located at Culross, did not originate there. If we could identify Lokencheinoch, that would be a help; but Professor MacQueen's suggestion, Lochwinnoch, cannot be accepted.[38] The name does seem to incorporate Gaelic *loch* or *lochan*, but is presumably in Fife.

III. Chapter 9. This story describes how Kentigern, having left Serf at the Forth, comes to *Kernach* where he meets an aged man called Fregus. Fregus dies in his presence, and Kentigern places his body in a cart to which he yokes two untamed oxen, who draw their burden 'as far as *Cathures*, which is now called *Glascu*'. Here Kentigern buries Fregus in a cemetery previously consecrated by St Ninian, but hitherto unused for burials, and here he establishes his hermitage. The traditional place of Fregus's burial was still recognised when Jocelin wrote, in a grove of shady trees near the church; it may have been the site of the Blackadder Aisle, where the incident is commemorated by a carving in the vault.

This very odd episode abounds in Gaelic names: *Fregus* (Gaelic Fergus), *Kernach*, *Cathures* (seeming to incorporate Gaelic *cathir*, a monastery), the otherwise unknown name of Glasgow. It is possible that this name reappears in the carving in the vault of the Blackadder Aisle mentioned above, where the inscription reads **THIS IS THE ILE OF CAR FERGUS**. *Car Fergus* is unlikely to mean 'Fergus's car', since the word order is incorrect in Middle Scots; it would, however, be perfectly correct Gaelic word order, and could represent *Cathir Fergusa*, 'the *cathir* of Fergus'. It has been suggested that this whole episode is an interpolation, since J introduces the reader to Glasgow, as if for the first time, and without the alternative *Cathures*, two chapters later. The story appears to be of Gaelic provenance, and is found in AK as well as in J. It appears to be separate from the preceding episode about St Serf, because it is not found in E.

Bishop Forbes, followed by Professor Jackson, identifies *Kernach* with a place called Carnock in St Ninian's, south of Stirling; this could have been on St Kentigern's route if he crossed the Forth near Alloa and proceeded southwest to skirt the Kilsyth Hills and travel down the Kelvin towards Glasgow, say along the Roman road. Professor Barrow has suggested to me, however, that Kernach may be intended to be Cairnoch in St Ninians, at the head of the Carron Valley.[39] By this reading Kentigern would have crossed the Forth and proceeded up through Strathcarron to Cairnoch and then over the Cró Road through Campsie Glen and down into Strathkelvin.

There is a possibility, although it is remote, that this story could have some basis in an actual event. There is some evidence that Aedán mac Gabráin, king of the Dál Riata from 574, had earlier had some kind of lordship on the upper Forth; some time during his reign, perhaps c. 582, he won a great victory over the *Miathi*, probably near Stirling.[40] The Dál Riata were driven out of central Scotland as the result of another great battle fought in Strathcarron in 642, in which their king Domnall Brecc was killed. So there may have been Gaelic penetration into the Forth valley in the late sixth and early seventh centuries. Unlike the episodes connecting St Kentigern with Serf and Columba, there is no attempt to link the subject of the *Life* with another famous personage; no claims are made for Fregus, and he remains (like Melchizadek) a curiously isolated figure. The story does not enhance the territorial claims of the church of Glasgow, and is relatively devoid of supernatural phenomena which would glorify Kentigern himself. We have seen in our analysis of St Ninian's chronology and sphere of activity that a burial ground or *cathir* founded by him but not used for burials before St Kentigern's visit is a possibility; the *eccles* place-name and the dedication at St Ninians are suggestive of great antiquity.

Set against this is the possibility that the story could be very much later. The image of two untamed oxen dragging a funeral cart without human guidance to a divinely-ordained location occurs in Muirchú's *Life of St Patrick* and is repeated elsewhere.[41] It is ultimately a biblical image, drawn from I Samuel, 6, which describes the return of the Ark of the Covenant from Philistia to Israel on such a cart. Since much of the S material in J is fantastic and demonstrably late, it may be dangerous to try to attach more weight to this episode than to any other.[42]

In either case, the story does not appear originally to have been about Glasgow at all. Dr Durkan has suggested that *Cathures* may be Cadder, the site of a Roman fort on the Antonine Wall, but covering a large area extending perhaps down as far as Glasgow itself.[43] Jocelin's gloss on *Cathures*, 'which is now called *Glasgu*', is suspect, principally because he reintroduces Glasgow in Chapter 11, as if for the first time, as the town where Kentigern established his cathedral seat after his consecration as bishop of the Cambrian region. When Jocelin visited Glasgow a site near the cathedral was pointed out to him as the place of Fregus's burial, 'encircled by a delicious density of overshadowing trees', possibly now occupied by the Blackadder Aisle; but the story may not originally have been a foundation legend for Glasgow itself.

IV. Chapters 10–11; Kentigern's early years in Glasgow. This describes how Kentigern abode in the place of Fregus's burial with two brothers, Telleyr and Anguen; the latter name, with its distinctive *gu-* spelling, is certainly Bretonnic, possibly indicating a written source. After a time Kentigern was elected bishop by the king and clergy of the Cambrian region and was consecrated by a single bishop from Ireland, as was then customary. He then fixed his cathedral seat 'in a town which was called *Glesgu*, which means 'dear family', and which is now called *Glasgu*'. His bishopric was co-extensive with the Cambrian kingdom, stretching, like the rampart of Emperor Severus, from sea to sea, 'as far as the *Flumen Fordense*' (a different name from *Frisicum litus* used above).

All indications are that this came from a Bretonnic source. The name Anguen and the interpretation of the name of Glasgow, as if it is here introduced for the first time, as Welsh *clas* + *cu* 'dear community', point to a British cultural background. In fact, the name is more likely to represent Welsh *glas cau*, 'green hollow', a name which could well describe the deep hollow through which the Molendinar flows between the cathedral and the Craigs (Necropolis Hill), now covered over by Wishart Street.[44] The popular etymology, 'dear green place', is the result of a mistaken compromise.

The mention of the Severan Rampart is of interest. There is no reason to believe that the kingdom of Strathclyde ever stretched as far as the Forth, or that the Antonine Wall (as Jocelin clearly understood it) ever formed part of its frontier. Jocelin appears to have misunderstood a statement in his original, possibly to the effect that the Cambrian kingdom stretched from sea to sea (i.e. from the Clyde to the Solway), as far as the Severan Rampart (meaning Hadrian's Wall, which Septimius Severus did repair).[45] This was the case for a period between c. 685, when, says Bede, 'a part of the Britons recovered their independence', and c. 725, when Northumbria pressed again into southwest Scotland.[46] Between two great sieges of Dumbarton in 756 and 870 there was a period of great obscurity when the kings may have been in control of only a small area round Dumbarton itself; in the late ninth century they may have restored the kingdom to something like its earlier size, though for part of the time at least as clients of the kings of Scots. From the mid-tenth century, Strathclyde or Cumbria seems to have extended further south, as far as the Yorkshire-Westmoreland boundary, due to the collapse of Viking York and the acceptance by the Wessex dynasty that they could not fill the vacuum.[47] This is the claim made by Fordun where he appears to quote from a lost portion of the *Historia Beati Kentigerni* which we have called H; but that is not what Jocelin is asserting here. Jocelin's source (F in this case, since it is pretty certain he is not quoting from S here) must refer to a period either before c. 725 or else after c. 900. Whichever it belongs to, we have here further evidence that J is independent of H.

A pointer to a possible early date for this passage is the reference to Kentigern's consecration by a single bishop. This is not an invention of Jocelin's, who clearly frowned on the practice; Professor MacQueen has pointed out that it is similar to Bede's criticism of the uncanonical practices of remote Christian churches, excused on the grounds that they did not know the better customs of the universal church.[48] Bede quotes Gregory the Great's comments on the practice of consecration by a single bishop as something which might be permitted under exceptional circumstances.[49] There exists a possibility that this passage could even be as early as the late seventh or early eighth century, the period to which the earliest surviving saints' Lives belong. If so, the first *Life* of Kentigern could belong to the period of the first flowering of hagiography in the British Isles; and we are reminded of the later tradition that connects this *Life* with St Baldred of Tynninghame (d. 756). But it is not definitely so early as this.

V. Chapters 12–20; Kentigern's deportment and assorted miracles. These chapters are largely devoid of proper names and 'career events', but are very generalised. They describe Kentigern's humble deportment, mode of dress, ascetic exercises (a stone bed, a bath in a freezing torrent while reciting the entire Psalter), the miracles which appeared while he was saying mass (without, as we have seen, any mention of levitation at the *Sursum corda*), and some other stock miracles (the yoking of a stag and a wolf under the plough, the sowing of sand and reaping of wheat). Much of this can be paralleled in Irish hagiography. The only place-name is a hill called *Gulath*, beside the water near his home, on which Kentigern sat while he dried himself after his aquatic psalm-singing. This name, with its characteristic *gu*-spelling, appears to be Bretonnic. Professor Jackson has shown that it cannot be for Welsh *wleth*, dew, which would offer a possible connection with the Dowhill north of the Gallowgate.[50] Dr Durkan has suggested that it could be connected with the name Cullochfauld, mentioned in 1738 'in Easter Craigs, not far from modern Whitehill' (Dennistoun).[51] Certainly it must be part of the Craigs.

Much of this material is summarised in AK, and therefore presumably came from S. The extremities of Kentigern's asceticism and the fantastic details of many of the miracles suggest a kinship with Irish hagiography. But the presence of an isolated Bretonnic place-name in such a part of J's narrative is a problem. It is not in AK, so it is not certain that Jocelin took this name from S; he could have found it in F, or borrowed it from the name of a likely hill in the Craigs area. These are possible explanations; but the name remains problematic.

VI. Chapters 21–23; Kentigern's encounter with King Morken and departure from Glasgow. This describes how Kentigern fell foul of a local tyrant called Morken, by miraculously transporting corn which the king had refused him from the royal barns beside the River *Clud* to Kentigern's own dwelling at the place known as *Mellingdenor* (i.e., the Molendinar, though not named as a burn in J); subsequently Morken kicks Kentigern and fittingly dies of gout. The king's friend Cathen, instigator of the king's hatred against Kentigern, dies by a fall from his horse. But Morken's family continue their hatred against the saint, who decides to leave Glasgow and go into Wales.

The Welsh genealogies name Morcant Bulc as a Northerner who was contemporary with Rhydderch Hael and Urien Rheged; he is said to have assassinated Urien at Lindisfarne c. 590, and he later entered Welsh folklore as a character of some notoriety.[52] He was not related to the dynasty of Strathclyde, and there is no historical evidence to suggest that he was ever king of Strathclyde. This episode is unhistorical as far as the authentic career of St Kentigern is concerned.

It may, however, relate to some local legend in the Glasgow area connected with the site of the cathedral and the royal barns. Professor

MacQueen suggests that the barns in question were the teind barns of Gorbals (Scots 'teind sheaves' translates *decima garbalia*, often anglicised as 'garbal tithes').[53] The problem here is that Gorbals was not part of Glasgow, but of Govan; the area round Gorbals Cross was formerly Little Govan,[54] and the rising ground to the south is still called Govanhill. Is Jocelin claiming that the teind barns of Govan belonged properly to Glasgow Cathedral? It seems unlikely. Besides, what he speaks of are royal barns, rather than the teind barns of a neighbouring church. The great royal centre in the area was at Rutherglen, where the king had a castle, and which became a royal burgh in David I's reign.[55] It is perhaps unlikely that what we have here is a story connecting Gorbals with Glasgow, as Professor MacQueen thought; but the motive behind the story remains obscure.

VII. Chapters 23–29; Kentigern's sojourn in Wales, and encounters with St David and St Asaph. Professor Jackson points out that the spellings of Welsh names in this section are all late forms, and he regards the episode as wholly unhistorical. The cult of St Kentigern is found in Wales, however, and it must be asked how it got there, since in 'triadic' tradition he is placed *yn y gogled*, 'in the North'.[56] There is good reason to believe that some Strathclyde aristocrats left Scotland and settled in Gwynedd c. 890, when they refused to conform with the increasing integration of Strathclyde into the kingdom of Scotia.[57] Presumably these aristocrats took the cult of St Kentigern with them, and subsequently legends about Kentigern developed in Wales; these could have been written up in the early twelfth century, transferred back to Glasgow, and have found their way into F. Their intention is to connect Kentigern with major Welsh saints, David and Asaph, and with Gwynedd, but the relationships described are not to be taken literally.[58]

VIII. Kentigern's recall to Strathclyde by King Rederech, sojourn at Hoddom and return to Glasgow. With the entry of 'Rederech king of Cambria' into J's narrative, we move from the shadows of uncertainty into a world of historical personages. For J's Rederech can only be Rhydderch Hael, king of Dumbarton, who is attested in a number of sources. Adomnán names him as a contemporary of St Columba in Scotland (563–597); the *Historia Brittonum* names him as a contemporary of Urien Rheged, Morgan, and Hussa of Bernicia (c. 590); a Welsh 'triad' names him as a contemporary of Aedán mac Gabráin, king of the Dál Riata (574–c. 608).[59] Taken together with

Kentigern's obit in the *Annales Cambriae* (s.a. [612], probably in fact
c. 614), we are in little doubt that Rhydderch Hael was king of
Dumbarton at the same time that Kentigern was bishop of Glasgow.
So it appears that here, at least, J is conveying an actual historical
fact.

That does not mean that all the circumstantial detail with which
J surrounds relations between Kentigern and Rhydderch is to be
unreservedly accepted, and it must be questioned whether Kentigern
spent an extended period at Hoddom. Hoddom is an ancient ecclesiastical centre with early stone crosses, an *eccles-* place-name and a
dedication to St Mungo nearby; but it is doubtful if it formed part
of the Strathclyde kingdom during Kentigern's and Rhydderch's
time. Still, we know of contact between the ecclesiastical centres of
different kingdoms and regions at this time. An extended stay by
Kentigern at Hoddom is inherently unlikely.

Some aspects of the story of Kentigern's 'recall' cannot be accepted: for example, that King Rederech gave the temporal power
into ecclesiastical subjection (a reflection of the church-state conflicts
of the late twelfth century), or that Kentigern converted the Picts of
Galweithia (who are spurious), or that he sent disciples to convert
the *Orchades, Noruagia* and *Ysalanda* (an attempt to improve upon
the missionary work of Ninian and Columba).

Proper names in this section suggest that it is Bretonnic: *Rederech*
may well be an early form of this name, and the name of his queen,
Languoreth, is also Bretonnic. But *Holdelm* for Hoddom may be
Anglian, and the name of the queen's son, Constantine, is found
among the Scots as well as the Britons. No progeny is credited to
Rhydderch in the Harleian genealogies, and the assertion that Constantine was his son born to Languoreth as a result of Kentigern's
intercession looks like an explanation for (or justification of) the fact
that during the twelfth century the great minster church of St
Constantine at Govan became subordinated as a prebend of St
Kentigern's cathedral church at Glasgow. The Aberdeen Breviary
lectiones for St Constantine connect him rather with Kilchousland
(*Cill Chostatin*) in Kintyre.[60] The *Cenél nGabráin* came from Kintyre,
and the name Constantine occurs frequently in the family of Cinaed
mac Alpín, who were increasingly influential in Strathclyde from the
late ninth century onwards – i.e., during the period when the Govan
school of stonecarving was most active.[61]

So this episode shows signs of coming from a Bretonnic source with some factual information and some overlaid material, not all of it Bretonnic. Jocelin repeats his Gaelic etymology for Kentigern's name, *Ceann tigearn*, 'chief lord', presumably from its previous occurrence. The most reliable and historical parts of this section could go back to a *Life* written in a Bretonnic cultural milieu, possibly as early as the late seventh or early eighth century, and be part of the oldest stratum in F.

IX. Chapters 35–38; assorted miracles at Glasgow. These describe how the saint's clothing was never dampened by rain, how he recovered for the queen a ring which she had improperly bestowed upon a lover, how he caused fresh mulberries to be produced in January for a visiting Irish *seanchaidh*, and how milk which the saint was sending for the refreshment of a workman fell into the Clyde and was transformed into a stone of cheese. The famous story of the queen's ring and the fish, which figures prominently in the arms of the city of Glasgow, has parallels in Irish hagiography, and the *seanchaidh* (*ioculator, hystrio* in J) who plays the harp and seeks rewards travelling around the courts of Irish kings points to a Gaelic origin for this episode. Most of this material is summarised in AK, and presumably came originally from S.

An interesting point, however, is that while J calls Rhydderch's queen Languoreth, the name by which he has first introduced her, AK does not name her, but calls her simply queen of *Cadyhow*, i.e. Cadzow, now Hamilton. This confirms that AK cannot be dependent solely on J, but abbreviates a source also used by J. The likelihood that this source is strongly Gaelic-orientated, and therefore identifiable as S, is strengthened by an examination of the next episode.

X. Chapters 39–40; Kentigern's meeting with St Columba. The great Gaelic saint is made to come from Iona (called *Yi* in J) to Glasgow and meet with Kentigern beside the Molendinar. In J it is not called a burn, but simply the place where the saint dwelt. AK, which also has this story linking Kentigern with a major Gaelic saint, makes the Molendinar a burn. Professor Jackson suggests that this episode may have an Anglian origin because J says that Columba is called *Columkillus* by the Angles and because of a mention that St Columba's pastoral staff was preserved at the church of St Wilfrid of Ripon.[62] Certainly neither of these details could have come from J's Gaelic source, S, but neither is integral to the story. No Anglian church would have had an interest in preserving a story about a meeting between a Gaelic saint of the Dál Riata and a British saint of Strathclyde, whereas Jocelin could have had other reasons for knowing about Columba's staff at Ripon and the Gaelic form of his name (which was known to Bede).[63] The story of the ram's head turned to stone in the hands of thieves is the foundation legend of the Ramshorn Kirk in Glasgow; Jocelin apparently saw it during his visit to the city.

The whole episode is concerned to forge links between Strathclyde and Gaelic Scotland; as such it is unlikely to be any earlier than the late ninth century. Saints' lives abound with meetings between famous contemporaries (and often non-contemporaries) which are not to be taken literally. Columba and Kentigern were at least contemporaries, but Adomnán does not mention that they met. He describes a meeting between Columba and Bridei king of the Picts beside the River Ness, but only speaks of secret messages passing between Columba and Rhydderch Hael of Dumbarton.[64] We should probably regard this meeting as unhistorical, and probably from J's Gaelic source, S.

XI. Chapter 41; Kentigern sets up crosses in several places. Among the many crosses which Kentigern is alleged to have set up, two are singled out: one at Glasgow and one at Lothwerverd. The former was miraculously erected in the cemetery of the church of the Holy Trinity at Glasgow 'in which his episcopal seat was located' when lifting machinery failed. Jocelin implies that it was still standing in his day. Recent excavations under the nave of Glasgow Cathedral have for the first time yielded early Christian remains; although nothing goes back to the sixth or seventh century, we now have evidence that the site was occupied before the twelfth.[65] Jocelin's description of the stone cross may be taken as supporting this.

The other cross mentioned, at Lothwerverd, refers to Loquhariot in Borthwick, Midlothian. The church there was dedicated to St Kentigern, and was acquired by Glasgow Cathedral in the mid twelfth century.[66] There appears to be no connection with E's mention of a stone monument at Lokencheinoch, which was probably in Fife.

XII. Chapters 42–45; Kentigern's old age and death. This describes how in extreme old age Kentigern caused a hot bath to be prepared 'on the octave of the Epiphany, when he used each year to wash many people in holy baptism', in which, when he entered the water, he died; and many of his disciples entering the bath while it was still warm also passed away. Mgr MacRoberts has suggested that this story may be early, because the practice of conducting baptisms at the Epiphany had passed out of use in the western church long before Jocelin's time, and had in fact been condemned in 517.[67] He further points out that the warm bath itself is suggestive of a baptismal font, which in a Glasgow winter would have been warmed for the comfort of the catechumens, while a hot bath would have been totally out of character for a great ascetic like Kentigern, accustomed as he was to recite the Psalter while plunged in an icy torrent. Since the date of the saint's death, now his feastday, 13 January, is a week later than the Epiphany, the usual date for baptisms, Mgr MacRoberts suggests that Kentigern may have collapsed during the ceremony and died a week later. In conclusion, he argues that the story could 'derive ultimately from some factual account of Kentigern's death' like the one incorporated in Adomnán's *Vita Columbae*.[68]

Although this argument is attractive, and there are signs of an early date for this passage, one must be cautious. For one thing, Adomnán's moving account of Columba's last hours may not be Diarmait's verbatim account, for it has been shown that the passage has many verbal echoes of the account of the saint's last days in Evagrius' *Life of St Antony*.[69] Jocelin's story is full of angelic visions and other supernatural events (e.g., the sudden death of all the disciples who entered the bath, the foreknowledge of the king's death within a year). But the curious detail of celebrating baptisms at the Epiphany is unlikely to have been invented later.

In J this story is followed by an account of the king's death which abounds in Bretonnic names: *Rederech, Pertnech* (= Partick, seemingly incorporating Bretonnic *pert*, a copse),[70] *Laloecen, Morthec*. It is stated that Partick was a royal residence of King Rhydderch, and later evidence confirms that Partick was royal demesne in the early twelfth century;[71] Jocelin would hardly have invented this detail. The date of King Rhydderch's date is not recorded, but it cannot have been too much earlier or later than c. 614; there may be grounds for accepting J's statement that he died within a year of Kentigern's own death. The Bretonnic names indicate that this material comes from F. Kentigern's death is only very briefly mentioned in AK, with none of the details about the hot bath or the king's death; so its source, S, may not have had an extended story about Kentigern's death. The last two chapters in J appear to come from the earliest stratum in F.

We can thus determine, if not with absolute certainty then at least with reasonable likelihood, which parts of J's narrative are derived from S and which are from F. The following table makes clear the likely relationship of episodes and sources. The sources on the left are the surviving documents, F and S on the right are their hypothetical sources.

Chapters in J	H	E	AT	AK	/	F	S
I. 1–3; East Lothian	★		★	(★)		★	
II. 4–8; Fife	(★)	★		★			★
III. 9; Fregus				★			★
IV. 10–11; Glasgow						★	
V. 12–20; Early miracles				★			★
VI. 21–23; King Morken					★		
VII. 23–29; Wales					★		
VIII. 30–34; Hoddom and Glasgow						★	
IX. 35–38; Later miracles			★			★	
X. 39–40; St Columba			★			★	
XI. 41; Crosses						★?	
XII. 42–45; Death						★	

This makes it possible to say something about Jocelin's two sources. F, the *vita* in regular use in Glasgow Cathedral c. 1180, was a source from a Bretonnic cultural background, which in its final form sought to connect Kentigern with East Lothian and Wales, with Welsh saints, and with the Strathclyde king Rhydderch Hael. It is not all of the same date of composition. The East Lothian material, devoid of Gaelic influence, is likely to be earlier than c. 950; the episodes of King Morken and the Welsh exile are not likely to be earlier than c. 890, and may not have reached their present form before the twelfth century. None of these can be regarded as certainly historical. But other episodes which we have identified as coming from F, describing Kentigern's consecration by a single bishop, his practice of baptising catechumens and the Epiphany, the name of the historical king Rhydderch Hael, the apparent statement that Strathclyde stretched from sea to sea, as far as the Severan Rampart, the statement that Partick was a royal residence, and some at least of the information about St Kentigern's death, appear to be much earlier. Some of it could reflect the conditions of the late seventh or early eighth century, after the Battle of Dunnichen (685) and before the Northumbrian advance beyond the Solway (c. 725) and the siege of Dumbarton (756) and subsequent eclipse of the Strathclyde kings' power. The East Lothian episode may belong to a period somewhere between then and c. 950, and the Welsh episode is probably not earlier that c. 890.

Jocelin's other source, the 'little volume dictated in a Gaelic style', which we have called S, may also have contained material of different dates. Much of it consisted of miracle stories, beginning with those performed at Culross (Chapters 4–8) and continuing with those performed at Glasgow (Chapters 12–20 and 35–40). The connections with St Serf and St Columba, and the string of miracles, appear to be unhistorical. The only part of S which might possibly contain an element of historical fact is the Fregus episode (Chapter 9), which could reflect the conditions of the late sixth century; but even this is very uncertain. Since Gaelic influence in Strathclyde was slight before the late ninth century, and reached its strongest in the eleventh, we should probably place S in the tenth-eleventh centuries.

Whether or not we can say very much about the career of Kentigern himself is questionable. His name is British (even though Jocelin was informed otherwise), but the stories of his conception in Lothian and his birth and education at Culross are clearly unhistorical. He seems to have been bishop of Strathclyde during the reign of Rhydderch Hael. It is not asserted that he was the first bishop of Strathclyde, and there is some slight evidence suggestive of Christianity in the area earlier.[72] He probably died c. 614 and was buried at Glasgow, which he is alleged to have founded. Other churches associated with him are Cadder, and possibly Hoddom. This is about the sum of our historical knowledge.[73]

Kentigern's hagiography, and the disentangling of the various threads in its makeup, help to provide some evidence about the development of the church of Glasgow, which is otherwise very obscure. We have seen that the earliest *stratum* in J could belong to a period c. 685 × 725, about a century after the saint's death, a time when founders' *vitae* were very much in fashion. This is the core of F. Of the additions to F, the East Lothian episode is unhistorical but probably before c. 950, the Welsh episode is also unhistorical and likely to be later than c. 890, and may not have entered F until the twelfth century.

During the tenth and eleventh centuries, when Gaelic influence was penetrating Strathclyde, a totally different *vita* was drawn up in a Gaelic style, replete with Irish-style miracles and ascetic feats, and concerned to connect Kentigern with saints of Scotia north of the Forth like Columba and Serf (Kentigern does not figure in Culross tradition about Serf).

By the first half of the twelfth century, F had achieved the form in which Jocelin found it.[74] This was unsatisfactory to the Anglo-Norman clergy of Glasgow Cathedral for a number of reasons, most notably its reference to a virginal conception. So Bishop Herbert commissioned a new *vita* (H), the surviving fragment of which is more elaborate and circumstantial than its equivalent in J, and seems to draw on Bretonnic folklore. This *vita* failed to dislodge F, and so some thirty years later Bishop Jocelin commissioned a new *vita* by Jocelin of Furness, which explained away the virginal conception much more discreetly and stitched together the partly factual narrative in F with the largely fantastic sequence of miracles in S. H's opening chapters were preserved because of their circumstantial information about Kentigern's mother Teneu, whose cult was developing in Glasgow. Fordun knew H as the *Historia Beati Kentigerni*, and appears to have had access to a more complete copy than the one which has survived.

The only independently attested 'fact' of Kentigern's career is the date of his death in the Harleian *Annales Cambriae*. These seem to have reached their present form soon after 950, although by this time they have long since ceased to carry northern material. The northern material is closely related to the northern genealogies, which extend down to the reign of Rhun map Arthgal in the 870s. As well as providing a pedigree for Rhun, these also provide pedigrees for two other important descendants of Dyfnwal Hen, Rhydderch Hael and Clynog Eidyn, who are sixth-century figures. Cumulatively, this suggests a compilation of northern historical material somewhere in southern Scotland down to the late ninth century, which found its way into Wales some time between the accession of Rhun in 872 and the last annal entries in the 950s. The supposed exile of Strathclyde aristocrats into Gwynedd c. 890 would be the obvious occasion for the transfer of such material, and the material, including the first written *vita* of St Kentigern (the core of F), could represent the productions of the *scriptorium* of Glasgow Cathedral.

These arguments contain an element of speculation. They differ to some extent from the views which I expressed in 1986 (perhaps due to the increasing caution of advancing middle age), and remain to some extent tentative. What is important is that Kentigern is a real historical figure, and that a small number of facts about him can, with patience, be teased out of the web of twelfth-century and later hagiography. It is a tribute to the care and skill of Jocelin of Furness in 'stitching together' the *Life of St Kentigern* that this is now such a difficult process.

NOTES

1. This is a substantial revision of my paper on this subject which appeared in the *Innes Review* in 1986 (see n. 7 below). Since I wrote it, I have become rather less optimistic about the amount of reliable historical information which can be extracted from the 12th-century hagiography. I have also taken the opportunity to correct some minor errors.

2. Edited by E Phillimore, '*Annales Cambriae* and Old Welsh Genealogies from Harleian MS 3859' *Y Cymmrodor*, ix (1888), 141–83; and more recently but less reliably in *Nennius: British History and the Welsh Annals*, ed J Morris (1980). The MS does not have AD dates, but *An[no]* to indicate each new year. This obit is entered 18 years after the death of Columba and the arrival of St Augustine in England (both 597), and 6 years after the death of Aedán mac Gabráin (c. 608–9).

3. R Bromwich, *Trioedd Ynys Prydein* (2nd edn 1978), 319–20. 'The name does not appear to be recorded in reference to any other person'.

4. Jocelin of Furness c. 1180 interpreted the name as Gaelic *Kyentyern*, i.e., *Ceanntigearn*, 'chief lord'. A P Forbes (ed.), *The Lives of SS Ninian and Kentigern* (Historians of Scotland, v, 1874), *Vita Kentigerni*, cap. 4 (hereafter *VK*).

5. Anderson, *ESSH*, i, 21, 125; J W M Bannerman, *Studies in the History of Dalriada* (1974), 77–8, 80–90; M O Anderson, *Kings and Kingship in early Scotland* (2nd edn, 1980)(hereafter Anderson, *KKES*), 145, 148–9, 228–9.

6. M Miller, 'Historicity and the Pedigrees of the Northcountrymen', *Bulletin of the Board of Celtic Studies*, xxvi (1976), 255–80, at 279–80; N K Chadwick, 'Early Culture and Learning in North Wales', in N K Chadwick et al., *Studies in the early British Church* (1958), 29–120, at 58–65.

7. K H Jackson, 'The Sources for the Life of St Kentigern,' in N K Chadwick et al., *Studies in the early British Church* (1958), 273–357; J MacQueen, 'Yvain, Ewen, and Owain ap Urien', *TDGNHAS*, xxxiii (1956), 107–31; J MacQueen, 'Reply to Professor Jackson', *TDGNHAS*, xxxvi (1959), 175–83; A Macquarrie, 'The Career of St Kentigern of Glasgow: *Vitae, Lectiones*, and Glimpses of Fact', *Innes Review*, xxxvii (1986), 3–24.

8. Ed. in Forbes, op. cit., 243ff., at 243. It is possible, but uncertain, that the MS reads *codicellis* rather than *codicello*; but even if it were the case, it might imply no more than that the author's source was not bound in a single volume. See Jackson, 'Sources', 275, 347ff.

9. Forbes, op. cit., 159ff.; Jackson, 'Sources', 274; *Glasgow Registrum*, p. xxv; *Chron. Melrose*, s.a. 1197.
10. *VK*, 159–61.
11. Jackson, 'Sources', 275, 347ff.
12. *VK*, 163–4.
13. Ibid., 252.
14. Ibid., 163–4.
15. Ibid., 249; Jackson, 'Sources', 289–91.
16. *Aberdeen Breviary*, PE., pt 3, f. 35v.
17. MacQueen, 'Yvain', esp. 112–21; *Aberdeen Breviarium*, Pars Hiem., 63v-64r; *Historia Dunelmensis Ecclesiae* (RS, lxxv, 18xx), i, 48; Anderson, *SAEC*, 56.
18. MacQueen, 'Yvain', 121.
19. *Aberdeen Breviary*, PH., 63v; Jackson, 'Sources', 344.
20. This paternity is asserted in *Bonedd y Saint*; see Bromwich, *TYP*, 320; Jackson, 'Sources', 286.
21. Even here H may reflect Bretonnic as well as Gaelic influence. The name Serf or Servanus is probably British or Pictish, and not Gaelic, as I previously argued; see below, Chapter 6, p. 155, and A Macquarrie, '*Vita Sancti Servani*: the Life of St Serf', *IR*, xliv (1993), 122–52, at 131–2. Likewise, the name Culross may be Bretonnic; see Watson, *CPNS*, 497.
22. *Aberdeen Breviary*, PE., f.34v-36r,PE. f. 15r-16r, PH. f. 63v-64r, PE., 117r-v; the Sprouston Breviary *lectiones* and canticles are edited in *VK*, pp. xciv-c.
23. *Chron. Fordun*, 94.
24. *VK*, 246.
25. *Chron. Fordun*, 115.
26. *VK*, 183.
27. *Aberdeen Breviary*, PE. f.34v-36r.
28. A Gibb, *Glasgow: the Making of a City* (1983), 15–16; see, for example, Vatican Archives, Reg. Supp., 919, 140v (8 July 1490).
29. J MacQueen, 'A Lost Glasgow Life of St Thaney (St Enoch)', *IR*, vi (1955), 125–30.
30. F J Byrne, *Irish Kings and High-kings* (1973), 97–102.
31. *VK*, 168–77; ibid., pp. xciv-c.
32. On the music, see J Purser, *Scotland's Music* (1992), 48.
33. I formerly argued (Macquarrie, 'The Career of St Kentigern of Glasgow: *Vitae, Lectiones*, and Glimpses of Fact', 8–9) that this episode came from a Gaelic cultural milieu, because at the time I believed that Serf and Culross were Gaelic names. However, in Macquarrie, '*Vita Sancti Servani*: the Life of St Serf', I argue that Serf is probably a British or Pictish name, and I now accept Watson's interpretation of the name

Culross. See below, chapter 7, pp. 147, 155; Watson, *CPNS*, 497; see also J MacQueen, 'Myth and Legends of Lowland Scottish Saints', *Scottish Studies*, xxiv (1980), 1–21.

34. *Aberdeen Breviay*, PH., f. 27r ff.
35. *VK*, 186–7.
36. Macquarrie, '*Vita Sancti Servani*', 126, 136, 144 n.; see below, Chapter 6, p.150.
37. Macquarrie, '*Vita Sancti Servani*', 125–6, 132–3, 140, 148–9nn.; see below, Chapter 6, pp. 147, 149.
38. MacQueen, 'Myth and Legends of Lowland Scottish Saints'.
39. Personal communication from Professor G W S Barrow in 1988.
40. See above, Chapter 4, Appendix II, pp 103–16.
41. In Bieler, *PT*, 120.
42. Daphne Brooke (*Wild Men and Holy Places*, 25–7) appears not to be aware that the story of the oxcart derives, directly or indirectly, from the *Book of Armagh*.
43. J Durkan, 'The Bishops' Barony of Glasgow in Pre-Reformation Times', *RSCHS*, xxii (1986), 277–301, at 284–6.
44. Watson, *CPNS*, 385–6; W F H Nicolaisen, *Scottish Place-names* (1976), 172.
45. Todd, *Roman Britain*, 174–80; *LSRB*, 30–2, 34, quoting Herodian and the *Scriptores Historiae Augustae*; above, Chapter 1, p 19.
46. *VK*, cap.11; *HE*, iv, 26; ibid., v, 23.
47. Macquarrie, 'Kings of Strathclyde', esp. p. 19.
48. MacQueen, 'Yvain', 18–20.
49. Bede, *HE*, i, 27.
50. Jackson, 'Sources', 311–12.
51. Durkan, 'Bishops' Barony', 294. There is a Golfhill Lane in the same area, but I do not know how old this name is.
52. Phillimore, '*Annales Cambriae* and Old Welsh Genealogies', 174; *Nennius*, 79; Anderson, *ESSH*, i, 13, 132.
53. J MacQueen, 'The Dear Green Place: St Mungo and Glasgow, 600–1966' *IR*, xliii (1992), 87–98, at 94–6.
54. Shown as such, for example, in Blaeu's map of Renfrewshire; *Illustrated Maps of Scotland from Blaeu's Atlas Novus of the 17th Century*, ed. J Stone (1991), pl. 24.
55. G S Pryde, *The Burghs of Scotland* (1965), 6–7; *RRS*, i, 170. Castle Street is on the north side of Rutherglen Main Street.
56. Bromwich, *TYP*, 1.
57. Macquarrie, 'Kings of Strathclyde', 13–14; idem, 'Early Christian Govan', 7–10; and see below, Chapter 8, p 190.
58. N K Chadwick, 'Intellectual Life in West Wales in the last Days of the Celtic Church', in *Studies in the early British Church*, 128–58.

59. Adomnán, *VC*, i, 15; *Nennius*, cap. 63; Bromwich, *TYP*, 147.
60. *Aberdeen Breviary*, PH., 11 March.
61. A Macquarrie, 'Early Christian Govan: the Historical Context', *RSCHS*, xxiv (1990), 1–17; idem in *Govan and its early Medieval Sculpture*, ed. A Ritchie (1994), 27–32; see below, Chapter 8, pp. 187–95.
62. Jackson, 'Sources', 326–7. See J MacQueen, 'The Name Molendinar', *IR*, viii (1957), 67–9.
63. *HE*, v, 9.
64. Adomnán, *VC*, ii, 33–35; i, 15; see above, Chapter 4, pp. 80–2.
65. I was shown a fragment of a disc-shaped crosshead, found under the nave, during the summer of 1993.
66. *Glasgow Registrum*, i, 13.
67. D MacRoberts, 'The Death of St Kentigern of Glasgow', *IR*, xxiv (1973), 43–50. See also *ODCC*, 2nd edn, s.v. 'Baptism', 126–7.
68. MacRoberts, 'The Death of St Kentigern of Glasgow', 45.
69. 2nd edn, iii, 23, nn., and p. lxviii.
70. Watson, *CPNS*, 386; Nicolaisen, *Scottish Place-names*, 164.
71. *Glasgow Registrum*, 9.
72. See above, Chapter 2, pp. 42–3.
73. In my earlier version of this paper (Macquarrie, 'Career of St Kentigern', 19–21) I tentatively suggested a fuller reconstruction of the career of the historical Kentigern; but I am no longer so confident.
74. The revival of the church of Glasgow under David c. 1112 could have provided the stimulus for its construction. There was interest in the traditions of *Cyndeyrn Garthwys yn y Gogled* in Wales in the second quarter of the twelfth century; cf. Bromwich, *TYP*, pp. cxi-cxii.

6

St Serf of Fife

A manuscript in Marsh's Library in Dublin, written in the thirteenth century and probably belonging originally to Glasgow Cathedral, contains a copy of Jocelin of Furness's *Vita Sancti Kentigerni*.[1] The first six folios also contain a *Vita Sancti Servani*, which was first edited by Skene and has recently been newly edited and translated.[2] The date of this *vita* (hereafter *VS*) is uncertain. It is similar in character to Lives of Scottish saints written in the twelfth century, such as Jocelin's *Vita Sancti Kentigerni*, the anonymous *Vita Kentigerni* of c. 1150, and the *Vita Niniani* attributed to Ailred of Rievaulx.[3] Professor MacQueen and others have assumed it to be the *vita* of Serf referred to by Jocelin in his *Vita Sancti Kentigerni* (cap. 8).[4] If that is correct, it must be earlier in date than c. 1180, when Jocelin's *Vita Kentigerni* was written. It is not certain, however, that the Marsh's Library *VS* is identical with the one mentioned by Jocelin; the *Aberdeen Breviary lectiones* for St Serf (1 July) come from a closely similar collection of miracles of St Serf which omit the legends of his Canaanite origins and his early career in the eastern Mediterranean.[5] The *Aberdeen Breviary lectiones*, curiously, also fail to mention his connection with Culross and Lochleven, but add at the end: 'Est et alius Sanctus Servanus nacione Israleticus qui temporibus Beati Adampnani abbatis in Insula Petmook multis miraculis claruit prout gesta per eum in eius vita lucidius complectuntur' (There is another St Serf, of Israelite nationality, who at the time of the abbot St Adomnán performed many miracles in the island of Portmoak; as is more clearly described in the deeds in his *vita*). It will appear that this *vita* mentioned in the *Aberdeen Breviary* is not likely to be our Marsh's Library *VS*. Likewise, it will be shown that Wyntoun's account of St Serf, although very similar to *VS*, is not identical with it; but all three are very closely related, so it is probably safe to assume that the *vita* referred to by Jocelin was also closely related to them.

The Marsh's Library manuscript of *VS* appears to have been copied from an exemplar. It contains a number of slips, and there are some other missing words: *Domini* after *verbum* on f. 1r; and the subject of *obtulerunt ei totius regni eorum regimen* ('the [?] of the whole kingdom offered him their rule') on f. 1v. Similarly for *quinquaginta et decem milibus* we should perhaps read *quinquaginta et centum milibus* (150,000) on f. 2r; and perhaps for *septem milibus milium* (7,000,000) on f. 3v. we should assume that the writer intended a more modest 700,000.

The Marsh's Library manuscript of *VS* is not quite the unique medieval copy. A manuscript in the National Library of Scotland, which c. 1500 belonged to Master James Gray, priest and notary of Dunblane diocese, contains the opening paragraphs of the *Vita* in a faded condition and in handwriting so tiny as to be in places almost illegible.[6] It appears that this manuscript never contained the whole of the *Vita*, but only the opening portion.

VS is short, occupying only six folios. Its account of the life of St Serf may be summarised as follows. St Serf's parents were Obeth son of Eliud, king of Canaan, and Alpia daughter of the king of Arabia. They were childless for many years until as a result of prayers and vigils (as well as her eating of mandrake root) she conceived twin sons called Servanus (i.e., Serf) and Generatius. On their father's death, Serf renounced his right to the kingship of Canaan to his brother, and instead studied arts and divinity at Alexandria, where he became a monk and a priest. Returning to Canaan, his own people elected him their bishop, a position which he held for twenty years. At the word of an angel, he left his own land and came to Jerusalem, crossing the Nile and making a dryshod crossing of the Red Sea on the way; on his arrival in Jerusalem, he was immediately made patriarch, and held that office for seven years. His angel instructed him to cut four staves from a tree growing on Mount Zion from which the true cross had been hewn, and thereafter he carried these with him on his journeys. Then the angel instructed him to leave Jerusalem.

He went from there to Constantinople and to an unidentified island called Salvatoris or 'Saviour's Island', and then to Rome. The papacy was vacant at the time, so he was immediately elected pope, and held that office for seven years. Again his angel instructed him to leave, and he said farewell to the Romans at an unidentified hill called the 'Hill of Tears' outside Rome; but many of the Romans refused to let him go, and insisted on accompanying him on his journey. While crossing the Alps they were assailed by demons in a place called 'the Black Valley or the Valley of Beasts'; many of his companions died of fright, but Serf put the demons to flight. They then crossed the English Channel (*Icteum mare*) dryshod and proceeded to the Firth of Forth. Here at last the restless pilgrim found a place suitable for the mortification of the flesh.

At Inchkeith Serf was met by St Adomnán, 'abbot in Scotland at that time', who assigned him 'the land of Fife, from the Hill of the Britons to the Ochil Hills' for his *familia*. Serf returned to Kinneil and threw his staff across the Firth of Forth, and where it landed it sprouted into a fruit-tree which later became known as Morglas (= sea-green?). Serf and his companions began to clear away the 'spines and thorn-bushes' from the area (Culross, *cuilen ros* = 'holly point'), but were hindered by spies sent by King Brude f. Dargart to kill them. The king was taken ill, healed by Serf's prayers on his behalf, and moved to grant him Culross as the site of his church and burial ground. The *vita* then records a second encounter with Adomnán, this time at Lochleven, which is also given to Serf.

There follows a series of miracle stories located at places in West Fife and the surrounding area. At Dysart Serf turned water into wine to help a sick monk; in the same place he disputed with the Devil one night on the creation, fall and atonement of man. At Tullibody he cured a man of an insatiable appetite for food. At Tillicoultry he revived dead twins born to a poor woman. At Alva a peasant slaughtered his only pig to provide a meal for the saint, and when he arose in the morning he found it alive in his sty. At Airthrey Serf's pet lamb was stolen, killed and eaten by a thief; when the suspect was brought before the saint and swore on his staff that he was innocent, the lamb bleated within his gullet. At Dunning Serf slew a terrible dragon with his staff. He cured three blind men, three lame men, and three deaf men when they came to him from the Alps. In old age and after a long illness, he died at Dunning on 1 July. His body was carried to Culross and buried there, 'where his merits and the powers thereof have flourished to the present day'.[7]

If we were basing our judgements about St Serf on this *vita* alone, we would probably conclude that he was active in west Fife and the surrounding area c. 700, that Culross was his principal church, the place of his burial and later cult centre, and that the other places mentioned in the *vita* were claimed as parts of Culross's *parochia*.

Unfortunately, the story is not so simple. There are other sources for St Serf's life which are totally irreconcilable with *VS*. Two other chronological patterns are set out in late medieval sources. According to one of these, Serf was a contemporary of St Palladius, and was found practicing the primitive rite of the Scottish church when (as Prosper of Aquitaine records) Pope Celestine sent Palladius 'to the Scots believing in Christ' c. 430. This version is found in the anonymous *Vita Kentigerni*, in the *lectiones* for St Kentigern in the Sprouston Breviary, in Fordun, and in the *lectiones* for St Serf (1 July) in the *Aberdeen Breviary*.[8] Since the supposed connection of Palladius with Scotland was based on a misunderstanding of what Prosper meant by *Scoti*, such an early date can be explained and therefore safely discounted.

By contrast, other sources would make Serf an early contemporary of St Kentigern, the founder of Glasgow who is said to have flourished at the time of Rhydderch Hael and probably died c. 614. The anonymous *Vita Kentigerni*, the *Sprouston Breviary*, and Jocelin's *Vita Sancti Kentigerni* all record the tradition that Kentigern studies under St Serf at Culross; Wyntoun also knows of this tradition, and it is alluded to in the title of *VS* in the Dublin manuscript (but not in the text of the *vita*).[9] Jocelin says that Kentigern took leave of Serf at the Forth near Alloa as he started west on the journey which would eventually bring him to Glasgow. This might place Serf c. 570. If one could accept Jocelin's assertion that Kentigern was 180 years old when he died, it would presumably have been possible for him to have studied under Serf soon after Palladius's arrival in Scotland c. 430 and to have died in the time of Rhydderch Hael c. 600. Such amazing longevity, although common enough in saints' lives, has none the less to be discounted. That does not mean that we should automatically reject a chronological scheme which would place St Serf c. 570; but it will be argued below that such a chronology is suspect.

Two other sources mention St Serf. There is an Irish genealogical tract concerning 'The Mothers of the Saints' which is included in a number of Irish compilations. In some versions of this there is an entry: '*Alma ingen ríg Cruithnech mathair Seirb m. Proic ríg Canandan Egipti 7 is esin in srúthsenoir congeibh Cuillennros hi Sraith Erenn hi Comgellaibh eter Sliabh nOcel 7 Mur nGiúdan.*' (Alma daughter of the king of the Picts was the mother of Serf son of Proc, king of Canaan in Egypt; and he is the venerable old man who holds Culross in Strathearn in Comgellaig, between the Ochil Hills and the Firth of

Forth.)[10] The date of the 'Mothers of Saints' is in some doubt, but it is unlikely to be as early as the early ninth century; Colgan's attribution to Oengus the Culdee is no longer accepted.[11]

Whatever its date, it has intriguing connections with *VS*. *VS* names the parents as Obeth son of Eliud king of Canaan and Alpia (Alixia, with long-tailed *x*, shaped not unlike *p*, in the NLS manuscript) daughter of the king of Arabia. The mother's names, Alma (or possibly read Alina or Alnia) and Alpia (or Alixia), are similar, and both sources agree that the father was king of Canaan, though they do not agree as to his name. Anderson suggests that the *Comgellaig* (hostage-lands?) of Strathearn were what was formerly a detached portion of Perthshire in which Culross stands.[12] The statement that he holds Culross 'between the Ochil Hills and the Firth of Forth' may find an echo in *VS*'s description of how Serf asked Adomnán for a place to dispose his *familia*; Adomnán replied 'Habitant terram Fif, et a Monte Britannorum usque ad montem qui dicitur Okhel.' The statement in *VS* reads like an agreement between the successors of Columba at Iona (here personified by Adomnán) and the house at Culross that it should have a *parochia* in Fife between the Ochils and the 'Hill of the Britons'.[13]

The other late source is the *Orygynale Cronykil* of Andrew de Wyntoun, who was himself prior of St Serf of Lochleven in the early fifteenth century.[14] Wyntoun's account, which was presumably based on materials which were available to him at Lochleven, is very closely related to *VS*, but does vary sufficiently to make us suspect that Wyntoun's source was not identical with our manuscript. It is probably Wyntoun's own editorial policy as a chronicler to try to harmonise the story of Serf's pontificate with historical events. He says that Serf was elected pope in succession to John III (561–574), although no person called Servanus or any similar sounding name occurs at this point in papal lists. Wyntoun knows the tradition that Serf was son of the king of Canaan and that he was in Alexandria and Jerusalem before coming to Rome, but he does not name his father or mother. When Serf resigns the papacy and leaves Rome for France, Wyntoun makes no mention of his conflict with the demons in the Alps. Nor does Wyntoun mention his dryshod crossing of the English Channel, for his account of Serf's arrival in Scotland is quite different: he says that when Serf came to the sea that divides England and France, he got ships ready for himself and a hundred companions, and set sail, allowing the wind to carry them whither it would.

It brought them into the Firth of Forth, and they landed at Inchkeith. Adomnán came to meet them there, and on his advice Serf sent his followers (*menyhe*) to Dysart, but he himself proceeded alone to Kinneil; from there he threw his staff across the water, from it sprouted an apple tree at a place long known as Morglas, and Serf then crossed to Culross. Wyntoun appears not to have been aware that Morglas was the name of the tree itself rather than of its location, or that it was at Culross. His account makes slightly better geographical sense than does *VS*, with Serf sailing up the Firth of Forth to Inchkeith, on to Kinneil, and crossing from there to Culross. The story of the attempt on his life by 'Brude Dargardys sowne', and the king's repentance and gift of Culross, follow as in *VS*. Wyntoun adds one detail about Serf's life at Culross which is not in *VS* (except in the title):

And thare he browchte upe Saynte Mongowe,
That syne wes bischape off Glasgowe.

From there he went to the Isle of Lochleven, and King Brude gave it to him (*VS* attributes this gift to Adomnán). He dwelt at Lochleven for seven years.

There follows a sequence of miracles located at Tullibody, Tillicoultry, Airthrey and 'Douyn' (=Dunning), much as they appear in *VS*. The story of his disputation with the devil is not located ('in till a stede', says Wyntoun; *VS* and the *Aberdeen Breviary* place it in the cave of Dysart); the questions and answers are given at length, as in *VS*. The miraculous cure of three blind, three deaf, and three lame men, which *VS* locates at Dunning, is not mentioned. After his debate with the devil, in Wyntoun's account, Serf returned to Culross and died there. (*VS* says that he died at Dunning and that his body was carried to Culross for burial.)

So it seems that by the late middle ages, there were several of versions of the life of St Serf, closely related but not identical. A number of these can be identified. First, there was *VS* itself, surviving complete in one manuscript and as a fragment in another. Second, there was a very similar *vita* at Lochleven Priory, used by Wyntoun in his *Cronykil*. Its divergences from *VS* are described above. Another closely related *vita* seems to have been used by the compilers of the *Aberdeen Breviary*, with many of the same miracles and some of the same topographical details, but omitting mention of St Serf's foreign origins and early travels, and of his connection with Culross and Lochleven. Finally, it is hard to reconcile the *Aberdeen Breviary* description of the *vita* of 'another St Serf', of Israelite nationality who performed many miracles in the island of Portmoak, with either of the first two named above. They speak of Canaanite rather than Israelite nationality, refer to the island of Lochleven rather than of Portmoak, and stress Serf's connection with Culross. So there may have been another Lochleven *vita* of St Serf, not identical with the one which was used by Wyntoun, which was known to, but not used by, the compilers of the *Aberdeen Breviary*. Its existence, however, is uncertain; the compilers of the *Aberdeen Breviary* may have had only a vague report of a Lochleven *vita* which they had not seen, corresponding either to *VS* or (perhaps more likely) Wyntoun's source.

At least the first three of the above are closely related and may well have a common origin. What was it, and where was it written? I have said above that *VS* gives the impression that Culross was St Serf's principal foundation and cult centre, the place of his burial and so presumably where his relics were preserved, and the other places mentioned in *VS* look like the churches claimed for Culross's *parochia*. The obvious inference to be drawn is that *VS*, or its ultimate source, was composed at Culross in order to set out the territorial and jurisdictional claims of an early Christian church or monastery there. The same appears to be true of Wyntoun's source; it too names Culross as Serf's first foundation in Scotland and the place of his death and burial.

Cowan and Easson's *Medieval Religious Houses: Scotland* does not suggest Culross as the site of an early Christian church foundation.[15] But unless such an early foundation had existed, it is inconceivable that *VS* could have been written in anything like the form in which it survives. The existence of an early Christian foundation at Culross is indicated, however, by the presence there of a number of carved stones apparently of early Christian date. These include a massive cross-base and a cross-shaft on which some decoration survives. The shaft has a panel of fret-pattern combined with spirals which could be as early as the ninth century; the surviving fragments, although slight and badly worn, may have been comparable in quality with, and close in date to, cross-shafts at St Andrews.[16] The site is on a steep slope which presented awkward problems for the builders of the medieval claustral buildings; those on the south of the church are all on two storeys because of the fall in the ground.[17] The inference is that this was not a 'greenfield site' which the Cistercians were choosing for themselves, but a place with ancient associations which they were re-using for a good reason.

The Cistercian monastery of Culross was founded by Malcolm earl of Fife in 1217, and none of the churches or places mentioned in *VS* had any subsequent connection with the Cistercian abbey; so *VS* cannot be a post-1217 concoction in favour of the Cistercian monks of Culross. Neither can it have been composed in order to put forward the claims of Lochleven, even though Wyntoun knew something very similar to it; both *VS* and Wyntoun's source concur that Culross was St Serf's first foundation and the place of his burial. Indeed, it is striking how little *VS* and its relatives have to say about Lochleven; *VS* and Wyntoun imply that it was a daughter or subordinate church of Culross, like Dysart, Dunning and other places. Jocelin's *Vita Sancti Kentigerni*, the anonymous *Vita Kentigerni* of c. 1150, and the *Sprouston Breviary*, in their description of Kentigern's tutelage under Serf at Culross, imply that Culross was Serf's chief church and the site of his monastic school.[18]

I have suggested elsewhere that the Fife material in Jocelin's *Vita Kentigerni* probably belongs to the mid-ninth to late-tenth century.[19] Can we suggest a similar date, or indeed any date at all, for *VS*? We have noted that a *vita* of Serf was known to Jocelin c. 1180, though we cannot be certain that it was *VS*. What does seem very likely, however, is that Jocelin's *vita* of Serf was at least something closely related to it. So something very similar to our existing *VS* was in existence before 1180. How long before?

The priory register of St Andrews contains copies of a number of early notes relating to the Céli Dé of Lochleven, which it claims are translations 'veteris voluminis antiquo Scotorum idiomate conscripti', i.e., from an old book written in Gaelic; these may possibly have been marginal notes in a gospel book, like those inserted in the *Book of Deer*.[20] The first of them states that the island of Lochleven was given to Serf by Brude f. Dergard, 'last king of the Picts', and that the Céli Dé of that place came to an agreement with Fothad f. Bran, bishop of St Andrews. A bishop of that name is recorded in the mid-tenth century; so we can reasonably conclude that Lochleven was in existence before c. 950, and Culross before that.

Many of the place-names in *VS*, such as Insula Keth, Fif, Okhel, Kinel, Morglas, Culenros, Desertum, Tuligbotuan, Tuligcultrin,

Alveth, Atheren, Insula Leuene, Cella Dunenensis, are close to their Gaelic forms. The name of the Pictish king, Brude f. Dergard, is in a form found in sources associated with Lochleven Priory;[21] the various spellings of Adomnán's name (Edaunanus, etc.) are also Gaelic. This is perhaps of little help in dating the *vita*, since we should probably assume that Gaelic would have been spoken and written in Fife from at least the tenth century until the twelfth. *VS* states that the apple-tree at Culross was called Morglas, a Gaelic name probably meaning something like 'sea-green', *apud modernos*, 'among men of the present time'.

That part of the *vita* which covers Serf's activities in Scotland, with topographical details of where his activities are supposed to have taken place (Clackmannanshire, south-west Fife, and the surrounding area, plus the outlier at Dunning), seems to be the most strongly Gaelic in character as well as the most significant for the claims of Culross. But there are two parts of *VS* which do not show such strongly Gaelic characteristics, and which do not contribute to the pretensions of Culross: they are the first section, dealing with Serf's continental origins and travels before his arrival at the Firth of Forth; and the curious scholastic digression of his theological disputation with the devil at Dysart.

The section dealing with Serf's Mediterranean career has a number of peculiarities. Serf's father is named as Obeth f. Eliud, king of Canaan. These are biblical names (Obed was the father of Jesse in Ruth 4, 17; Eliud is named among the ancestors of Jesus in Mt. 1, 14–15), but it is worth noting that the name Eliud occurs also in Welsh genealogies.[22] It is difficult to see how 'Obeth king of Canaan' relates to the Irish tract's 'Proc rí Canandan'. Canaan, of course, was the territory occupied by the Hebrews after the Exodus, but it is not clear that this is how it was understood by the writer of *VS*. He implies that Serf came from Canaan, passing through Egypt (crossing first the Nile and then the Red Sea) and continuing on to Jerusalem; and he also seems to regard being bishop of Canaan as being something different from being patriarch of Jerusalem. The implication in this is that the writer thought of Canaan as lying to the west of Egypt, perhaps in Libya. On the other hand, he seems to have regarded Heliopolis (an ancient city near the Nile, about 10km. NE of Cairo) as lying in or near Obeth's kingdom. The Irish tract speaks of *Canandan Egipti*, 'of Canaan in Egypt'. Again, the angel warned Serf to leave Jerusalem and press on to Constantinople 'because this place (i.e., Jerusalem) is near to your nation and family'. From Constantinople Serf went to the island of Salvator (which I cannot identify) and thence to Rome. *VS* says simply that the papacy was vacant on his arrival, but Wyntoun supplies the detail that his predecessor was Pope John III (561–574); I would suggest that this was the work of Wyntoun's tidy historical mind, but it has no factual basis.

There is nothing specifically Scottish about any of this, but it could perhaps be argued that Serf's adventures in the Alps and across the English Channel find an echo in the exploits of Irish saga-heroes (for example in *Tain Bó Fraích*)[23] and of protohistoric kings such as Níall Noigíallach and Nath Í, both of whom are alleged to have fought battles in Britain and on the continent, and to have crossed the Alps.[24] A P Smyth has suggested, however, that 'the Near Eastern origins of Serf ... emanated from the pro-Roman party in Pictland in the aftermath of the Easter Controversy', and should be compared with similar stories surrounding Curetan/Boniface of Rosemarkie and Regulus of St Andrews.[25] It is doubtful, however, that these legends can have developed into their later medieval form until much later.

We have also to consider the other seemingly non-local element in *VS*, Serf's scholastic disputation with the devil in the cave of Dysart. This is perhaps the most alien part of the *vita*. The disputation covers questions about the Creation, the Fall of Man, and Christ's Redemption and Atonement. Although perhaps not of any great intellectual weight, it contrasts strikingly with the hotchpotch of miracles which surrounds it. It belongs rather to the theological and philosophical world of men like Anselm of Bec, and in a modest way it echoes the great disputation carried through in *Cur Deus Homo*. If the author was influenced by St Anselm (d. 1109), this helps us to place *VS* as it stands in the twelfth century, with *termini* c. 1100 × 1180. The *Aberdeen Breviary lectiones* record simply that the devil tempted Serf with questions, omitting the disputation itself; but it cannot be determined whether this is the result of abbreviation or whether this part was not in the *Aberdeen Breviary* writer's original.

Can we draw any conclusions, however tentative, about the person of St Serf himself? Perhaps the first thing to be said is that a personage of this name probably did in fact exist. The combined testimony of *VS*, Wyntoun, the Kentigern traditions, the *Aberdeen Breviary* and the 'Mothers of the Saints', together with all his dedications, seem to indicate a concrete personage. A twelfth-century thane of Clack-mannan called Gille-Serf points in the same direction.[26]

Where did he come from, and what was his nationality? The *Aberdeen Breviary* claims he was Scottish, but that the 'other St Serf' was an Israelite; *VS*, Wyntoun and the 'Mothers of the Saints' call him a Canaanite. Exotic oriental origins are claimed for a number of Scottish saints, and (whatever the motives behind them) probably should be rejected as unhistorical in every case.

Serf's name, however, presents interesting questions. Wyntoun presumably searched in vain for a Pope Servanus; the name is not that of a Roman pope, but it is not clear where it does come from. We have seen that the Irish form is Serb or Serbh, whence English Serf, but the name is not a common Gaelic one. One possibility is that Serf was British. The name Seruan or Serguan occurs in Welsh genealogies.[27] So one possibility is that Serf was himself British, that his name was Seruan, latinised as Servanus and gaelicised as Serbh.

An alternative, and perhaps more likely, possibility is that Serf was a Pict. The 'Mothers of the Saints' entry states that his mother was *ingen ríg Cruithnech*, daughter of the king of Picts. A rare example of the name occurs in Irish heroic literature, in the tale called *Tochmarc Émire la Coin Culainn*.[28] In an episode in this tale Cú Chulainn visits the court of Ruad, king of the Western Isles, whose daughter he rescues from the Fomori, thereby freeing the Isles from their tribute to them. One of his companions on his ship going from Alba to Eire *via* the Isles is called Drust mac Seirb, whose name, according to Carney, 'appears nowhere else in Irish literature'.[29] Since Drust is a name with a strong Pictish flavour, we may assume that the writer used it to give his Hebridean episode local colour; and if so, that suggests that the writer used the name Serb for the same reason, believing that it was a Pictish name as well.[30]

Can we hope to date St Serf with any degree of precision? We have rejected the suggestion that he could have been active in Scotland at the time of St Palladius, c. 430. The other possibilities offered by hagiographical literature are contemporaneity with St Kentigern (c. 570) and with St Adomnán (c. 700). Neither can be firmly ruled out. It could be suggested, however, that the association with St Kentigern arose because it was believed that Kentigern had come to Strathclyde from the east; it would have been natural to claim for him an association with a well-known (though obscure) east coast British or Pictish saint.

In the case of the supposed association with Adomnán and King Brude f. Dergard, these were again well-known historical figures whose inclusion as contemporaries in a *vita* has to be received with caution. St Adomnán was very famous and became the subject of his own mythology; Brude/Bridei was the brother and predecessor of King Nechtan, well-known from Bede, and his name, in the form *Bruide mac Derilei ri Cruithintuathi*, appears on the guarantor-list of Cáin Adomnáin.[31] The tradition that Brude f. Dergard (mistakenly called 'last king of the Picts') was the founder of Lochleven seems to have been in existence by the mid-tenth century, however, so it may have some substance. If so, the connection with Adomnán remains a possibility. A date of c. 700 might appear more likely than one of c. 570, especially considering that Curetan of Rosemarkie, whose traditions have much in common with St Serf's, seems to have flourished at this time.[32] St Andrews, supposedly founded by St Regulus under King Onuist f. Urguist c. 750, has a similarly exotic foundation story; and the sculpture at Culross appears to be comparable in style and date to that at St Andrews. But an early eighth-century date cannot be accepted without caution.

A firm *terminus ante quem* for the historical St Serf is probably provided only by the Lochleven notes, which indicate that the church there was in existence by c. 950. If, as appears virtually certain, the church at Culross was in existence before that at Lochleven, then St Serf must have lived and worked before the mid-tenth century. The Early Christian fragments of sculpture at Culross, of ninth- or tenth-century date, point in the same direction. If, as appears likely, he was Pictish or (less likely) British, then he must have been ninth century or earlier. It has been remarked that most Celtic hagiography relates to figures of the sixth and seventh centuries;[33] this might incline us to place St Serf within this period, but of course we cannot know if he is an exception to a general rule. He is unknown to Bede, which may not indicate anything; but it must be remembered that Bede's friend Trumwin was an Anglian 'bishop of the Picts', operating from a cathedral at Abercorn, for a few years up to 685. His 'bishopric of the Picts' had probably consisted of those Pictish lands most easily accessible from Abercorn, i.e., southern and western Fife. If we could be confident that *VS* is right in making Serf a contemporary of St Adomnán and King Brude f. Dergard, then we could see St Serf, with his church at Culross and a *parochia* in and around west Fife with outliers at Dysart and Dunning, filling the vacuum left by the flight of Trumwin in 685 and reorganising the church there along Columban lines. It may not be possible to date him more precisely than to the seventh, eighth, or ninth century; but of the dates offered by hagiography, c. 700 seems the most likely.[34]

NOTES

1. Dublin, Marsh's Library, MS Z 4.5.5 (D). An inventory of the books of Glasgow Cathedral drawn up in March 1432/3 mentions a small book containing the *Vitae* of St Kentigern and St Serf which sat on the precentor's stall in the Choir of Glasgow Cathedral; *Glasgow Registrum*, ii, 335.
2. W F Skene, *Chron. Picts-Scots*, 412–420. See A Macquarrie, '*Vita Sancti Servani*: the Life of St Serf', *Innes Review*, xliv (1993), 122–52. This chapter is a revision and expansion of the introduction to that article.
3. *Lives of SS Ninian and Kentigern*, ed. A P Forbes (Historians of Scotland, v, 1874).
4. J MacQueen, *St Nynia* (2nd edn 1990), 84 and n on p 133; idem, 'Myth and the Legends of Lowland Scottish Saints', *Scottish Studies*, xxiv (1980), 1–21, at 8–11.
5. *Aberdeen Breviary*, PE, 1 July.
6. Edinburgh, NLS, MS Adv. 34.7.3 (E). Described in M O Anderson, *Kings and Kingship in early Scotland* (1st edn 1973), 64–5. Skene knew this MS and transcribed parts of it in *Chron Picts-Scots*, but he did not collate this fragment with the Marsh's Library MS. I cannot determine whether the fragment was copied from the Marsh's Library MS. The grammatically wrong 'Ite rex' where the Dublin MS has 'Ite [uo]s' on f.1r might indicate that the reading of D was obscure at a time when Mr James Gray copied it; on the other hand, the Edinburgh MS's probably correct 'verbum Domini', where D has simply 'uerbum' on f. 1r, could either be a silent correction of D or could indicate that Gray was copying from a different MS.
7. Summarised from my own edition and translation in Macquarrie, '*Vita Sancti Servani*', 136–52.
8. For *VK*, see footnote 3 above; *Chron. Fordun*, iii, c. 9.
9. *Chron. Wyntoun*, ed F J Amours (STS, 50, 53, 54, 56, 57, 63, 1903–1914), iv, 76–91; see p 150 below.
10. P O Riain, *Corpus Genealogiarum Sanctorum Hiberniae* (Dublin Institute for Advanced Studies, 1985), 181; W Reeves, *On the Céli-Dé, commonly called Culdees* (1860), 242n. See also A O Anderson, *Early Sources of Scottish History, AD 500–1286* (1922) (hereafter Anderson, *ESSH*), i, 127–8.

11. O Riain, *Corpus*, 220, believes that 'the sources for the tract ... were probably very varied,' if not always as ancient as sometimes assumed; 'one must suspect the presence of some *ad hoc* fabrication'. Colgan is responsible for attributing it 'most implausibly' to Oengus the Culdee.

12. Anderson, *ESSH*, 127–8.

13. On the 'Hill of the Britons', see Watson, *CPNS*, 207–8, 208n.; *St Andrews Liber*, 27.

14. See n. 9 above. Wyntoun may himself have been a native of Portmoak.

15. I B Cowan and D E Easson, *Medieval Religious Houses: Scotland* (2nd edn London, 1976), 46–54, makes no mention of Culross.

16. Illustrated in W Douglas, 'Culross Abbey and its early Charters, with Notes on a fifteenth-century Transumpt', *PSAS*, lx (1925–6), 67ff., at 68. The shaft has connections with a panel on the Dupplin Cross, and with decoration in the Book of Armagh (early 9th century) and the Gospel of Mac Durnan (see J Anderson and J R Allen, *Early Christian Monuments of Scotland* (1903), ii, 345). I am grateful to Mr Ian Fisher of RCAHMS for most of this information.

17. *Royal Commission for the Ancient and Historical Monuments of Scotland: Inventory of the Monuments of Fife and Clackmannan* (Edinburgh, 1933), 70–7. The cross-base and shaft which are described as lying to the north of the west door of the church have now been moved inside and lie in the north transept. The stones are not described in *ECMS*, iii.

18. *Lives of SS Ninian and Kentigern*, *VK*, c. ivff.

19. A Macquarrie, 'The Career of St Kentigern of Glasgow: *Vitae, Lectiones* and Glimpses of Fact', *Innes Review*, xxxvii (1986), 3–24, at 10; above, Chapter 5, pp. 127–8.

20. *St Andrews Liber*, 113ff. They are also printed in Reeves, *Culdees*, 242ff, and in A C Lawrie, *Early Scottish Charters prior to AD 1153* (1905), 4ff. On the Gaelic notes in the Book of Deer, see K H Jackson, *The Gaelic Notes in the Book of Deer* (1972).

21. For Brude/Bridei, see Anderson, *KKES*, 64, 66, 100. The spelling Dergard seems to be unique to a group of MSS connected with Lochleven.

22. E Phillimore, '*Annales Cambriae* and Old Welsh Genealogies from Harleian MS 3859' *Y Cymmrodor*, ix (1888), 141–83.

23. *Táin Bó Fraích*, ed. F Byrne and M Dillon (DIAS, Medieval and Modern Irish Series, v, 1933). Fróech is said to have gone to Britain, across the Channel to the Alps, and finally to Lombardy in pursuit of his stolen cattle.

24. Nath I, for example, is said to have led 'an expedition across the English Channel and to the Alps' (*ceim dar Muir nIcht dochum nElpa*); *VS*'s name for the English Channel, *Icteum Mare*, would be the natural latinisation of *Muir nIcht*. Cf. T F O'Rahilly, *Early Irish History and Mythology* (1946), 212ff.

25. A Williams, A P Smyth and D P Kirby, *A Biographical Dictionary of Dark Age Britain* (1991), 94–5, 213; A P Smyth, *Warlords and Holy Men: Scotland, AD 80–1000* (1984), 127–8, 134.

26. Lawrie, *Early Scottish Charters*, no. clvi; Watson, *CPNS*, 333, for other examples of the name Gille-Serf.

27. R Bromwich, *Trioedd Ynys Prydein* (2nd edn 1978), 5, 238, 508; Phillimore, '*Annales Cambriae* and Old Welsh Genealogies', 175.

28. In *Compert Con Culainn and other Stories*, ed. A G van Hamel (Dublin Institute for Advanced Studies, Mediaeval and Modern Irish Series, iii, 1933, reprinted 1968), 16–68, at 60–1. The tale *Tochmarc Emire la Coin Culainn* is not of a single date, displaying both Old Irish and early Middle Irish features. This episode in its present form must post-date the Viking invasions, since in it the Isles are called *Innse Gall*. The episode is a version of the Perseus and Andromeda legend; another version of this legend, that of St George and the Dragon, is not found before the 12th century.

29. J Carney, *Studies in Irish Literature and History* (1955), 240–1. The occurrence of the name Drust in Irish heroic literature is of particular interest to scholars seeking the origins of the Tristan (= Drestan, Drostan, etc) story.

30. The names Drust and Drusticc (with a feminine suffix) are also found in a 'scholiastic' tale relating to Whithorn in the *Liber Hymnorum*, presumably with the same purpose of providing local colour by using Pictish-sounding names. Cf. *The Irish Liber Hymnorum*, ed. J H Bernard and R Atkinson (Henry Bradshaw Society, 1898), i, 22; Anderson, *ESSH*, i, 7–8; chapter 3 above, pp. 64–5.

31. M Ní Dhonnchadha, 'The Guarantor List of Cáin Adomnáin', *Peritia*, i (1982), 178–215, no. 91.

32. Ibid., no. 22; Williams et al., *Biographical Dictionary*, 94–5.

33. R Sharpe, *Medieval Irish Saints' Lives* (1991), 8–10; see below, Conclusions, p 235.

34. I am grateful to a number of scholars for their help and advice: to the editor of the *Innes Review*; to Dr Richard Sharpe of Wadham College, Oxford; to the late Professor Emeritus Gordon Donaldson; to Mr Ian Fisher of the RCAHMS; to Dr John Durkan of the University of Glasgow; and to the staff of Marsh's Library, Dublin.

7

St Adomnán of Iona: St Maelrubai of Applecross

The saints discussed in the preceding chapters all form the subjects of *vitae*. It is true that there is a tenth-century Irish *vita* of St Adomnán, but in it the author of *Vita Columbae* is largely unrecognisable.[1] When we come to churchmen of a period after AD 700, we are moving away from the 'age of saints' in the sense of people commemorated in saints' *Lives*; but they are important figures nonetheless. This chapter concerns two important saints of the Western Isles who lived about a hundred years after Columba's time, whose names have not become as well known as his. The first of these is St Adomnán, who was abbot of Iona a century after Columba's death. Almost everything we know about Columba we owe to Adomnán, because he wrote the oldest surviving *vita* of the great saint, based on a combination of written sources and oral tradition. It is thanks to him that we possess such a vivid and compelling picture of Columba. Part of the importance of this *vita* springs from the fact that it is preserved in a very early MS, written on Iona within a decade of Adomnán's death.

Adomnán is, however, a fascinating personage in his own right. He was born in the north-east of Ireland sometime in the 620s.[2] He belonged to the same aristocratic family as Columba himself, and in his childhood there would have been people still living who remembered the great saint; for example the northern Irish high-king Domnall son of Aed, who died in 642, had as a child been baptised by Columba at the Convention of Druim Cett.[3] Of Adomnán's childhood and early years we know very little, except that he received a thorough training at one of the great religious schools of Ireland in Latin and the Latin Bible, with perhaps a tiny smattering of Greek; certainly he at least knew the Greek alphabet.[4] Part of his training may have been at Columba's foundation of Durrow (now in County Offaly), which was probably the most important of Columba's Irish houses, second in importance only to Iona itself. These houses were monasteries in which unmarried clergy lived according to a rule laid down by the founder; they were great centres of art, education and medicine as well as houses of prayer and praise. Most of them were presided over by an abbot who belonged to the same family lineage as the founder. The abbots were often presbyters rather than bishops.

At some uncertain stage in his career, possibly when he was already of mature years, Adomnán moved to Iona. Iona was at the time at the height of its prestige and authority. Among its most famous abbots in succession to Columba himself (d. 597) had been Ségéne (abbot 623–652), who had first sent Columban missionaries to found the church of Lindisfarne in Northumbria in 632, and who self-confidently rejected appeals from the clergy of southern Ireland to conform to the Roman method of calculating the date of Easter a few years later;[5] and Cumméne (abbot 657–669), who wrote a book 'On the Virtues of Saint Columba', the first written collection of stories about Columba's life and actions.[6] The earliest abbot of whom Adomnán claims to have had personal knowledge was Failbe (abbot 669–679), who continued Iona's tradition of cultural and scholarly excellence. Like most of the abbots of Iona, and like Adomnán himself, these men were all members of Columba's own family, the royal house of Tír Conaill (Tirconnell) in County Donegal, one of the principal branches of the Northern Uí Néill.

His family connections, as well as his scholarship and blameless personal life, made Adomnán ideally suited to succeed Failbe on the latter's death in 679. The abbacy of Iona was an office with important secular contacts as well as religious duties. Adomnán found himself immediately drawn in to the 'Paschal Controversy' or argument about the method of calculating the date of Easter. The calendrical arguments involved were technical and complex, and need not concern us here.[7] What is important is that the question was a major one, because Easter was the most important feast of the Christian year, and from it were calculated other important days in the church calendar – Ash Wednesday, Palm Sunday, Good Friday, and Pentecost. It is also important to point out that the Celtic churches were not in any way 'heretical' or divergent in doctrine from the universal church on this issue; merely, they observed old-fashioned practices and based their calculations on methods and tables which had gone

out of use in the rest of the western world. It may be that the heat
generated by the Paschal controversy has been to some extent
exaggerated by Bede, who was himself an expert on chronology and
calendrical calculation, and from whom much of our information
about this period derives. On the other hand, Cummian's 'Paschal
Letter' of c. 633,[8] and to a lesser extent Adomnán's own cryptic
allusion to the problem,[9] may suggest that Bede was not alone in
taking it seriously.

Be that as it may, the controversy came to a head for the monks
at Iona in 664, when the kings of Northumbria decided to go over
to the Roman method of calculating Easter, expelled the Columban
abbot of Lindisfarne, and upset the connection between Lindisfarne
and Iona which had lasted a generation.[10] From then on, Northumbria ceased to be a bridge between Iona and continental Europe. But
the monks of Iona had other outlets and sources of information. A
few years after Adomnán became abbot, he describes how a bishop
from Gaul, Arculf, was driven off course while returning to his own
land from a pilgrimage to the Holy Land; his ship was blown
northward into the uncharted ocean, and finally made landfall in the
Western Isles. Arculf was brought to Iona where he was given
hospitality by Adomnán. While he was staying at Iona, waiting for a
favourable wind to take him back to Gaul, Arculf described to the
monks the sights he had seen in and around Jerusalem; and while he
did so, Adomnán eagerly copied down his account on wax tablets.
Later, he made a fair copy from his notes, and called the resulting
book *De Locis Sanctis*, The Holy Places, to be a guide to pilgrims and
a work of reference for scholars.[11] Adomnán's book on the Holy
Places deserves to be better known, if only because it is the oldest
book to have been written in Scotland whose text has survived (apart
from one brief fragment, Cumméne's book on *The Virtues of St
Columba* has been lost).

In 685 the Pictish king Bridei son of Bile defeated the English of
Northumbria in a great battle fought at Dunnichen in Angus, and
the Gaels, Britons and Picts were able to throw off the yoke of English
servitude which the Northumbrians had imposed on them.[12] The
previous year the same English army had raided in Ireland, devastat-
ing Brega and taking many captives back to be slaves in England. In
686, the year following the English defeat, Adomnán went on a
diplomatic mission to the court of the Northumbrian king Aldfrith
at Bamborough, in an attempt to negotiate the release of the Irishmen

captured two years earlier. The English defeat in 685 made his task easier, but Adomnán also used his considerable tact: he took with him a copy of *The Holy Places*, which he dedicated to King Aldfrith with a suitably laudatory preface. The king remitted all the captives, and Adomnán returned with them in triumph to Ireland.[13] The manuscript of *The Holy Places* was lodged in the library at Wearmouth, and Bede later made an edited version of his own. Where Bede quotes passages from *The Holy Places* in his *Ecclesiastical History*, he is in fact quoting from his own revision.[14]

While in Northumbria Adomnán visited the monastery of Wearmouth and Jarrow, and two years later he returned to Northumbria and stayed for some time visiting the churches there.[15] Bede's account of his visit is written from an intensely partisan point of view. He describes how Adomnán was exhorted by many who were better informed than himself to abandon his erroneous traditions and accept the customs of the universal church; Adomnán was so impressed by what he saw that he was persuaded by their arguments. Bede heaps praise on Adomnán for this receptiveness, describing him as 'a good and wise man with an excellent knowledge of the Scriptures' and 'a man who greatly loved unity and peace.'[16]

It would be wrong to interpret Adomnán's 'conversion' as bowing to English cultural imperialism. Iona and its abbot were too self-confident for that, and it must be remembered that the Gaels and Picts had broken free of English political domination only three years before. If Adomnán's decision has sometimes been portrayed as a 'sell-out' of the Columban churches, that is perhaps largely due to Bede's rather smug interpretation of his change of mind. Adomnán will also have been aware of the arguments adduced by Cummian and others in Ireland, and these will have weighed with him as well as the opinions of the monks of Wearmouth.

If Bede has misled us about the reasons for Adomnán's 'conversion' to the Roman camp in the Paschal Controversy in 688, he has led us further astray by his description of subsequent events. Bede describes how after his visit to Northumbria, Adomnán returned to Iona and tried to persuade his own monks of the rightness of the English practice in the Paschal controversy; in this, we are told, he was unsuccessful. The monks of Iona refused to conform, and insisted on continuing their outmoded traditions. Adomnán was so discouraged by his failure that he withdrew to Ireland, and passed most of the rest of his life there, returning to Iona only once in the last year of his life (704), but he again failed to convert his monks, and died before he witnessed the 'scandal' of Easter being celebrated on two separate days in Christian disunity.

This is Bede's account of Adomnán's last years, but it has been shown that it contains certain difficulties.[17] Recent research has shown that it is more likely that Adomnán continued to spend much of his time on Iona after 688. A chronicle being kept contemporaneously on Iona speaks of him going into Ireland in 692 and again in 697, implying that he was going from his normal residence on Iona on both occasions.[18] In his own writings Adomnán describes himself making a journey from one of the islands in the Firth of Lorn to Iona 'in the summer after the meeting of the Synod of Ireland'; this can only be a reference to the Synod of Birr held in 697.[19] It is clear from the text that Adomnán was still living on Iona when he wrote his second book, the *Life of Columba*.

This book is arranged by categories into three books, describing miracles of prophecy (Book i), miracles of power (Book ii), and angelic visions (Book iii). In some ways it does not greatly appeal to modern taste which is sceptical about the miraculous and looks for chronological continuity. It has been pointed out, however, that Book iii does form something of a chronological narrative, beginning with pre-natal miracles, then tales from Columba's childhood, maturity, his old age and death, and ending with his funeral.[20] The whole of the *Vita Columbae* vividly portrays Columba's own character and the daily life and work of his monks, performing divine service, working in the fields, writing, studying, and travelling far and wide. Adomnán emphasises Columba's humane concern for the well-being of people in all walks of life, the great and the humble; and he stresses Columba's love of animals in his picturesque stories of his care for an exhausted migrant bird which flopped down on Iona one day and his final blessing given to his pack-horse when it came to visit him on the day of his death. The *Life of Columba* stands apart from all other Celtic saints' lives as a faithful and honest portrait of a great and saintly man. The majority of saints' lives read like a collection of the title deeds of the founder's church; but Adomnán had no such acquisitive purpose in view.

Apart from his writings, Adomnán's most remarkable achievement came in 697. At the synod of Birr in that year he proposed a new law, the *Cáin Adomnáin*, exempting non-combatants from military service and extending to them the protection of the abbots of Iona.

Transgressions against this 'Law of the Innocents' were punishable by a fine to be collected by Iona Abbey. The law was guaranteed by the kings of Ireland and Scotland, whose names appear as witnesses to it.[21] Although the text of the *Cáin Adomnáin* contains much later material, it has been demonstrated that the list of guarantors is probably largely authentic.

Adomnán died in 704. He must have been approaching eighty years of age, and had served as abbot of Iona for twenty-five of them. The qualities of kindness and humanity, especially to the weak and oppressed, of broad-mindedness, and of scholarship and learning, make him stand out above all his contemporaries.

We know as much as we do about Adomnán because of his writings. Some contemporaries have not left as full a record of themselves, but were none the less important; and perhaps none was more important than St Maelrubai of Applecross, who revived Christianity in the northern Hebrides after a gap of half a century. Thanks to Adomnán's *Life of Columba*, we have plenty of evidence regarding the early development of Christianity in the Western Isles south of Ardnamurchan and on the adjacent mainland. Much more poorly documented is the early development of Christianity further north, in the northern Hebrides and on the West Coast north of Ardnamurchan. But it may be that by a careful analysis of scraps of evidence we can build up some picture of developments there.

Two incidents in Columba's career which took place in Skye are recorded by Adomnán; they include the baptising of a pagan, so presumably there had been little or no missionary activity there before his time. The first describes how, during a visit to Skye, Columba was praying in a wood, apart from his companions, when a wild boar approached. As the boar rushed towards him Columba raised his hand and forbade it to come further, but commanded it rather to die on the spot; and so it happened.[22] Modern scepticism might attribute the boar's sudden death more to the actions of huntsmen than to the power of Columba's word; but whatever the cause of the animal's sudden death, we may well believe that Columba had some communication with the hunters after his narrow escape.

Adomnán also describes how Columba was beside the sea-coast when a boat came to shore bearing in it an old man named Artbranan, 'leader of the war-band of Geona', to whom he preached through an interpreter, and whom he baptised; the old man then died and was buried in his presence, and his followers raised a cairn over his body.

This cairn was still visible in Adomnán's time, and the place was called *Dobur Artbranain*.[23]

There is nothing in Adomnán's account to suggest that Columba visited Skye more than once, so probably the two incidents are close in time as well as place. We might speculate that his encounter with Artbranan was a later consequence of his meeting with a boar-hunt.

We have no record of Columba visiting Eigg or the Small Isles, but we do know that Baithéne, his second in command and 'foster-son', was once detained on Eigg at a time when Columba was on Hinba.[24] It is unlikely, however, that Hinba was near Eigg or is to be identified with any of the islands north of Iona. Perhaps Baithéne's visit was made at the time when he was prior of the Columban monastery of Mag Luing on Tiree, but we cannot be certain of this or of Baithéne's reason for visiting Eigg.

St Donnan of Eigg, who died c. 617,[25] has dedications in Skye and the adjacent mainland (e.g. Eilean Donan),[26] and so presumably had undertaken missionary work in the area. Later traditions connect his death with opposition from the local lay aristocracy, presumably Picts; they also record reluctance on Columba's part to get involved with Donnan.[27] Obits of abbots of Eigg are not recorded again until 725 and 752.[28] It has been suggested that the christianising of this area stagnated for more than 50 years following the death of St Donnan.[29]

A certain amount of a factual nature is known about St Maelrubai. His dedications and the form of the name are discussed at length by Watson; they are concentrated in the north-west, but with a scattering down the west coast, in the north-east, and in the central Highlands.[30] He was a monk of Bangor, who according to the Irish annals came to Scotland in 671, founded the church of Applecross two years later, and died in 722 at the age of eighty.[31] The late tradition in the *Aberdeen Breviary* that he was martyred by Vikings at Urquhart cannot be accepted, since he is not called a martyr in earlier Irish sources and the Viking raids in Scotland did not begin until the 790s.[32] His feast-day in late medieval Scottish calendars, 27 August, differs from that in earlier Irish sources, 21 April; it has been suggested that a later saint of the same or a similar name, associated with Urquhart, has been confused with the monk of Bangor who settled at Applecross.[33]

It has been suggested that Maelrubai was deliberately reviving the mission of Donnan which had ended in tragedy fifty years earlier.[34] But an alternative possibility is that Maelrubai's arrival in the north-west in 671 is to be connected with the activities of the local Pictish aristocracy. It may be that we know more about the native (Pictish) family of Skye in the seventh century than is often assumed, and this in turn may cast light on early Christianity in the region and Maelrubai's mission.

A member of this family, Cano son of Gartnait, became the subject of an Irish pseudo-historical romance, *Scela Cano meic Gartnáin* (hereafter *SCMG*). This tale is perhaps less well-known than it deserves to be, probably because it has never been completely translated into English.[35] Although the story purports to deal with historical characters such as the sons of Aed Sláne, Guaire Aidne, Illand mac Scandláin, Marcán mac Tommáin, and Aedán mac Gabráin, it is full of anachronisms and chronological impossibilities;[36] it is therefore best to treat it as a pseudo-historical romance rather than as a true historical source. But its characters are mostly people who are otherwise known to have existed (although not all at the same time), so it may be accepted as supporting evidence for the existence of a hero called Cano mac Gartnait from Skye, though not necessarily for his chronology or for the facts of his career.

The genealogical compilations known as the *Genelaig Albanensium* include what appears to be a pedigree of the family of Cano mac Gartnáin:[37]

Con[gus]
mac Consamla [*lege* Conamla, gen. of Conamail]
mic Canai [= *Cano*] Gairb
mic Gartnait
mic Aedáin
mic Gabráin.

This is at variance with the pedigree in *SCMG*:

Cano
mac Gartnáin
meic Aeda
meic Gabráin.

Senchus Fer nAlban mentions a son of Aedán called Gartnait:[38]

Gabrán had five sons: Aedán [and four others named.] Aedán had seven sons: [six named] and Gartnait. Four sons of Gartnait mac Aedáin, namely [no names follow.]

Possibly two generations have been omitted in the *BB* pedigree between Cano and Gartnait. If we accept that Aedán's grandson

Domnall Brecc had a son Gartnait, who is the Gartnait f. Donuel of
the Pictish Chronicle and Gartnait mac Domnaill of the Irish Annals,
the pedigree could be reconstructed to read: Congus mac Conamla
(d. *AU* 705) mic Canonn/Canai (d. *AU* 688) mic Gartnait (d. *AU*
663) [mic Domnaill (d. *AU* 642) mic Echdach Buidi (d. *AU* 630)]
mic Aedáin (d. *AU* 608) mic Gabráin (d. *AU* 559).

On the other hand, the rivals of the descendants of Aedán are
called descendants of Gartnait mac Acithain; Acithan appears to be
a masculine name, so it cannot be a matronymic. *AT* has a record
of the death of Tolar Aithicain, (presumably for Talorc son of
Athican), s.a. [685], which is immediately followed by an account of
the death of Domnall Brecc. The death of Domnall Brecc is certainly
misplaced, and should belong to c. 642; probably the other entry is
also misplaced and belongs to about the same year. A record of
Domnall Brecc's defeat at the battle of *Calathros* is entered in *AU*
678, and the record of his death s.a. 685; these appear to have been
misplaced, because they are also recorded at their apparently correct
dates s.a. 635 and 642. So there are good reasons for believing that
the death of Talorc f. Acithan probably belongs correctly c. 642.

It is not impossible, of course, that Cano mac Gartnait was
descended from Gabrán through Domnall Brecc; this would fit the
Irish pedigree, although it appears to have lost two generations. If so,
his inheritance must have been in part at least maternal. On the other
hand, it is perhaps more likely that Cano was a member of an
(apparently patrilineal) Pictish dynasty in Skye, descended from
Acithan and unrelated, except perhaps through females, to the Cenél
nGabráin.

There seem to have been two persons called Gartnait, roughly
contemporary, one the son of Donuel/Domnall (Brecc?), the other
son of Acithan. It is also possible that an Irish copyist could have
mistaken the unfamiliar (presumably Pictish) *mac Acidain* for the
familiar Irish *mac Aidáin*. Further confusion could have arisen
because Aedán mac Gabráin did have a son called Gartnait.[39]

Neither the *BB* pedigree or *SCMG* may be in fact a true record of
this family's lineage. The Annals contain a number of references to
the dynasty of Skye and to other persons named in *SCMG*, the most
important of which are set out below:

AT [642?] The death of Talor[c mac] Athicain.

AU 649. War between the descendants of Aedán and [those] of
Gartnait mac Acithain.

AU 668. Voyage of the sons of Gartnait to Ireland, with the people of Skye.

AU 670. The family of Gartnait came [back] from Ireland.

AU 673. The capture of Eliuin mac Cuirp and of Conamail mac Canonn.

AU 688. The murder of Cano son of Gartnait.

AU 690. Coblaith daughter of Cano died.

AU 705. The slaying of Conamail mac Canonn.

AU 731. A battle between the Picts and the Dál Riata in Muirbolg, and the Picts were defeated. This was fought between the son of Aengus and the son of Congus; Brude conquered Talorc, who fled. [i.e., Bridei f. Aengus defeated Talorc f. Congus.]

AU 734. Talorc son of Congus took his own brother and gave him into the hands of the Picts; and he was drowned by them.

AU 740. Cubretan son of Congus died.

This is the last mention of the family in the Annals. Since the Iona Chronicle appears to have been being kept contemporaneously between about 670 and 740, these references may be taken as reasonably trustworthy. They allow us tentatively to reconstruct the pedigree of the family as follows:

Pedigree of the Pictish Dynasty of Skye
c. 600–740

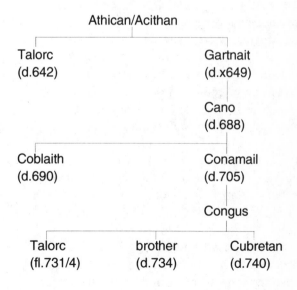

Gartnait son of Acithan was probably dead by 649, when his descendants were fighting against the Cenél nGabráin; Gartnait son of Donuel/Domnall died in 663. On balance it seems more likely that our Cano was the son of Gartnait mac Acithain.

Any slight historical basis that *SCMG* has relates to the war between the Cenél nGabráin and the descendants of Gartnait mac Acithain of Skye in 649 and the exile of Gartnait's sons in Ireland 668–70. One of these sons was called Cano (indeclinable in *SCMG*; treated as an N-stem, gen. *Canonn*, in *AU*; *Genelaig Albinensium*'s gen. *Canai* reflects a different inflection).[40] But Cano's romantic adventures are set in an earlier generation: Marcán died in 653, Illann mac Scandláin died in 656, Guaire Aidne and the two sons of Aed Sláne died in the great plague of the mid-660s. Aedán mac Gabráin was earlier still, and had been dead for 60 years. He may have been included simply as the personification of his dynasty, which did in fact fight against the sons of Gartnait. The pedigree which relates Cano's family to the Cenél nGabráin may be artificial, like the pedigree in *SCMG* (Cano mac Gartnáin mic Aeda mic Gabráin; 'Aed mac Gabráin' is spurious). There are two alternative possibilities: either intermarriage between the Skye dynasty and the Cenél nGabráin, and a connection through a female; or genuine confusion arising from the fact that there were two persons called Gartnait, one king of Fortrenn, the other king of Skye, roughly contemporary.

The exile of the sons of Gartnait may have a bearing on the ecclesiastical developments of this period. They may have become Christians during their exile in Ireland 668–670, and thereafter invited the monks of Bangor to re-establish Christian churches in the north-west. Maelrubai was a monk of Bangor, and Applecross appears to have belonged to the *familia* of St Comgall of Bangor. For what it is worth, *SCMG* says that Cano came first to *Collmag hi Crich Ulad*, 'the hazel-plain on the borders of the Ulaid', before continuing his adventures further south and west in Meath, Connacht and Munster. Collmag has not been identified, and one does not want to rely too much on a tale which is largely unhistorical. But the arrival of Maelrubai of Bangor in Scotland just a few years after the exile of the sons of Gartnait might suggest that the two events were in some way connected.

Certainly Christianity became well established in Skye; there are more than a dozen place-names incorporating the element *cill-*, with the greatest concentration in northern Trotternish. These are probably all or mostly pre-Viking.[41] Although from 795 onwards the Vikings were raiding and later settling in Skye,[42] the church there seems to have survived and continued as an important focus for the northern Hebrides; a person calling himself bishop 'of the holy church of Skye' is mentioned in the 1130s, apparently claiming to be bishop of the Isles.[43] Although in the medieval period before the Great Schism (1387) the bishops of the Isles seem to have been based normally in Man, the loss of Man to the Scots in 1331 created a crisis, and at the same time we find the clergy of Skye electing a bishop of the Isles; by the 1430s the church of Snizort (Skeabost) had emerged as a cathedral, possibly reviving a much earlier practice.[45] Its use as a medieval cathedral does not seem to have been continuous, however; it had been forgotten by the time of Donald Monro in the 1540s, and he had been parson of Snizort.[46] Monro stated that there were twelve parish kirks in Skye, of which eleven have been identified.[47] But he also believed, wrongly, that Iona Abbey church had been used as the cathedral of the Isles since the 1330s.[48]

The cumulative evidence suggests that Christianity in Skye is very ancient. St Columba may well have been the first Christian to visit the island and make converts there; but the task of missionary activity in Skye was not mainly carried out by monks from Iona. St Donnan's achievements on Eigg and the surrounding islands were ephemeral, but the conversion of Skye was made permanent by the work of St Maelrubai from the 670s onwards; it may be worth speculating that monks from Bangor were invited to Skye and supported there by Cano mac Gartnait and his family following their exile in Ireland in the late 660s. The re-emergence of abbots of Eigg in the early eighth century is probably connected with this activity. Skye had a good number of kirks, reckoned as twelve in the middle ages. There was also a hazy episcopal tradition connected with Skye, but it is not certain that it can be pushed back beyond the twelfth century.

Adomnán and Maelrubai were contemporaries; the poorly-documented career of the latter is a reminder that much activity was taking place beyond the orbit of Iona even while the successors of Columba were at the height of their influence. During this period, the consolidating or secondary phase of Scottish Christianity, there was much saintly activity throughout Scotland; but saints later in time than Serf and Adomnán were not the heroes of hagiography to the same extent.

NOTES

1. R Sharpe, *Medieval Irish Saints' Lives* (1991), 23. M Herbert, *Iona, Kells, and Derry* (1988), 158–71.
2. The known facts of Adomnán's life are assembled in *Adomnán's Life of Columba*, ed. A O and M O Anderson (Edinburgh, 1961; 2nd edn Oxford, 1991)(hereafter *VC*), pp. xxxix ff., in R Sharpe, *Adomnán of Iona: the Life of St Columba* (1995), and in Herbert, *Iona, Kells, and Derry*.
3. *VC*, i, 10.
4. *Adomnán's De Locis Sanctis*, ed. D Meehan (Dublin, 1958).
5. M Walsh and D O Croinín, *Cummian's letter De controversia Paschali, etc.* (Toronto Pontifical Institute of Mediaeval Studies, Texts and Studies, 1988); text also in Migne, *PL*, lxxxvii, 969–78.
6. A fragment is quoted in *VC*, iii, 5.
7. A good summary is in H Mayr-Harting, *The Coming of Christianity to Anglo-Saxon England* (1972), 103ff.; and since this was written, cf. also Adomnán of Iona, *Life of St Columba*, trans. R Sharpe (1995), 36–8.
8. Walsh and O Croinín, *Cummian's letter De controversia Paschali*.
9. *VC*, i, 3.
10. Bede, *HE*, iii, 25, 26; much of his information is drawn from *Eddius' Life of Wilfrid*, ed. B Colgrave (1927).
11. See n. 3 above.
12. *AU* 685; Bede, *HE*, iv, 26.
13. *AU* 687; *HE*, iv, 26; v, 15.
14. Ibid., v, 16–17.
15. In *HE*, v, 15, Bede mentions only one visit by Adomnán to Northumbria; but Bede was still very young at the time. *VC*, ii, 46 makes it clear that Adomnán visited Northumbria in 686 and again in 688.
16. *HE*, v, 15.
17. J M Picard, 'The Purpose of Adomnán's *Vita Columbae*', *Peritia*, i (1982), 160–77.
18. Bannerman, *Dalriada*, 9ff., demonstrates the provenance of these annalistic entries.
19. *VC*, ii, 45; cf. Picard, op. cit. On the identification of this island, cf. Chapter 4 above, Appendix I, pp 91–102.
20. J Marsden, *The Illustrated Columcille* (1991), 143.
21. *Cáin Adomnáin*, ed. K Meyer (1905); M Ní Dhonnachada, 'The Guarantor list of Cáin Adomnáin', *Peritia*, i (1982), 178–215.
22. *VC*, ii, 26.
23. Ibid., i, 33. The name means 'Artbranan's Water'; Watson, *CPNS*, 75.

24. *VC*, iii, 18   On the identification of Hinba, see above, Chapter 4, Appendix I: Hinba, pp 91–102.
25. *AU*, s.a.
26. Watson, *CPNS*, 283.
27. Discussion in Smyth, *Warlords and Holy Men*, 107–12.
28. *AU*, s. annis.
29. Smyth, *Warlords and Holy Men*, 109–10.
30. Watson, *CPNS*, 287–9.
31. *AU*, s. annis.
32. *Aberdeen Breviary*, PE., 27 August.
33. Boyle, 'Notes on Scottish Saints', 72–3.
34. Smyth, *Warlords*, 107–11.
35. There is a good edition of the OI text (*Scela Cano meic Gartnáin*, ed. D A Binchy, Dublin Institute for Advanced Studies, Medieval and Modern Irish Series, xviii (1963)). The best English summary remains M Dillon, *The Cycles of the Kings* (Oxford, 1946), 79–83. Parts of the Irish text are very obscure. The tale is of interest to scholars looking for the origins of the medieval legend of Tristan and Iseult. The name Tristan is apparently Pictish in origin: cf. Pictish Drestan, Drustan, Drostan. Cano's beloved is called Cred; she is the daughter of Guaire Aidne, king of Connacht, and is married to Marcán mac Tommáin, one of the sub-kings in Connacht. The name of Marcán is strikingly similar to that of King Mark of Cornwall, who occupies the same role in the Tristan legend; but there are no other echoes of this kind, although the broad outline of the two stories is similar.
36. Reference to a few annal entries will show how wayward the tale's chronology is: *AU* c. 608. The death of Aedán mac Gabráin [*AT*. adds, in the 37th year of his reign and 74th of his age.] *AU* 649. The battle of Carn Conaill in which Guaire fled, and Diarmait mac Aedo Sláne was victor.   *AU* 653.   A battle in Connacht, in which Marcán mac Tommáin fell.   *AI* 656. The death of Illann mac Scandláin.   *AU* 663. The death of Guaire Aidne.   *AU* 668.   Diarmait and Blathmac, [sons of Aed Sláne,] joint kings of Ireland, died of the 'yellow plague'.
37. Bannerman, *Dalriada*, 66.
38. Bannerman, *Dalriada*, 41–2, 48.   We have seen that Gartnait mac Aedáin is probably identifiable with Gartnait f. Dome(l)ch, king of Picts c. 584–599; see above, Chapter 4, Appendix II, p 111.
39. *AU*, 601. The death of Gartnait, king of the Picts. *AU* 663. The death of Gartnait mac Domnaill, king of the Picts.
40. Cf. R Thurneysen, *A Grammar of Old Irish* (1980), 217.
41. Nicolaisen, *Scottish Place-names*, 142–3.
42. *AU*, 795.

43. J Raine, *Historians of the Church of York* (RS, 71), ii, 372; Anderson, *SAEC*, 224n; Anderson, *ESSH*, ii, 97.
44. *Diplom. Norv.*, xvii, no. 10.
45. *CSSR*, iv, no. 105; Watt, *Fasti*, 203ff.
46. D Monro, *The Western Isles of Scotland and Genealogies of the Clans*, ed. R W Munro (1961), 62–3.
47. Ibid., 37; I B Cowan, *The Parishes of medieval Scotland* (Scottish Record Society, 1967), 183.
48. Monro, *Western Isles*, 62–3.

8

St Brigit, St Peter, St Andrew and St Constantine

Most of the earliest church foundations of which we have record seem to have reflected the initiative of saintly founders rather than of laymen. We know that Iona was given to Columba for the foundation of his monastery; we know that he 'commended' the monk Cormac to the Pictish king of the Orkneys and thus made it possible for him to found a hermitage there. We know of hostility between St Donnan of Eigg and the local Pictish laity, resulting in his martyrdom in 617. The story of St Kentigern records that the saint sought a place to found his church and that Rhydderch Hael gave him the 'green hollow', *glascau*, just a few miles away from the royal residence at Partick. Bur for the most part, we have no record of the active involvement of laymen in the establishment of religious houses until a later period. We do not think of Iona or its contemporaries as 'royal monasteries', because they were founded on the saint's own initiative, albeit with royal approval or a royal grant. But from the eighth century onwards, as religious foundations became more numerous and records of them more abundant (although still sparse), we seem to find more involvement on the part of laymen in their foundation, with kings and others actually taking the initiative.[1] The houses founded by them were often near royal centres, and some at least do not seem to have been strictly or solely monastic in purpose. As the title of this chapter implies, they are dedicated to a variety of patrons, both Celtic and continental, rather than founded by individual 'saints'; although saintly founders are still claimed in some cases.

Although the foundation legends of Abernethy claim a very early date for its origins, the earliest religious house founded by a Pictish king of which we have knowledge is that established by Nechton f.

Derilei c. 710.[2] It is likely, however, that there were Columban churches in Pictland before this, for Columba and his monks had been active there for over a century, and the Annals record the expulsion of Columban monks *trans dorsum Britanniae* in 717.[3] But the location of their houses on the Pictish side of Drumalban cannot be certainly determined. In a famous passage Bede describes how, a few years before the expulsion of the Columbans, King Nechton had written to Ceolfrith, abbot of Wearmouth and Jarrow, requesting information on the catholic calculation of the date of Easter and on the Roman tonsure. 'He also asked for masons to be sent to build a church of stone after the Roman fashion in his land, promising that it should be dedicated in honour of the blessed prince of the apostles.'[4] The identification of this church with an ancient tower incorporated within the later priory church of St Peter at Restenneth is attractive, but specialist opinion does not favour so early a date.[5] Whether Restenneth really is Nechton's foundation or not, we can see in his action the first certain example of a religious foundation by the initiative of a Pictish king. The main purpose was to reduce the importance of Iona and its monks in Pictish affairs.

The Northumbrians had already attempted to do this by the establishment of a short-lived bishopric of the Picts based at Abercorn; this attempt came to an abrupt end after the Battle of Dunnichen in 685, when Bridei f. Bile king of the Picts defeated and drove out the Angles from southern Scotland; these included 'the reverend man of God Trumwin, who had been made their bishop, who fled with his companions who were in the monastery of Abercorn, situated in the land of the Angles, but close to the firth which separates Anglian from Pictish territory.'[6] We have seen that St Serf's activities in southern Fife, perhaps c. 700, could possibly represent an attempt to replace the Anglian mission with a church modelled on Columban lines, perhaps encouraged by Adomnán and fostered by his ally King Bridei f. Derilei.[7] But Bridei's brother Nechton was beginning a trend which was to have a much longer history.

The identification of Restenneth as Nechton's foundation must remain doubtful. Also uncertain is the nature of the new foundation. Bede does not mention a bishop at the new church, and does not state explicitly that it was a *monasterium*. Yet his words, 'All ministers of the altar and monks were tonsured in the shape of a crown, and the corrected nation rejoiced to submit to the discipleship of Peter... and under his protection', might be taken to imply that Nechton's foundation was staffed by priests and monks and had an extensive jurisdiction throughout the Pictish kingdom.[8]

The different accounts which survive of the foundation of Abernethy cannot be readily reconciled; all they have in common is the assertion that Abernethy was founded by a Pictish king and dedicated to St Brigit of Kildare. In one version, embedded in a Pictish king-list copied into a fourteenth-century manuscript, it is stated that Darlugdach, abbess of Kildare, came to Britain in the third year of 'Necton Morbet filius Erip', who in the following year gave Abernethy to God and St Brigit in her presence; and Darlugdach 'sang Alleluia over that offering.'[9]

This account is followed by what purports to be the foundation charter of Abernethy. Documents of this kind are rare, so it is worth quoting it in full: 'Necton the great son of Wirp, king of all the provinces of the Picts, gave Apurnethige to St Brigit until the Day of Judgement, with its boundaries: from the stone at Apurfeirc to the stone beside Cairfuill (i.e., Lethfoss), and from there upwards as far as Athan. The reason for the gift is this: Necton had been expelled by his brother Drust and was living the life [of an exile] in Ireland. He begged St Brigit to intercede with God for him. She prayed for him and replied, "If you come to your own land the Lord will have mercy on you; you will hold the kingship of the Picts in peace." '[10] This charter certainly looks very ancient, though probably not as early as the time of Abbess Darlugdach (who succeeded Brigit as abbess of Kildare; Brigit's death is recorded in *AU* 526).[11]

The Pictish king-list enters a 'Nectu nepos Uerb' with a reign of twenty years at a point which makes him possibly identifiable with the 'Nechtan mac Canonn' whose death is entered in *AU* 621. Nechton, though apparently not an uncommon Pictish name, is the name of only one other king in the king-list, Nechton f. Derilei (c. 705–724), mentioned above as the founder of a church dedicated to St Peter.[12] It seems unlikely that the later Nechton could have been the founder of Abernethy, since his policy of co-operation with the Romanizing churches of Anglian Northumbria is not easy to reconcile with a foundation in honour of St Brigit of Kildare.

One version of the Pictish king-list attributes the foundation of Abernethy to Gartnait f. Domelch (or Domech).[13] A more elaborate account of this version of the Abernethy foundation legend is incorporated by Walter Bower in his fifteenth-century copy of John of Fordun's version of the Pictish king-list.[14] This states that 'Garnard filius Dompnach sive Makdompnach' founded and built a collegiate church at Abernethy after St Patrick had brought Brigit and her nine virgins into Scotland; he gave Brigit and the nine virgins all the lands and teinds which the canons of Abernethy now (c. 1440) hold. The nine virgins all died within five years and were buried in the north part of the church. At this time, says Bower, there was only one bishop in Scotland, and three episcopal elections were held in this church; it was the principal royal and episcopal (*pontificalis*) seat of the Picts for a long time. It was founded 226 years before Dunkeld, or, *in alia cronica*, 244 years. In a later revision of the Scotichronicon Bower adds that Dunkeld was founded by Constantine f. Fergus, a Pictish king who is dateable c. 789–820.[15] On these calculations the foundation of Abernethy would have been c. 570–590. The Pictish king Gartnait f. Domelch appears to have had a reign covering part of the 590s, and he is presumably the king intended in Bower's version of the foundation legend. Other kings named Gartnait died in *AU* 635 and *AU* 663. At 649 *AU* records the 'warfare between the descendants of Aedán and [those] of Gartnait f. Accidan' (*Cocath hUae nAedáin ⁊ Gartnait mic Accidain*), presumably between the Dál Riata and the Picts, possibly of Skye. A Pictish hero called Cano mac Gartnait from Skye, who entered into Irish romantic legend, is recorded as having died in *AU* 688.[16]

These accounts of the foundation of Abernethy seem to be irreconcilably muddled. They appear to indicate that Abernethy was founded by a Pictish king, possibly called either Nechton or Gartnait, at or near a centre of Pictish royal power, and that it was in some way associated with the *familia* of St Brigit of Kildare. It seems to have been in existence considerably earlier than the church of Dunkeld.

There is evidence at the site itself for what appears to have been an early ecclesiastical foundation close to a royal centre. A Class I Pictish symbol-stone bearing the Pictish 'tuning-fork' and 'crescent and V-rod' symbols flanked by a hammer and anvil has been found close to the tenth- or eleventh-century round tower. Several fragments of later sculpture have also been uncovered at Abernethy, mostly re-used for building purposes. Above Abernethy stands a hill 'crowned by an iron-age fort that may have been re-used by the Picts.'[17] There are other examples, such as Craig Phadric near Inverness, of iron-age forts that were reoccupied during the Pictish period.[18]

These indications, taken together with the dedication to St Brigit, suggest that an ecclesiastical foundation existed at Abernethy in the seventh century. We have seen that Columban monks were extensively settled in Pictland before their expulsion in 717. The activities of St Donnan of Eigg and later of St Maelrubai of Applecross (a house of the *familia* of St Comgall of Bangor) show the work of Irish founders outwith the *familia* of Columba in Pictish territories,[19] and the probable association of Eileach an Naoimh in the Garbh Eileach group with St Brendan of Clonfert may show that work within the territories of the Dál Riata.[20] The link between Abernethy and Kildare may be part of the same phenomenon, and so could well belong to the seventh century or possibly even earlier.

Both versions of the foundation legend stress royal involvement in the foundation of Abernethy. It is posible that this may be an anachronistic reflection of the conditions of the eighth century and later, but the proximity of the hill-fort just to the south is suggestive of a connection with a royal centre.

One possible, and perhaps the most likely, contender as the founder of Abernethy is Gartnait mac Domnaill, whose death is recorded *AU* 663; in the Pictish king-list he is styled Gartnait f. Donuel.[21] It is possible, though not certain, that he was a son of Domnall Brecc, king of the Dál Riata, who died in 642.[22]

If Gartnait f. Domnall was the founder of a church of the *familia* of Kildare at Abernethy, what does this tell us about political and cultural conditions in Pictland at the time? The disastrous career and death (642) of Domnall Brecc (possibly his father) had gone far towards reversing the remarkable expansion of Dalriadic power under Aedán mac Gabráin and his son Eochaid Buide 'king of the Picts'.[23] Cumméne abbot of Iona recorded that in his time (abbot 657–669) the Dál Riata were 'held down by foreigners', but without saying who these were.[24] Bede states that after the Battle of Dunnichen (685) 'the Picts regained possession of their lands which the Angles had occupied, and the Scots dwelling in Britain and a part of the Britons recovered their freedom.'[25] Oswy and Ecgfrith seem to have established some sort of hegemony in the north, and it may be that the domination described by Cumméne was Anglian rather than Pictish.[26] If so, the foundation of a religious house with Irish cultural links by a Pictish king who possibly had a Dalriadic father might be seen as a counter-move to the establishment of an Anglian bishopric of the Picts based at Abercorn. The strong Gaelic leaning of such a

foundation strengthens the possibility that Gartnait's father was a
Gael; but that, of course, depends on the assumption that Gartnait
Domnall/Donuel was the founder. The form Donuel could well be
the Pictish form of Celtic *Dumno-Ualdos* (Gaelic Domnall, Welsh
Dumnagual > Dyfnwal), with the *w* of the second element still
sounded as in Bretonnic whereas it had become silent in Goidelic.
The fact that Abernethy was not a dependency of Iona may reflect
the weakening of Columban influence in the years leading up to the
Synod of Whitby.

On the other hand, we cannot ignore the possibility that Abernethy
was founded by Gartnait f. Dome(l)ch (c. 584–599). It has been
shown by Dr Bannerman that he was probably a son of Aedán mac
Gabráin; his reign over the Picts appears to have followed Aedán's
victories in the 580s.[27] If, as some of the sources suggest, Abernethy
was a royal foundation of the 590s, it must represent the spread of
Gaelic culture into this area immediately after Aedán's successes. If
the seventh-century Gartnait f. Donuel seems the more likely candidate, the late-sixth-century Gartnait f. Domelch cannot be excluded
as a possibility.

What sort of religious centre was Abernethy? Clearly it was later
regarded as a place of great antiquity and continuing importance, but
beyond that it is not easy to say. There was a tradition of stone-carving
going back probably to the seventh century, and there was an
imposing Irish-style round tower of tenth- or eleventh-century date.
The tradition that there had been three episcopal elections held at
Abernethy at a time when there was only one bishop in Scotland
indicates that it was probably an episcopal centre with a succession
of bishops. In 721 a certain Fergustus, *episcopus Scotiae Pictus*,
attended a council in Rome held by Pope Gregory II.[28] He was
perhaps one of the three successive bishops resident at Abernethy
mentioned in Bower's source. In the mid-tenth century 'the house
of blessed Brigit' was an important church, visited by King Constantine II, thronged with nobles and peasants, and filled with relics of
the saints.[29] An abbot called Maelodair who was with the king at the
time of his visit may have been abbot of Abernethy; the source does
not mention an episcopal seat there.

In the central Middle Ages, Abernethy was a detached parish
belonging to the diocese of Dunblane. The episcopal centre at
Dunblane was probably moved there from an earlier episcopal site
at Muthill, and it may be that a bishopric based at Abernethy was

ancestral to that at Muthill and so ultimately to the medieval diocese of Dunblane.[30]

In the early twelfth century a community of *Céli Dé* apparently shared the house with ordinary *clerici*, but were distinct from them; both communities included *sacerdotes* (i.e., priests).[31] By the end of the twelfth century the *clerici* had disappeared, and revenues were divided equally, with half going to the family of the lay abbot and half belonging to the *Céli Dé*.[32] These later became canons regular. In the twelfth century there is also mention of a *rector scholarum*.[33] Abernethy also seems to have had dependent churches or chapels, including Dron, Dunbog, Abdie (?), Flisk and Coultra (now in Balmerino), forming a compact group stretching in a straight line along the southern shore of the Firth of Tay.[34] Such a group of churches or chapels within easy reach of a major religious centre is a phenomenon encountered again and again; perhaps this is how we should understand the typical *parochia* of a major church. One point worth stressing about Abernethy with its episcopal and royal connections, its *clerici*, and its dependent churches and chapels, was not an isolated eremitic community, but had in part at least a public function.

The sources relating to the foundation of Abernethy are so uncertain as to require an element of guesswork; those relating to St Andrews allow for greater confidence, while still involving an element of uncertainty. There are two twelfth-century versions of the St Andrews foundation legend, to the longer of which is appended a description of the constitution of the church of St Andrews at the time of its erection into an Augustinian priory c. 1160.[35] The shorter version attributes the foundation to a Pictish king, Ungus son of Urguist, who had a vision of St Andrew while campaigning in Mercia with his seven *comites*. After his subsequent victory, he resolves to give a tenth part of his kingdom to God and St Andrew, but he and his council cannot decide where to make the principal grant. Meanwhile a monk called Regulus in Constantinople has a vision urging him to take the relics of St Andrew and set sail with them, until he should come to a place called *Rigmund*, the royal mount. Here he is met by King Ungus, who grants him the locality, one third of his kingdom, and the headship over all the churches in the lands of the Picts.[36]

The longer version is equally fantastic, but differs in a number of respects. The Pictish king is called Hungus son of Forso (read

Forguso) or son of Ferlon. He is fighting against Athelstan at the
Tyne. The monk Regulus arrives with Andrew's relics at Kylrimont,
which was at that time called Muckros. Here Hungus meets him and
gives to St Andrew a huge *parochia* from the sea called Ishundenema
(the Firth of Forth) to the sea called Slethenma (the Firth of Tay),
from Largo by way of Ceres to Naughton. Hungus confirms his grant
by laying earth upon the altar of St Andrews before an assembly of
Pictish nobles; the list of these witnesses is a credit to the ingenuity
of a twelfth-century forger, who has freely quarried the names from
a copy of the Pictish king-list. Regulus sings the Alleluia over this
offering, as Darlugdach had done at Abernethy.[37]

There are two kings called Unuist son of Urguist or Uurguist in
the king-list, with dates c. 729–761 and c. 820–834 respectively.
Neither, then, is a contemporary of Athelstan (924–41). Although a
gloss in some manuscripts of the list states against the name of the
later Unuist that *Hic aedificavit Kilrymont*,[38] the king intended must
be the earlier king of the same name. The death of Tuathalán abbot
of Cinrighmona (i.e., *Ceannrighmonadh*, now St Andrews) is recorded
in the Irish annals in 747, indicating that St Andrews was in existence
by that date.[39] This date accords well with the wealth of carved stones
at St Andrews, which appears to date from the mid-eighth century
onwards.[40]

The most spectacular of all the carved stones at St Andrews are
the fragments of a magnificent sarcophagus or tomb-shrine, carved
probably in the second half of the eighth century. Is there a possibility
that the great figure of David on the St Andrews sarcophagus is a
portrait of Unuist f. Urguist? We know that St Andrews was in
existence before the end of his reign, and tradition attributes its
foundation to him. Typologically, the sarcophagus and its art could
be as early as c. 760. The equation with David makes it virtually
certain that this is a portrait of a king. There is no other obvious
candidate for the portrait with a known devotion to St Andrew. It is
likely that the founder would have commissioned a shrine to house
the church's most holy relics, and easy to believe that the sculptor
would have flattered him by putting his royal image on it, with the
attributes of David, the greatest biblical king.

Why the dedication to St Andrew? The foundation legend offers
a reason, but it is obviously fantastic. Bede tells us that one of Unuist's
eighth-century predecessors, Nechton f. Derilei, founded a church
in honour of St Peter the apostle in opposition to the Columban

domination of Christianity in northern Britain, after correspondence with the abbot of St Peter's monastery at Wearmouth/Jarrow.[41] It has been suggested that the importation of the cult of St Andrew into Pictland may have been connected with the exile of Acca, bishop of St Andrew's church at Hexham, in 732.[42]

The foundation of Abernethy represents the presence of Gaelic culture among the Picts in the late sixth or seventh century. The foundations of Nechton f. Derilei and Unuist f. Uurguist show the limitations of Gaelic influence at a later date. For the first half of the eighth century, the kingdom of the Dál Riata seems to have been in a state of internal unrest, with a contest for the throne between the old ruling dynasty of the Cenél nGabráin (for the most part the descendants of Aedán mac Gabráin) and the Cenél Loairn in the person of Ferchar Fota (k. c. 676–697) and his descendants. Dr Bannerman has suggested that disputes over the abbacy of Iona in the same period may reflect this situation, rather that being a result of the Easter controversy.[43] Whatever the reason, there seems to have been considerable internal turmoil both at Iona and among the lay rulers of the Dál Riata, until Unuist subjected the kingdom to Pictish overlordship in the 730s.

But the eclipse of the Gael, although marked, was not final and permanent. In the second half of the eighth century the fortunes of the Dál Riata seem to have been revived in the person of Aed Finn, a king of the Cenél nGabráin (c. 748–778). At the same time, there seems to have been a cultural renaissance at Iona under Abbot Bressal (c. 770–801). Probably the great standing crosses of Iona, Islay, and Knapdale belong to the second half of the eighth century, and the 'Pictish boss style' of Nigg and Hilton of Cadboll reflects its influence in northern Pictland. The Book of Kells, widely believed to be an Iona manuscript, probably belongs to the same period. Although we are sadly ignorant of the historical events of the period (the 'Iona Chronicle' embedded in the Irish Annals comes to an end c. 740), there can be no doubt that there was Gaelic cultural and political revival in the second half of the eighth century.

The savage fury of the Viking raids from the 790s onwards brought this to an end in the Western Isles. The period that follows is one of particular obscurity, with disagreement in the king-lists, few historical records, and no saints' lives to guide us. But the first half of the ninth century witnessed an event which was later regarded as being of crucial importance for the development of a unified kingdom of Scots and Picts: the arrival of the dynasty of Cinaed mac Alpín. A major ecclesiastical development of this period which may cast some light on this is the foundation of the church of Dunkeld.

According to some versions of the Pictish king-list, the church of Dunkeld was founded by the Pictish king Constantine f. Fergus, who is assigned a reign of about thirty years c. 789–820.[44] It is virtually certain that this Constantine was son of Fergus son of Eochaid, a brother of Aed Finn (king of the Dál Riata c. 748–778). Aed Finn is a sadly obscure but undoubtedly important Dalriadic king, who revived the fortunes of the Dál Riata after a long period of obscurity; he claimed descent from the Cenél nGabráin, a Dalriadic dynasty based in Kintyre and Knapdale.[45]

The church of Dunkeld has also been identified as the church built in the land of the Picts by Cinaed mac Alpín c. 849. We are told that in the seventh year of his reign (which began c. 842) he brought relics of Colum Cille to this church; Dunkeld later had a dedication to St Columba.[46] The annals record a major translation of Columba's relics to Kells in 849, so it may be that Cinaed received a share of the relics as compensation.[47] Part of this was probably the Monymusk Reliquary or *Brecbennoch Coluim Chille*, a silver and enamel reliquary which may be as early as c. 700.[48]

The translation of Columba's relics into Pictland to a great church built there by Cinaed must have been a potent symbol, in cultural and ecclesiastical terms, of the dynastic and political mastery which he had established. A Pictish king had expelled the *familia* of Columba across Drumalban in 717, and now the Gaelic saint was making a triumphant return.[49]

The importance of Dunkeld from this time onwards is indicated by the record of the death of Tuathal, abbot of Dunkeld and *prímepscop Fortrenn*, in 865.[50] It has been pointed out that the term *prímepscop*, 'chief bishop', implies that there were other bishops; although in its narrowest sense *Fortrenn* means Strathearn and Gowrie, it also has a wider meaning embracing the whole kingdom ruled by the king of Scots.[51] We may assume that at this time other Scottish bishops, e.g. the bishops of St Andrews and Abernethy, were of lower status than the bishop of Dunkeld.

In the tenth century and later, the abbots of Dunkeld were important secular figures. An abbot was killed in a battle between two rivals for the Scottish kingship in 965. Crinan, abbot of Dunkeld, was son-in-law of Malcolm II, and when Malcolm died (1034) was able to have his own son Duncan made king. After Duncan had been killed by Macbeth, mormaer of Moray, in 1040, Crinan rebelled against Macbeth and was himself killed in battle in 1045.[52] Clearly the abbots of Dunkeld had become hereditory administrators of the church's properties.

Late traditions that there had been *Céli Dé* at Dunkeld have been regarded as doubtful.[53] A strong indication that there probably were *Céli Dé* at Dunkeld is provided by a cross-slab of ninth or tenth century date, now kept in the chapter-house.[54] On the front is a cross in relief with curving cusped arms; carved on the cross-head is a battle scene with two horsemen, footsoldiers, and a jumble of decapitated corpses; beneath this on the shaft is a scene of Daniel in the lions' den. On one side of the slab is another horseman, a large figure with a halo (St Columba?), and below him three small figures, who may represent the three children in the fiery furnace. On the back is a scene of the feeding of the multitude by multiplication of loaves and fishes, and below that the twelve apostles in two rows of six. The slab has had other carvings, which are now too worn to be discernable.

Some of these scenes, notably the multiplication of loaves and fishes and the twelve apostles, are very rare on Scottish cross-slabs. They occur frequently, however, on the granite high-crosses of the Barrow Valley school in Ireland, of which the best examples are at St Mullins, Graiguenamanagh, Ullard, Castledermot, Moone, and Old Kilcullen. The great pyramidal base of the cross of Moone, probably a subsequent addition to the cross itself, has the best arrangement of scenes illustrating the theme of divine aid, known also from *Céli Dé* literature: the fall of man, the sacrifice of Isaac, Daniel in the lions' den, the three children, the flight into Egypt, the multiplication of loaves and fishes, the twelve apostles, the crucifixion, St Paul and St Antony in the desert, and the temptation of St Antony.[55] The Dunkeld slab is an interesting and unusual translation of some of these images onto the typically Pictish medium of a cross-slab in high relief. In some ways its closest affinities may be with the south cross at Castledermot: the rather unsystematic arrangement of the imagery, the juxtaposition of the apostles and the miracle of loaves and fishes, the representation of the multitude, and the similar treatment of rows of featureless standing figures, are features which they share in common. Castledermot was an early ninth-century *Céli Dé* foundation, while Moone (Irish *Maoine Choluim Chille*) belonged to the *familia* of Colum Cille. Thus the

Dunkeld slab, with its free use of *Céli Dé* imagery related to that of
Castledermot and vicinity, may be taken as evidence of a community
of *Céli Dé* at Dunkeld in the ninth or tenth century.[56]

An odd feature of the medieval diocese of Dunkeld, which it shares
also with the dioceses of St Andrews, Dunblane and Brechin, is the
large number of detached parishes scattered within the boundaries
of other dioceses. These look like remote churches which constituted
parts of the *parochia* of an early Christian monastery which were
counted as parishes within its diocese when regular diocesan boundaries were defined in the twelfth century. In the diocesan boundaries
of central Scotland in the middle ages we can see preserved part of
the fossilised remains of a pre-diocesan system of 'parochial' juris-
dictions.[57]

The foundation of Dunkeld perhaps helps to cast some light on
the very obscure circumstances under which Cinaed mac Alpín came
to power c. 849. The Dunkeld cross-slab may not be as early as his
time, but its battle-scene could be a commemoration of a military
event held in special significance by the lay patrons of Dunkeld, the
MacAlpín dynasty.[58]

If in the late seventh and eighth centuries there was a development
of interest in 'cosmopolitan' saints such as Peter and Andrew, and a
decline in the prestige of Columba and other local saints, this process
was reversed after c. 800. The cult of Columba had never really faded,
and the crisis of the Viking raids turned the Scots in upon themselves.
The new dynasty, however it came to power, identified itself with
Gaelic Celtic tradition. This was detrimental to the Mediterranean
interests promoted by Pictish kings from c. 715 onwards, and
ultimately to the culture of the Picts themselves. But perhaps by their
promotion of non-indigenous culture during the eighth century the
Picts were in some way contributing to the destruction of their own
culture.

The late ninth and tenth centuries are a very poorly documented
period in early Scottish history. This is particularly unfortunate,
because this period witnessed an event which had far-reaching
consequences for the shaping of the later kingdom of Scotland: the
beginning of the integration of Strathclyde into the kingdom of the
Scots. Although documentary evidence here is scanty, it is possible
to assemble some evidence from ecclesiastical sources which helps
to cast light on these developments. In particular, the foundation and
early history of the church of Govan in Strathclyde is significant.

Cinaed mac Alpín's takeover of the kingship of the Scots and Picts c. 849 is poorly documented and has become the subject of an accretion of later legend.[59] Only slightly better documented is his dynasty's other great coup in the ninth century, the acquisition of the kingdom of Strathclyde.

There is documentary evidence about what was happening in Strathclyde in the ninth and tenth centuries (whereas there is virtually nothing for the period 750–850), though it is sparse, sometimes very late, and difficult to use. None of it, however, mentions the church of Govan. What Govan does have is its own very rich 'literature' graven in stone: the 'Govan school' of stonecarving, about which we hear much from art historians.[60] This puts Govan into a category with such great stone-carving centres as Meigle and St Vigeans, early Christian churches which are virtually unknown to documentation; with the difference that Govan is an even more extreme example than these others. If the Govan stones did not exist, there would be almost no evidence that this was an important early Christian site. The dedication, admittedly, would be a puzzle; but the place-name (which I take to be OI *gobán*, 'little beak', indicating the promontory sticking out into the Clyde on which the church stands, viewing modern Gaelic *Baile a'Ghobhainn* as a back-formation) gives nothing away, except perhaps that the place seems to have been named by Gaelic speakers rather than Britons.[61]

Most of the discussion about the Govan material, up to and including C A R Radford's important article in 1966,[62] was concerned to set the stonecarving in its artistic context. This has been much discussed, and I am not competent to do more than make a few general observations. My concern, rather, has been to set the 'Govan phenomenon' in a historical context: i.e., to look at what was going on in Strathclyde at the time when these stones were most probably being produced, and to see if this helps us towards a better understanding of the material itself and the motivation which lay behind its production.

The Govan and area stones consist of cross-shafts, fragments, and complete crosses, as at Govan itself, Barochan, Inchinnan, Arthurlie, Cambusnethan, Lochwinnoch, Old Kilpatrick, Mountblow (possibly originally from Old Kilpatrick?), Capelrig, Cadzow, Kilwinning, and elsewhere. There were also stone sarcophagi, of which the famous example at Govan is the most complete; there is a sarcophagus lid at Inchinnan, and a fragment has been found at Kilmahew. Recumbent cross-slabs appear in profusion at Govan, there is a similar example at Inchinnan, fragments at Dumbarton Rock, and stones with incised crosses at Luss. Apart from the fine group of five hogback tombstones at Govan, there are late examples at Luss and Dalserf.[63]

This is not the place to do more than summarize the main characteristics of the school and arguments about their probable date. The most common form of abstract ornament is interlace, much of it repetitive and naive, some of it botched; it is often of 'double-beaded' type. There is some 'ring-twist' ornament and some more complex knots. There is a little key-pattern, a few swastikas and swastika-like designs, and a few spirals. There are two or three serpent bosses. Figure sculpture takes the form mainly of horsemen riding from left to right across the upright slabs, but there are some other human figures as well: a crucifix on the Lochwinnoch cross; a standing figure on top of the cross-head at Cadzow; Daniel in the lions' den on the Inchinnan sarcophagus; and a scene on the Cambusnethan shaft. The crosses were not, as Radford thought, of 'Anglian' type (Ruthwell, Hoddom, Thornhill, etc.), but were thin and slablike in section, with in some cases an unpierced ring (Barochan and Lochwinnoch; Inchinnan and Arthurlie had rings, but it is impossible to tell whether they were pierced or not). The rather crude Cadzow cross is the only example that was definitely ringless; its general shape reminds one more of the Viking-age crosses of Inishowen in Co. Donegal, e.g. Carndonagh and Cloncha, but its very poor quality might simply suggest that the sculptor did not have the technique to shape a ringed head. The hogbacks have been expertly described by others.[64]

Stylistically, Govan represents a fusion of styles: there are 'Pictish' horsemen and beasts, 'Gaelic' ringed crosses (but cf. Viking-age examples from the north of England), 'Anglian' knots and interlace, and 'Scandinavian' hogbacks. This wide range of influences seems to point to a date later than the eighth and early ninth centuries, and the Anglo-Scandinavian hogbacks seem to confirm this. But the hunting scene on the Govan sarcophagus would not be too out of place on late Pictish slabs, and might not be too long after 900 AD. There is general agreement that the Govan hogbacks are probably tenth-century, though the romanesque ornament on the Luss example cannot be so early. The best of the crosses, at Barochan and Govan, could be early in the sequence (though I suspect that few would agree with J B Stevenson, 'could be as early as the eighth century'), and the most debased examples, like Cadzow, could be late. The Lochwinnoch crucifix reminds one of the large figures on late Irish crosses, e.g. Cashel, Drumcliffe, Kilfenora, etc., showing that ring-headed crosses were still being produced late in the sequence; but it also has affinities with the 'sun-stone' at Govan and the Cadzow cross. Perhaps the serpent-bosses at Lochwinnoch, Cadzow and the 'sun-stone' are part of a late fashion. It is generally accepted that the material shows a fusion of artistic styles, Pictish, Gaelic, Anglian and Norse, and that it belongs mostly to the tenth and eleventh centuries, with the possibility of some being slightly earlier and some slightly later.[65]

The presence of such a rich collection of stonework at an otherwise unrecorded site at this date is something of a puzzle. The suggestion that Govan was the true site of St Kentigern's 6th-century church has never been advanced with much conviction.[66] The Govan stones are so remote in time from St Kentigern (d. c. 614) as to preclude any definite connection; and the evidence suggests that Glasgow was in existence in the early Christian period as well.[67]

The stonecarving tradition of Govan and its neighbours seems to be continuous from the time of its emergence down to the early twelfth century, when Earl David revived the church of Glasgow 1113 × 1124. There is no clear evidence to suggest that the church at Govan was in existence earlier than the late ninth century, and the absence of anything earlier might be taken (cautiously) as evidence that the church's importance dates from this time and not earlier.

So what was the historical context of the emergence of the stonecarving school? Before the mid-eighth century, the British kingdom of Strathclyde had been one among a number of kingdoms jockeying for power in central Scotland with Scots, Picts, Angles, and other British kingdoms. But after a damaging succession dispute in the early 750s and a serious defeat by a combined Pictish-Anglian army in 756, the kingdom of Strathclyde and its rulers disappear from record almost completely for nearly a century. The Dumbarton king who surrendered in 756 died in exile, fighting in Gwynedd, in 760. Thereafter names of the kings and their reign-lengths are lacking until 872. The Harleian MS pedigree of a Strathclyde king who died in 878 names his ancestors in the male line through this century, but does not make clear that they were all kings or the only kings during this period. With one exception, they are all so obscure as to be otherwise unknown.[68]

That exception is Arthgal f. Dyfnwal. It may have been under his leadership that the Britons burned Dunblane in 849, their first recorded aggressive exploit for nearly a century. But if Arthgal's reign represented a revival, it brought Strathclyde unwelcome attention, for in 870 the Norse kings of Dublin, Olaf and Ivar, besieged Dumbarton Rock for four months and reduced it when they cut off the defenders' water supply. In the following year they returned to Dublin with much booty and many prisoners, including Arthgal, who was put to death a year later 'by counsel of Constantín mac Cinaeda', king of Scots. King Constantine (the name is noteworthy – to my knowledge the first recorded person so called who had a connection with Strathclyde) was, or soon became, brother-in-law of Rhun map Arthgal. Rhun died c. 878, round about the same time that Constantine was killed in battle by the Norse; he may have been fighting in Constantine's army, for the indications are that he was his client. He is the last king named in the Welsh genealogy of the Strathclyde kings; names of later kings have to be assembled from other sources.

The next of these is Eochaid f. Rhun, the first Strathclyde king to bear a Gaelic name. Confused accounts of his reign suggest that he may have reigned jointly with Giric mac Dúngaile c. 878–889, and been expelled with him in the latter year.

According to the late and unreliable Welsh 'Chronicle of the Princes' (*Brut y Tywyssogion*), 'the men of Strathclyde, those that refused to unite with the English, had to depart from their country and go into Gwynedd' c. 890. There they were settled by Anarawd king of Gwynedd, whom they aided in defeating the Saxons. It is doubtful how much reliance can be placed on this source, but if it can be trusted at all we should probably agree with AP Smyth that the threatened union which was unacceptable to these Strathclyde aristocrats was with the Scots rather than the English; the dynasty of Cinaed mac Alpín represented a much more serious threat to Strathclyde's autonomy than any English dynasty at this time.[69]

So what appears to have happened was something like this. Constantín mac Cinaeda was in some way allied or associated with the Dublin Norse attack on Dumbarton in 870, with the removal of Arthgal and with his supplantation by Rhun, Constantine's brother-in-law and (presumably) client. Rhun and Constantine both died c. 878, possibly in the same battle. Eochaid f. Rhun then attempted to assert his own kingship of Scots, perhaps through his descent from Cinaed; but was unsuccessful, having to accept joint status with or (more likely) client status under Giric mac Dúngaile. C. 889 Giric was expelled, and presumably Eochaid too, and replaced by Domnall mac Constantín. The date of Eochaid's death is not recorded. It cannot be ascertained whether he led his war-band into exile in Gwynedd, or whether their supposed migration took place after his death.

The migration of a group of displaced Strathclyde aristocrats into Gwynedd c. 890 could explain a number of phenomena: (1) The appearance of the cult of St Kentigern in North Wales, as evidenced by dedications to him at St Asaphs and elsewhere, and by the curious story about a period of exile in Gwynedd told in Jocelin's *Vita Kentigerni*; (2) the preservation of the pedigree of Rhun map Arthgal in Welsh lore, and possibly other traditions relating to the 'Men of the North' (*Gwyr y Gogledd*); (3) the obscurity of the cult centre of St Kentigern at Glasgow for a long period before its revival under Earl David c. 1113 × 1124. How long this period was cannot now be determined; the wording of the *Inquisitio David* hardly implies a stretch of 200 years plus, but the causes of Glasgow's obscurity could well have gone back to the ninth century. I have argued above that the earliest stratum in Jocelin's *Vita Kentigerni* could go back to the eighth century.[70] It is tempting to see in some of these documents the tattered remnants of the work of a Glasgow scriptorium which was active up until the late ninth century, but nor thereafter.

After c. 890 some at least of the Strathclyde kings were clients of the kings of Scots. Some of them, such as Domnall mac Aedo (acceded c. 908 × 916, died × 934), can be identified as members of the Scottish royal dynasty. It has been argued, most notably by A P Smyth and A A M Duncan, on the basis of this and Fordun's 14th-century attempt at systematization, that all Strathclyde kings in the late ninth and early tenth century were *tanaise* (second, i.e., heir-designate) to the king of Scots. But some tenth-century kings had native names, Ywain, Dyfnwallon, and (if it is the correct reading of a corrupt form in Scottish sources) Rhydderch. D P Kirby has argued that the effective independence of the Strathclyde kingdom continued up to the time of Ywain (or Owen) the Bald who died in 1018.[71] My own view, which has been argued at length elsewhere, is that in the late ninth and early tenth centuries Strathclyde fell under the control of the dynasty of Cinaed mac Alpín, but that later in the tenth century a native dynasty, possibly descended from the old ruling dynasty, reasserted a measure of independence which lasted into the early eleventh century.[72] It cannot be asserted that all Strathclyde kings of the tenth century were *tanaise* to the king of Scots; but the practice was known, as we see in the granting of Strathclyde to Earl David by his brother c. 1113, and possibly in the ephemeral granting of Lennox to a later Earl David by his brother in 1174; twelfth-century attempts to secure the earldom of Northumbria for the heir to the Scottish throne may point in the same direction.

We have seen that the church of St Kentigern at Glasgow was patronized by Strathclyde aristocrats who were displaced both by the great siege of 870 and by subsequent upheavals, such as the probable migration of some of them into Gwynedd c. 890. It is to this period that probably belong the beginnings of the Govan school of stone-carving; so, in the last quarter of the ninth century, we can see lay patronage and increased activity surrounding the church of St Constantine at Govan.

Who was St Constantine? The first Christian Roman emperor? The West Country tyrant named by Gildas c. 540? Or a descendant of his who entered religion about 50 years later? Or, following Jocelin of Furness, a son of Rhydderch Hael (d. c. 614) born to his queen late in life? Or the British saint cited in the Irish martyrologies on 11 March? Or, following the scholiastic notes appended to *Félire Oengusso*, 'Constantine f. Fergus, king of Alba'? Or an Irish saint, martyred in Kintyre according to the *Aberdeen Breviary*, presumably venerated at Kilchousland (i.e., *Cill Chostatin*)? The name appears in British and Irish hagiography.[73] Can we ever hope to identify the person really referred to?

I think it is unlikely. It is probably more profitable to look at occurences of the personal name Constantine during the period to which the Govan carving belongs, and see if they can tell us anything about the sort of people among whom devotion to St Constantine was popular.

The first occurrence of the name that I am aware of is Constantine f. Fergus, king of Picts c. 789–820. (One may safely ignore the fact that the scholiastic notes appended to *Félire Oengusso* speak of 'Constantine f. Fergus king of Alba'; this martyrology was compiled c. 800, when this Constantine was still alive.) It would be wrong to assume that because he is named as king of Picts, his name had earlier been current among the Picts; in fact, the name nowhere else occurs in the Pictish king-list. It is virtually certain that this Constantine was son of Fergus son of Eochaid, a brother of Aed Finn (king of the Dál Riata c. 748–778). Aed Finn is a sadly obscure but undoubtedly important Dalriadic king, who revived the fortunes of the Dál Riata after a long period of obscurity; he claimed descent from the Cenél nGabráin, a Dalriadic dynasty based in Kintyre and Knapdale.

Another Scottish king who claimed descent from the Cenél nGabráin, rightly or wrongly, was Cinaed mac Alpín. The name Constantine was frequently used in his family. He had a son who bore it; Constantín mac Cinaeda was king 862–878. A grandson of Cinaed, Constantín mac Aeda, was king for nearly half a century (900–943) and continued to influence political events from his monastic retirement at St Andrews. There was a king Domnall mac Constantín 889–900. As late as the twelfth century the name was in use in the branch of the royal dynasty which became earls of Fife. (One version of the king-list credits to Giric mac Dúngaile, Eochaid f. Rhun's co-reigner, a brother called Constantine.) An inscription commemerating a Constantine has recently been discovered on the Dupplin Cross at Forteviot.[74]

An earlier king of the Dál Riata was also called Domnall mac Constantín (c. 781–810). He is chronologically too early to have been a son of Constantín mac Fergusa (k. of Picts, c. 789–820). If his father's name was Constantine, he is not otherwise known, but he looks like a member of the dynasty of Aed Finn. I have suggested that he may be in fact a son of Aed Finn whose patronymic has been miscopied. If this suggestion is not accepted, then we have another holder of this popular name among the Dál Riata in the late eighth century.

The important point is that the name was commonly used in the Dalriadic dynasty (the Cenél nGabráin) from the late eighth century onwards. It is otherwise extremely rare. This dynasty originated in Kintyre. There was a dedication to St Constantine at Kilchousland (*Cill Chostatín*) in Kintyre. The *Aberdeen Breviary*, presumably on the suggestion of this dedication, states that St Constantine was martyred in Kintyre.[75] This points us in the direction in which we should be looking for the explanation of the dedication at Govan.

Equally significantly, the king of Scots at the time of greatest political upheaval in Strathclyde was himself called Constantine (Constantín mac Cinaeda, k. 862–878). He was in some way involved in the death of Arthgal at the hands of the Dublin Norse in 872, and was brother-in-law of Rhun map Arthgal. Rhun must have been his client, and may have been fighting in his army when both died in 878. His son Domnall mac Constantín reasserted MacAlpín dynastic control in 890 after the period of Eochaid f. Rhun and Giric mac Dúngaile, and was possibly responsible for the expulsion of Strathclyde aristocrats into Gwynedd in 890.[76]

In the space of 30 years, 870–900, we can detect a Norse-Scots carve-up of Strathclyde. Apart from their part in the siege of Dumbarton and the death of Arthgal, the role of the Dublin Norse in all this is poorly documented. A A M Duncan may be right to argue that Dumbarton 'for a time was (like Dublin) a Viking headquarters', although the evidence is sparse. The Govan school stonecarving is eloquent evidence of Norse influence, as its presence at Dumbarton Rock is evidence of continued occupation of that site after 870.

Radford argued that Govan was founded in order to translate St Constantine's relics from an exposed coastal site in Kintyre, threatened by Vikings, to a safer inland site. The obvious parallel is the translation of St Columba's relics to Dunkeld by Cinaed, c. 850. I would argue that these were not negative, defensive moves, but assertions of political and cultural mastery. The reimposition of the cult of the Gaelic saint Columba in the lands of the Picts, who had rejected Iona's authority in the eighth century, was a powerful symbolic gesture. We should probably view the origins of Govan, the importation of the Dalriadic saint Constantine into Strathclyde, in the same light.[77]

Sadly, the lections for St Constantine in the *Aberdeen Breviary* (1509–10) are of no help to us here. They do not appear to derive from a *vita* written in the interest of a particular cult centre, and they are wholly independent of the traditions mentioned in Jocelin's *Vita Kentigerni*. The author knew of traditions linking Constantine with the kingship of Cornwall, with Ireland, with Kintyre and Galloway, and with the Glasgow/ Strathclyde area. The lections do not associate St Constantine's relics with any particular kirk or place, nor do they mention a *vita* from which they are drawn; this seems to indicate that there was no strong local cult of Constantine by the time the *Aberdeen Breviary* was drawn together. Galloway and Kintyre are mentioned, as are St Columba and St Kentigern; but there is nothing to indicate the existence of a *vita* setting forth the pretensions of a particular kirk.[78]

Perhaps, given the probable date of the foundation of Govan, this is not surprising; hagiography seems to have been out of fashion in the ninth century. For this reason it is very difficult to put together a history of the Scottish church in this period. Other churches, such as Meigle and St Vigeans, have fine collections of (probably slightly earlier) carved stones, but no foundation legends. Not until later is there a revival in the fashion of collecting legends of the saints.

NOTES

1. Since this was written, see now also T O Clancy, 'Iona, Scotland and the *Céli Dé*', in B E Crawford (ed.), *Scotland in Dark Age Britain* (1996), 111–30, at 120–1.
2. Bede, *HE*, v, 21.
3. *AU*, s.a. 717. Cf. Bede, *HE*, iii, 4.
4. Ibid., v, 21.
5. G Donaldson, 'Scotland's earliest Church Buildings', *RSCHS*, xviii (1973), 109; reprinted in his *Scottish Church History* (1985), 1–10; A Ritchie, *Picts* (1989), 34.
6. Bede, *HE*, iv, 26.
7. Cf. chapter 6 above, pp. 155–7.
8. Bede, *HE*, v, 21.
9. Anderson, *KKES*, 247; *Chron. Picts-Scots*, 6–7.
10. Apurfeirc = the mouth of the River Farg, perhaps nearer to Calfargie (Dron) than to Aberargie (Abernethy). Cairfuill = Carpow. Athan = (?) Ayton.
11. W Davies, 'The Latin Charter Tradition in Western Britain, Brittany, and Ireland in the early Medieval Period', in *Ireland in early Medieval Europe: Studies in Memory of Kathleen Hughes*, ed. D Whitelock et al. (1982), 258–80, at 273 and n. 55.
12. *AU*, s.a. 621; K H Jackson, 'The Pictish Language' in *Problem of the Picts*, 129–60, at 140–1, 145; Anderson, *KKES*, 231–3.
13. Anderson, *KKES*, 266, 287.
14. *Chron. Bower* (ed. Watt), iv, 12 (vol. ii, 302 and 458–9).
15. Ibid., nn. on pp. 458–9; Anderson, *KKES*, 192–4, 233.
16. *AU*, s.a. Bannerman, *Dalriada*, 92–3; Byrne, *Irish Kings and High-Kings*, 105, 243. For *Scela Cano meic Gartnáin*, see above, chapter 7, pp. 167–70.
17. Ritchie, *Picts*, 16, 44. The only other surviving round tower in Scotland is at Brechin. There are a number of square towers of similar or slightly later date in east central Scotland.
18. L Alcock, 'Pictish Studues: present and future', in *The Picts: a new Look at old Problems*, ed. A Small (1987), 80–92, at 82. For Columba's visit to Bridei's fort at Inverness, see above, Chapter 4, pp. 80–1.

19. Smyth, *Warlords*, 107–11. The arrival of St Maelrubai at Applecross in *AU* 671 may be in some way connected with the return of the tribe of Gartnait from Ireland in the previous year. 'The sons of Gartnait with the people of Skye' had fled to Ireland in *AU* 668, probably under pressure from the Cenél nGabráin. See above, Chapter 7, pp. 167–70.

20. *RCAHMS, Argyll Inventory*, v, 170–82.

21. *AU*, s.a. 663; Anderson, *KKES*, 231, 248.

22. *AU*, s.a. 642. On Pictish succession, cf. Anderson, *KKES*, 165–79, 231–3; Smyth, *Warlords*, 57–73; W D H Sellar, 'Warlords, Holy Men, and Matrilineal Succession', *IR*, xxxvi (1985), 29–43.

23. Eochaid Buide is so called at his death in *AU*, s.a. 629. On the achievements of Aedán mac Gabráin, cf. above, Chapter 4, Appendix II, pp 103–16.

24. *VC*, iii, 6.

25. Bede, *HE*, iv, 26.

26. Cf. Smyth, *Warlords*, Chapter 4, esp. 119–21.

27. See above, Chapter 4, Appendix II, pp. 107, 111; Bannerman, *Dalriada*, 92–4.

28. P Labbé, *Sacrosancta Concilia* (1671–3), vi, 1458; Donaldson, 'Bishops' Sees', 14.

29. Life of Catroe (*Vita S Kaddroe*) in *AASS, Mar.*, i, 476. See below, Chapter 9, pp 199–210.

30. The origins of the diocese of Dunblane are discussed in A Macquarrie, 'Early Christian Religious Houses in Scotland: Foundation and Function', in J Blair and R Sharpe (eds.), *Pastoral Care before the Parish* (Leicester, 1992), 128–9.

31. Lawrie, *Charters*, 11–12.

32. *Arbroath Liber*, 25–6.

33. Lawrie, *Charters*, 11–12.

34. Ibid.; *RRS*, ii, 342–3.

35. *Chron. Picts-Scots*, 138–40, 183–93; M O Anderson, 'The Celtic Church in Kinrimund', in *The Medieval Church of St Andrews*, ed. D MacRoberts (1976), 1–10, at 1, n., dates the descriptive section 1144 x 1153. Cf. also M O Anderson, 'St Andrews before Alexander I', in *The Scottish Tradition: Essays in Honour of R G Cant*, ed. G W S Barrow (1974), 1–13, at 7–13.

36. *Chron. Picts-Scots*, 138–40.

37. Anderson, *KKES*, 99–100; *Chron. Picts-Scots* 183–8.

38. Anderson, *KKES*, 273; cf. the *Scalachronica* version: *Cesty edifia Kelrymonech, ore saint Andrew, quel temps vient saint Regulus od sez disciples al eglis de saint Andrew*, ibid., 287.

39. *AU*, s.a. 747. An interesting counter-argument is advanced in Clancy, 'Iona, Scotland and the *Céli Dé*', 114–5.

40. Allen and Anderson, *ECMS*, iii, 350–63.
41. Bede, *HE*, v, 21.
42. W F Skene, 'Notice of the early ecclesiastical Settlements at St Andrews', *PSAS*, iv (1860–2), 300–21.
43. J W M Bannerman, Appendix to K Hughes, 'The Church and the World in early Christian Ireland', *Irish Historical Studies*, xiii (1962–3), 113–16.
44. Anderson, *KKES*, 266, 273, 287; and cf. 192–4.
45. Ibid., 189–90.
46. Ibid., 250.
47. *AU*, s.a. 849.
48. F Henry, *Irish Art in the Early Christian Period* (1940), 70.
49. Since this was written, cf. now C P Wormald, 'The Emergence of the *Regnum Scottorum*: a Carolingian Hegemony?' in Crawford, *Scotland in Dark Age Britain*, 131–60, esp. 143.
50. *AU*, s.a. 865.
51. Donaldson, 'Bishops' Sees', 15–17; Anderson, *KKES*, 139–42.
52. Anderson, *Early Sources*, i, 472–3, 576–7, 583–4.
53. Cowan and Easson, *MRHS*, 47.
54. Allen and Anderson, *ECMS*, iii, 317–9.
55. F Henry, *Irish High Crosses* (1964), 25–6; Idem., *Irish Art in the Early Christian Period*, 138, 147–9; Idem., *Irish Art during the Viking Invasions*, (new edn, 1967), 137–40; M and L de Paor, *Early Christian Ireland* (1958), 146–50; E de Bhaldraithe, *The High Crosses of Moone and Castledermot* (Bolton Abbey, 1987), esp. 8–9; M Herity, 'The Context and Date of the High Crosses at Dísert Diarmata (Castledermot), Co. Kildare', in *Figures from the Past: Studies in Honour of Helen M Roe*, ed. E Rynne (Dublin, 1987), 111–30, esp. 121; Stevenson, 'Pictish Art', 128.
56. Clancy, 'Iona, Scotland and the *Céli Dé*', 120, now advances further evidence which seems to confirm this view.
57. See the map in A Macquarrie, 'Early Christian Religious Houses in Scotland: Foundation and Function', in *Pastoral Care before the Parish*, ed. J Blair and R Sharpe (Leicester, 1992), 110–33, at 124.
58. This theme has been taken up in Wormald, 'Emergence of the *Regnum Scottorum*'.
59. Anderson, *KKES*, passim, esp. 196–9; Mac Cana, *Learned Tales of Ireland*, 107–8, 142–5.
60. C A R Radford, 'Early Christian Monuments at Govan and Inchinnan', *Trans. Glasgow Archaeol. Soc.*, n s xv (1966), 177–88; cf. A Macquarrie, 'Early Christian Govan: the Historical Context', in *RSCHS*, xxiv (1990), 1–17. A Ritchie (ed), *Govan and its early Medieval Sculpture* (1994), passim.

61. Ritchie, *Govan*, 19, 27. It has been pointed out to me that intervocalic *b* *p* should not normally lenite, whereas lenition is attested in the 12th century (*Guuen, Guuin*); but these forms also indicate first syllable stress, as in the modern pronunciation, and make it extremely unlikely that this could be a compound involving the British prefix *gu-*. The problem remains.

62. See n. 60 above.

63. D Craig, 'The early medieval Sculpture of the Glasgow Area', in Ritchie, *Govan*, 73–90.

64. See the essays by R M Spearman, Ian Fisher, Rosemary Cramp, Derek Craig, and James Lang in Ritchie, *Govan*.

65. Cf. Macquarrie, 'Early Christian Govan: the Historical Context'. This view is largely supported by the wide measure of consensus in Ritchie, *Govan*.

66. G and A Ritchie, *Scotland: Archaeology and early history* (1981), 147.

67. See above, Chapter 5, p. 136 and n. 35; Ritchie, *Govan*, passim.

68. The evidence is assembled in A Macquarrie, 'The Kings of Strathclyde, c.400–1018', in A Grant and K J Stringer (eds), *Medieval Scotland: Crown, Lordship and Community* (1993), 1–19; see also Macquarrie, 'Early Christian Govan: the Historical Context'.

69. Ibid.; see also Smyth, *Warlords and Holy Men*, 217–8.

70. See above, chapter 5, p 130–1.

71. D P Kirby, 'Strathclyde and Cumbria', *TCWAAS*, new ser. lxii (1962).

72. Macquarrie, 'The Kings of Strathclyde, c.400–1018'.

73. For the sources, see A Macquarrie, 'The historical Context of the Govan Stones' in Ritchie, *Govan*, 27–32, at 31.

74. K Forsyth, 'The Inscription on the Dupplin Cross', in From the Isles in the North: Medieval Art in Ireland and Britain (1995), 237–44.

75. A Macquarrie, 'Lections for St Constantine's Day (11 March) in the Aberdeen Breviary', *Annual Report of the Society of Friends of Govan Old*, v (1995), 25–32.

76. I MacIvor, *Dumbarton Castle* (HMSO, n.d.), 8; Ritchie, *Govan*, 82.

77. On the use of the cults of saints and their relics, cf. S Airlie, 'The View from Maastricht', in Crawford, *Scotland in Dark Age Europe*, 33–46, at 36–41; Wormald, 'Emergence of the *Regnum Scottorum*', 143.

78. *Aberdeen Breviary*, PH., 11 March; Macquarrie, 'Lections for St Constantine's Day (11 March) in the Aberdeen Breviary', 25–6.

9

St Catroe of Metz

We have seen that the *vita* of St Serf is set in a period later than almost any other. It might seem that between him and the subject of Thurgot's *Vita Margaretae Reginae* in the late eleventh century information about Scottish history from hagiographical sources dries up almost entirely before beginning in a new fashion. This is not quite totally the case, however; but we have to look to the continent for our next example of a *vita* of a Scottish saint. The *vita* which is the subject of this chapter bears some curious resemblances to that of St Serf, but that is chiefly because both contain a number of verbal echoes from Sulpicius' *Life of Martin*.

During a period from the seventh to eleventh centuries, many wandering *Scoti* made journeys of self-imposed exile to continental Europe. The vast majority of them were Irish; but late medieval Scottish writers like Walter Bower, and post-medieval controversialists like Thomas Dempster, were anxious to claim all *Scoti* as Scots. To some extent they were successful, insofar that Scottish Roman catholic monks were able to establish themselves in the *Schottenkloster* of Franconia;[1] but their efforts greatly annoyed Irish scholars like John Colgan and, much more recently, Tomas Ó Fíaich. The true identity of most of these wandering monks and scholars is now established beyond doubt; but there was a small number of Scots among them, and one of them has won a place in the pages of tenth-century continental hagiography.

In the tenth century, the dynasty of Cinaed mac Alpín became firmly entrenched during the long reign of Constantín, son of Aed mac Cinaeda, nephew of his namesake Constantín mac Cinaeda, and ruler of Scotland for most of the first half of the tenth century. Here again the cult of saints is able to enlighten an otherwise obscure period, in the shape of a near-contemporary *vita* of a Scot, Kaddroe or Catroe,[2] who settled in Lorraine and became abbot of Metz. This is the *Vita Kaddroe Abbatis Metis in Lotharingia*, from the Legendary of St Hubert in the Belgian Ardennes region, a manuscript which no longer survives. This MS has received attention from continental historians because of the light it casts on the reign of Emperor Otto II and on secular and ecclesiastical developments in Lorraine in the mid- to late-tenth century; but since A O Anderson translated parts of it into English in his *Early Sources of Scottish History* (1922),[3] it has not been much studied by Scottish historians.

It is of interest, however, in that it is a near-contemporary *vita* of a native Scot, Kaddroe (Cadroe, Catroe), compiled on the continent within a few years of his death (c. 971). The writer was called Ousmann, or perhaps more likely Reimann or Erimann;[4] he was a monk of St Clement (also called St Felix) of Metz. The *vita* was addressed to Immo, abbot of Gorze from 982;[5] it was written while Emperor Otto II was still living (d. December 983). The date of composition is thus fixed with some precision. The text is replete with verbal echoes and direct quotations from Sulpicius' *Life of St Martin*. On the internal evidence of the *vita* Catroe appears to have been a native of somewhere in Scotland, and a kinsman of 'Dovenald king of the Cumbrians'. His death can be placed with confidence c. 971, and he is said to have died in the seventy-first year of his age and the thirtieth year of his pilgrimage;[6] in other words, he was born c. 900 and left Scotland in 941. The spelling of his name, with -dd- consistently, indicates that the dental was unlenited; so it is unlikely that the first element in his name was Gaelic *cath*, 'battle' (as Colgan thought), but more probably its Bretonnic cognate, *cat, cad*, with the same meaning.[7]

Catroe therefore bore a name which may show Bretonnic influence; he is also described as a kinsman of the king of the Cumbrians (i.e., Strathclyde). It might be assumed therefore that he is a native of Strathclyde; but the picture appears not to be so simple. His name may indeed be British or Old Welsh, but might perhaps equally be Pictish. A number of persons and places alluded to in the text appear to belong to central and east-central Scotland.[8] His father's name is given as *Fochereach*; this may be a misreading of a Gaelic personal name. Whatever its original form, the first syllable *fo-* appears to show Gaelic influence.[9] Fochereach is said to have been, echoing Sulpicius's description of St Martin's family, 'of royal blood and notable wealth'. I am not sure if any deduction can be made from the name given to Catroe's mother, *Bania*, described as 'equal to him (i.e., Fochereach) in riches and nobility'. His relation to Dovenald king of the Cumbrians may have been through her. St Bean or Beoan is described as his *patruelis*, 'paternal uncle'; he seems to have been associated with a church which held relics of St Columba. The identity of St Bean and the church in question are discussed below.

Both parents are credited with devotion to *beatus Columbanus* and to have prayed at his *sepulchrum*, 'tomb'. If this is a reference to St Columba, it must be borne in mind that his tomb-shrine and relics had been removed from Iona to Kells in Ireland in 878 'in flight from the foreigners' (i.e., the Norse).[10] We know that in 825 the bones of St Columba still rested at Iona in a shrine of gold and precious metals which sat upon 'pediments', and which was sufficiently portable that it could be quickly removed and hidden in a hole in the ground when Vikings attacked.[11] There was a major division of Columba's relics c. 849 between Kells and Cinaed mac Alpín's church at Dunkeld.[12] The translation of 878 is the last on record, and thereafter the *familia* of St Columba may have maintained only a small community on Iona itself.[13] So we are not to understand that the parents of Catroe went to Iona, or for that matter to Kells; Dunkeld is perhaps the most likely possibility.

The *vita* describes how after Catroe's birth a 'noble throng' (*vulgus nobile*) approached his parents, demanding the right of fosterage of the child. However, despite their pressure, Catroe was eventually fostered by a priest, Bean (*Beanus*, or once *Beoanus*), his *patruelis*, 'paternal uncle'. Kirkbean in Kirkcudbrightshire (for an earlier *Cill Beoain*) is St Bean's most obvious dedication, but he has others as well;[14] we cannot be certain that this Bean was a figure of the south-west, because a personage of the same name has associations with Perthshire and the north-east. Most significant is a cluster of dedications and place-names in Strathearn and Glen Almond, at Kinkell, Fowlis Wester, and Buchanty.[15] Catroe's father is said to have consented to his fosterage of the boy after his wife had given birth to another son, called Mattadán, which appears to be a Gaelic name.

The *vita* also mentions in passing that Catroe had also spent a period in secular fosterage before coming under Bean's charge. When his former foster-parents were plundered by marauders, they appealed to Catroe to avenge them; *moris namque est patriae ut si quis nobilium infantem nutriat deinceps non minus genitoribus eius in omnibus auxilium exquirat* ('it is the custom of the land that if nobles foster a child he is required thereafter to provide them with help in every way, no less than to his parents'). Catroe and his companions set out in pursuit of the despoilers, and were close to catching up to them, when Bean sent a message to him urging him to desist. Catroe was torn between his duty to his former and his present fosterers; he agreed to renounce his violent intentions only when Bean persuaded him to open a gospel-book three times at random, and he found passages which dissuaded him from retribution.

When Catroe was given to Bean for fosterage his parents brought him *ad tumulum beati Columbani* and handed him over to the old man (Bean) to be instructed in divine law. This seems to indicate that Bean was a cleric, probably a monk, at the church which held Columba's relics. Bean sent him to study at the cathedral school at Armagh, where he was taught both divinity and secular literature. The latter was justified on the grounds that the Greek philosopher Plato had gone to Alexandria 'drawn by the fame of Jeremiah', from whom he learned the principle of monotheism. Later biographers of Plato record that he travelled to Egypt following the death of Socrates (399 BC), but this is not mentioned by his immediate disciple Hermodorus. If Plato did visit Egypt early in the fourth century he might well have met Jews; but Jeremiah's lifetime was some two centuries earlier, and his sojourn in Egypt followed the fall of Jerusalem in 586 BC.

It is of great interest, nonetheless, that the study of Plato at Armagh is recorded in the tenth century. The great ninth-century Irish philosopher John Scotus Eriugena had a knowledge of Greek and of classical and neo-Platonist writings, which enabled him to translate the works of Dionysius the Areopagite and to write his own *Periphyseon*.[16] It is uncertain where he acquired these skills, although it must have been before he obtained the patronage of King Charles the Bald and a position lecturing at the palace school at Laon. The suggestion that Greek was known and taught at Armagh in the following century points to it as one of the possible sources of Eriugena's learning.

After his return to Scotland, Catroe himself became a teacher, apparently at Bean's monastic school. After a while Catroe, still described as a youth, formed the desire to go abroad on pilgrimage, like so many Celtic scholars before and after him. An attempt to dissuade him uses a quotation from Sulpicius's Life of Martin (which coincidentally is also found in the Scottish *Vita Sancti Servani*): *Cur nos pater deseris,* 'Wherefore, father, do you leave us?'[17] As a result, Catroe remained in Scotland a while longer.

The *vita* describes how he spent the winter before his departure reciting Psalms 119–134 nightly while immersed in a swift and freezing torrent and clinging to a rope made fast to an overhanging tree. This was perhaps the Earn,[18] or possibly the Almond, if St Bean's activity is to be located in Glen Almond.

From this place, wherever it was, Catroe began his pilgrimage, and came to an important church (*aedes*) dedicated to St Brigit. St Brigit's most important dedication in Scotland was at Abernethy, which in the eighth century was the seat of a bishopric.[19] An identification with Abernethy would be consistent with identifying St Bean's church and school with one of his dedications in Strathearn or Glen Almond, and the tomb of St Columba with Dunkeld. It would also fit in well with the description in the *vita* of an encounter here with King Constantín, who had a major palace complex at Forteviot, some 12 km. to the west.[20] The Scottish kings may have continued to occupy a hill-fort south of Abernethy into this period as well.[21]

The narrative records that King Constantín had with him an abbot 'of just counsel', called *Mailedarius* or *Mailodarius,* i.e. Maelodair, who argued that Catroe should not be prevented from his journey, but rather aided in it. This person is not otherwise recorded, but if we can identify the house of St Brigit with the monastery of Abernethy, then it is not unreasonable to assume that Maelodair was its abbot.

Persuaded by his words, King Constantín conducted Catroe to the land of the Cumbrians (*usque terram Cumbrorum*), at the time ruled over by Dovenald, who was a relative of Catroe (*propinquus viri*). Anderson believed that this was Domnall mac Aeda, Constantín's brother, who succeeded another Donald or Dyfnwal 908 × 916.[22] But there are very good reasons for doubting this identification. First, the king of the Cumbrians who was defeated along with Constantín by Athelstan in 934 is named as Ywain, and the same king of the Cumbrians was still with Constantín when Athelstan again defeated them at the Battle of *Brunanburh* (unidentified; possibly = Burnswark on Solway?) in 937.[23] So Ywain must have succeeded Domnall mac Aeda sometime between 908 × 916 and 934.

Secondly, the Dovenald mentioned in *Vita Kaddroe* is unlikely to have been related to Constantín, while Domnall mac Aeda was his brother. This Dovenald was *propinquus viri*, a relative of Catroe, but no similar claim is made for Constantín. If Dovenald and Constantín had been brothers, the *vita* would presumably have claimed that Constantín also was *propinquus viri*. The absence of such a claim being made for Constantín leads to the conclusion that he and Dovenald were unrelated.[24]

The death of *Domnall mac Eoain* (or *Eogain*) *rí Bretan*, on pilgrimage, is recorded in the Irish annals s.a. 975.[25] Welsh sources record the pilgrimage to Rome of *Dunguallaun* king of Strathclyde under the same year. *Domnall* in Irish sources is clearly a gaelicisation of British *Dyfnwal*, perhaps shortened from an original *Dyfnwallon*. *Eoain* (genitive) in *AT* for the Gaelic *Eogain* may reflect the influence of British *Ywain*.[26] The Ywain in question is undoubtedly the Ywain who was with Constantín at his defeats by Athelstan in 934 and 937, and Dyfnwallon was his son. Dovenald mentioned in *Vita Kaddroe* can only be the same person, and *Vita Kaddroe* is our only evidence that he succeeded his father before Constantín's retiral into religion at St Andrews c. 943. He may have abdicated before his departure on pilgrimage; a king called Dufnal (= Dyfnwal) is named among those who allegedly rowed King Edgar on the Dee at Chester in 973, but the king of the Cumbrians at this time was Malcolm, called 'Malcolm son of Donald, king of the Britons of the north' in the Irish annals.[27]

It is uncertain if the spelling *Dovenaldus* in *Vita Kaddroe* represents Gaelic *Dom(h)nall* or British *Dyfnwal*; but his identification as the son of Ywain and father of Malcolm is not in doubt.

After keeping him with him for a time, Dovenald brought Catroe south as far as the town of *Loida*, which is the border between the Northmen and the Cumbrians (*quae est confinium Normannorum atque Cumbrorum*). The Bollandists would identify this with a town in the region of the Forest of Lowes, in Northumbria;[28] Anderson suggests Leeds, which seems to be too far south.[29] Stainmore Common in the Pennines, on the border of Westmoreland and Yorkshire, was by the tenth century recognised as the southern boundary of the Cumbrian kingdom and of the diocese of Glasgow;[30] possibly the lost town of *Loida* was in this area.

Wherever this place was, it was occupied by a Norse nobleman called Gunderic, who conducted Catroe to York (*Euroacum urbem*, for *Evoracum*) to a king who is named as Eric (*rex Erichius*), because 'the king had a wife who was a relative of the lord Catroe' (*rex habebat coniugem ipsius domini Kaddroe propinquam*). Eric 'Bloodaxe' was king of York for two brief periods, 947–8 and 952–4, but it is not certain that this is the person referred to here. For a start, on the basis of the calculation from the date of his death, Catroe's pilgrimage must have commenced in 941, some years before Eric was king of York. The dates of other persons named, Constantín (abdicated c. 943), King Edmund of Wessex (940–946), and Archbishop Oda of Canterbury (from 941), serve to confirm a date 941 × 943. Eric Bloodaxe's wife, moreover, was a Danish lady called Gunnhild Gorm's daughter, who is described in Norse sagas as 'very guileful and cruel', 'an evil-doing and most wicked woman', loathed both in Norway and Northumbria for her 'excessive insolence' and 'pestilential madness'.[31] Anderson comments that 'if ... Gunnhild was related to Catroe, she was strangely different in character'.[32] There is no suggestion, however, that Catroe had Danish connections. Besides, Catroe came from a Christian family with a tradition of devotion to St Columba, whereas Eric's wife and children were unbaptised until c. 937, when baptism was forced on them by Athelstan. If Eric was the king in question and this *coniux domini Kaddroe propinqua* is Gunnhild, it is not clear how she could have been related to Catroe.

It is possible, however, that the writer has erred in naming the king of York as Eric. Eric's immediate predecessor as king of York was Olaf Sigtrygg's son, who was king of Dublin, ally and son-in-law of Constantín. He became king of York in 941 or 942 in succession to another Olaf, Gothfrith's son, who had also been allied with Constantín and was defeated with him and Ywain of Strathclyde at Brunanburh in 939. It may be that one or other of these Olafs is the king of York referred to here, and that his name has been given in error as Eric. How he was related to Catroe by marriage is not known.

Catroe proceeded from York to London, where he stayed with a man called Ecgfrith; while he was there there was a fire in the city, part of which was preserved by Catroe's prayers. This brought him to the attention of King Edmund of Wessex (940–46) at Winchester, who had him conducted to the Channel by Archbishop Oda of Canterbury (941–958).[33] He came to the Channel port of Lympne,[34] and sailed from there with other pilgrims[35] to Boulogne. They proceeded from there first to the shrine of St Fursey at Péronne (dép. Somme) in Picardy.

The monasticism of eastern and north-eastern France, especially Lorraine and the surrounding regions, had experienced a period of decadence in the ninth century, and in the early tenth there was a move towards reform. The foundation of Cluny in Burgundy (909) was the spur for reform further north, and in 933 the abbey of Gorze near Metz was reformed by Adalbero, bishop of Metz, prompting a new wave of reform. The abbeys of the 'Gorzian' reform contrasted to some extent with the Cluniac houses, in that ecclesiastical control remained with the local diocesan bishops, while lordship and advocacy remained with the lay patrons. In these houses there was practiced rigorous monastic discipline, a common life, and efficient estate management, in the tradition of St Benedict of Aniane. The houses of the 'Gorzian' reform were much favoured by pious layfolk, including the Ottonian dynasty itself.[36] It was into this atmosphere of piety and reform that Catroe and his companions entered on their arrival on the continent; and it was not long before they began to attract the attention of pious founders looking for exemplary monks to lead their new communities.

A noble matron of the area called Hersent[37] was impressed by the sanctity of the pilgrims and, being childless, proposed to bequeath her goods to them. A group of thirteen pilgrims was established at a place dedicated to St Michael in the forest of Thierache, where they enlarged the church and built dwellings. Catroe was elected superior, but declined; and the choice then fell on his companion, called Maccalan.[38] Although the pilgrims were living as a religious community, they were not yet professed monks; so Hersent sent Maccalan to Gorze and Catroe to Fleury to make their monastic professions to the abbots of these houses (Agenald and Erkembald respectively). Both of the new monks spent some time at the monasteries where they had been received, but soon Hersent recalled Maccalan to St Michael in Thierache to resume his duties as superior there; when Catroe returned from Fleury, Hersent brought him to a place on the Meuse whose ancient name was Wassor or Waulsort (*prisco vocabulo Walciodorus nominatus*), where she appointed him as prior.[39] Soon after, Maccalan decided that the rule of both houses was too much for him, and persuaded Catroe to accept the title of abbot of Waulsort; his appointment was confirmed by King Otto I (later emperor).

Monastic life increased and developed at Waulsort, and many new monks were received there. Catroe's fame spread, especially when it was reported that he had healed a monk called Girerus, wounded in the hand. Meanwhile his benefactress Hersent was moved to found a 'choir of virgins' at a place called Bucilly; during the course of a visit Catroe cast out an evil spirit from one of the nuns. This brought him to the notice of Adalbero, the reforming bishop of Metz, who, on the advice of abbots Agenold of Gorze and Anstée of St Arnould of Metz, summoned him to the cathedral city. Near Metz there lay the ruins of a once famous abbey, 'noteworthy for the bones and relics of many saints', but now reduced to nothing; the bishop put Catroe in charge of its revival.

Catroe still held the cure of souls at Waulsort, and brought some of his monks from there to Metz. The remainder chose one of their number as his successor, and Catroe installed him as abbot at Waulsort. This man (unnamed) fell away from the way of righteousness (*via rectitudinis*), and Catroe's efforts to recall him to it were in vain.

He was more successful, however, in his new charge at Metz. During his abbacy he travelled widely and performed a number of miracles, producing a spring of water at Waulsort, causing his abbatial staff to glow like the sun's rays,[40] and healing the damaged eyes of a youthful companion. He healed John, abbot of Gorze, when he was sick, and cast out a demon from one of the nuns of St Peter of Metz.

When Bishop Adalbero died, he was succeeded by Theodore, a member of the imperial family; he transferred Catroe to the abbacy of St Felix of Metz. His fame reached the ears of the Empress Adelaide, mother of the future Emperor Otto II (973–983), and he was summoned to her at a place called Neierstheim[41] on the Rhine. Before his departure for her court he predicted his death before he could return, fearing that the Empress would want to keep him with her; and he comforted all his friends in Metz. As he had predicted, the Empress kept him at her court, and here he performed his last living miracle, healing a man who had fallen from a height and broken many bones. His own body was now enfeebled with age, and he besought the Empress to let him return to his monastery and die there. Reluctantly she let him go, but too late, and he died on the homeward journey between the Rhine and Metz. His remains were brought back and interred in his church of St Felix at Metz.[42]

This narrative is of great interest for a number of reasons. It sheds light on Scottish church and politics in the first half of the tenth century, a period for which we have very few sources; it is clear that the writer had access to material probably related by Catroe himself referring to his parentage and early life in Scotland. It casts light on a whole range of aspects of society, from the obligations required of a foster-son towards his foster-parents to the educational curriculum available at Armagh. It reveals also how Celtic monks were regarded on the continent at the height of the 'Gorzian' reform, showered with endowments by a pious matron, summoned by bishops, dukes and even the empress, and building reputations as powerful miracle workers. There can be no doubt of the impression made by Catroe and his companions, which lasted well into the high Middle Ages.

Most of our native Scottish hagiography comes from earlier and later periods, and relates to personages of earlier and later dates. *Vita Kaddroe* is a fortunate continental survival[43] from the obscure time in between. The following centuries witnessed a revival of interest in hagiography, as exemplified in the *vita* and career of Queen Margaret, to whom we turn in the next chapter.

NOTES

1. M Dilworth, *The Scots in Franconia* (1974).
2. Spelt *Kaddroe* consistently in his *vita*. The double -*dd*- probably indicates an unlenited dental stop; accordingly, I have accepted the familiar spelling Catroe.
3. 431–443; the whole text is edited with introduction and commentary in *AASS, Mar.*, i (1865), 468–80.
4. On the form of his name, cf. M Coens, 'Le Premier Tome du legendier de Saint-Hubert', *Analecta Bollandiana*, vii (1939), 109ff., at 117–8 nn; A Dierkens, *Abbayes et Chapîtres entre Sambre et Meuse* (1985), 167 and n; *AASS, Mar.*, i (1865), 473. Colgan may have misread a name he did not recognise.
5. There was also an Immo abbot of Waulsort at about the same time; cf. Coens, op. cit., 118n.; Dierkens, op. cit., 167n., identifies him as the abbot of Gorze, citing the unpublished researches of Dom D Misonne.
6. *AASS, Mar.*, i, 480, cap. 36.
7. Anderson, *ESSH*, 432n: 'The form of the name is probably Welsh'.
8. See below, p 201.
9. A king of Ireland called Fogartach is noted in the Irish annals; cf. *AU*, s.a. 714, 716, 724, with cognate entries in *AT*.
10. *AU*, s.a. 878.
11. Walafrid Strabo's 'Life of Blathmac', edited in *MGH Poetae Latini Aevi Carolini*, ii, 299–301; translated by Anderson, *ESSH*, i, 263–5.
12. Anderson, *ESSH*, i, 288; M O Anderson, *Kings and Kingship in Early Scotland* (1st edn, 1973), 249–50.
13. A Macquarrie and E M MacArthur, *Iona through the Ages* (2nd edn,

1992), 12–13. On 9th-century Iona, see now T O Clancy, 'Iona, Scotland and the *Céli Dé*', in B E Crawford (ed.), *Scotland in Dark Age Britain* (1996), 111–30, at 111ff.; J Bannerman, '*Comarbe Coluim Chille* and the Relics of Columba', *IR*, xliv (1993), 14–47, at 29–33. 'St Matthew's Cross' on Iona indicates 9th-century artistic activity. In *AU* 986 'the abbot and fifteen monks' were slaughtered by Vikings; this may be typical of the community in the 10th century.

14. Anderson, *ESSH*, i, 433n.
15. Watson, *CPNS*, 310–12.
16. Johannes Scotus Eriugena, *Periphyseon or De Divisione Naturae*, ed I P Sheldon-Williams et al. (DIAS, 1968-); also, with the rest of Eriugena's works, in Migne, *PL*, cxxii.
17. A Macquarrie, '*Vita Sancti Servani*: the Life of St Serf', *Innes Review*, xliv (1993), 122–52, at 143
18. As suggested by Archer in *DNB*, viii, 188.
19. A Macquarrie, 'Early Christian Religious Houses in Scotland: Foundation and Function', in J Blair and R Sharpe (eds.), *Pastoral Care before the Parish* (Leicester, 1992), 110–133, at 114–8; and see above, chapter 8, pp. 177–81.
20. L Alcock, *Survey and Excavation at Forteviot, Perthshire, 1981* (University of Glasgow Dept of Archaeology, 1982). A recently discovered inscription on the Dupplin Cross on the hillside above Forteviot may commemorate this Constantín, or an earlier holder of this name: cf. K Forsyth, 'The Inscription on the Dupplin Cross', in *From the Isles of the North: Medieval Art in Ireland and Britain* (1995), 237–44.
21. A Ritchie, *Picts* (1989), 16.
22. Anderson, *ESSH*, i, 441, 445–6.
23. Anderson, *SAEC*, 68, 70–1.
24. Macquarrie, 'Kings of Strathclyde', 14–16 and nn.
25. Anderson, *ESSH*, 480.
26. *AU* has *Hoan rege Britonum* s.a. 642; *AT* has *Ohan reghe Britonum* for its cognate entry. S.a. 694 *AU* and *AT* both call his son *Domnall mac Auin*, implying a nominative **Aun*. Cf. the apparently Pictish name *Tolarggan maphan* in *AU* s.a. 726; perhaps *lege Tolarggan map h-An*, 'Talorgen son of An', i.e., 'son of Owen'? But if Gaelic writers treated the name as an *o*-stem, we should expect a genitive **Auin*.
27. Macquarrie, 'Kings of Strathclyde', 15–16 and nn.
28. *AASS, Martii*, i, 476n.
29. Anderson, *ESSH*, i, 441.
30. A P Smyth, *Warlords and Holy Men: Scotland, AD 80–1000* (London, 1984), 227–30; D P Kirby, 'Strathclyde and Cumbria', *TCWAAS*, n.s. lxii (1962), 77–94.
31. Anderson, *ESSH*, i, 455–6n, 461n, 462n.

32. Ibid., 441n.
33. On the dates of these persons, cf. *Biographical Dictionary of Dark Age Britain*, snn.
34. 'It is near the mouth of the Rother, 2 miles from Hythe'; Anderson, *ESSH*, i, 442n.
35. The writer mentions in passing that one of Catroe's companions was his nephew, whom he persuaded to remain behind in Britain. Cap. 19.
36. Cf. *ODCC*, s.n. Gorze.
37. Hersent was wife of a nobleman called Eilbert, who is associated with her in the foundation documents of Waulsort, but is not mentioned in *Vita Kaddroe*; cf. Dierkens, op. cit., 166-7.
38. *Machalanus* in *Vita Kaddroe*; Flodoard calls him *Maccalinus* (*AASS, Mar.*, i, 476-7).
39. The foundation of Waulsort was confirmed by King Otto I (later Emperor) to 'the servants of God coming from *Scotia* on pilgrimage, desiring to live under the Rule of St Benedict' on 19 Nov. 946. Anderson, *ESSH*, i, 443; Dierkens, op. cit., 166.
40. This miracle took place in the presence of Duke Frederick of Lorraine, brother of Bishop Adalbero; Dierkens, op. cit., 171.
41. Anderson says this is a place called Erstein in Alsace. The Bollandists (*AASS*, loc. cit.) suggest that it lay between Mainz and Speier.
42. This narrative is based on the text of *Vita Kaddroe* in *AASS, Mar.*, i and the comments in Anderson, *ESSH*, i, and in Coens and Dierkens, opp. cit. Cf. also *Biographical Dictionary of Dark Age Britain*, s.n. Catroe.
43. Bearing in mind that the Legendary of St Hubert survives only in part, and that only in transcripts; the MS is lost. Cf. Coens, op. cit.

10

St Margaret of Scotland

Our last saint is also the only woman among them. Perhaps for this reason among others Margaret has always been popular in her adopted homeland, in spite rather than because of the portrait painted of her in her late-eleventh-century *vita* by her chaplain Thurgot.[1] It is appropriate that she should come at the end of our series, for more than anyone else she represents the transition from the old Celtic individualism of earlier centuries to the uniformity of Christendom in the High Middle Ages. Her son David has been called 'ane sair sanct for the croun', but unlike her, and in spite of Ailred's hagiographic eulogy,[2] he was never canonised; his reign (1124–1153) has been described as a skilful and successful balance of old and new,[3] but it may be that this description applies equally, if not better, to his mother's career (c. 1046–1093). She is rightly credited with bringing Benedictine monks to Scotland and beginning the process of ecclesiastical reform; on the other hand, we shall see that many traditional features of Celtic church and culture continued largely unaffected up to her death and beyond.[4]

'Many abuses which had grown up contrary to the rule of faith and the institutions and observances of the Church, she ... succeeded in condemning and expelling from the kingdom.' These words from Thurgot's *vita* of Queen Margaret,[5] addressed to her daughter Edith (or Matilda) within a few years of the queen's death,[6] have coloured our impression of Margaret for 900 years. Thurgot's portrait is of a strong-willed, severe and ascetic colonial incomer, who found uncivilised and barbaric practices everywhere and everywhere reformed and improved them. She improved the quality of the vessels and vestments of the churches of Dunfermline and St Andrews; she fostered overseas trade so that hitherto unknown luxury goods became available in Scotland; she improved the quality of the king's retainers, so that he travelled in state and style throughout the kingdom; the royal wardrobe and tableware similarly underwent her improvements.

But the impression presented by the *Vita* leaves difficulties. There is an element of contradiction in some of Thurgot's statements about the queen's attitudes and way of life, of which the author seems occasionally to be conscious. Thus, although 'she began to lead a life of great strictness, to love God above all things, and to occupy herself with the study of holy Scripture', she still consented to marry the king of Scots, 'compelled to do these things which are of the world... yet delighting more in good works than in abundance of riches'.[7] When he describes the magnificent improvements which she wrought in the trappings of the royal court, Thurgot adds: 'this the queen did not because the honour of the world delighted her, but because she felt compelled to do that which royal state demanded of her.'[8] The writer likens her to a second Esther, claiming that 'in the midst of her exalted dignity, she took very great care to preserve lowliness of mind.'[9] Clearly Thurgot found it difficult to reconcile royal dignity with his conception of humble sanctity.

Although Margaret is often thought of as an English incomer in Scotland, it is important to remember that she was in fact Hungarian by birth, and was thus a foreigner both in England and Scotland. Her grandfather Edmund Ironside had been defeated by Cnut and died in 1016, following which his two young sons, Edmund and Edward, fled abroad. Edmund died in exile a few years later, but Edward settled at the Hungarian court and married Agatha, a daughter of King Stephen of Hungary. Margaret was born c. 1046 or a few years later, and spent her early years at the pious court where Stephen's reign was still a recent memory. When she was not much more than ten (possibly younger), her father was recalled by Edward the Confessor, and died in obscure circumstances immediately after his return to England in 1057.[12] Margaret spent the next eleven years of her life in England, at a court increasingly dominated by the family of Earl Godwin until that dynasty was effectively wiped out in the disasters of 1066. Thereafter Margaret's young brother, Edgar Atheling, became the focus of opposition to the new Norman dynasty, and he and his mother and two sisters were forced to flee to Scotland in 1068.

So when she arrived in Scotland Margaret was already a foreigner twice over and a political exile, landless and penniless, without hope or prospects. It has been speculated that her mother intended to take her children (Margaret was the eldest, possibly in her late teens or early twenties) back to Hungary,[13] but the truth of this will never be known. At any rate, King Malcolm quickly spotted the advantages of a marriage alliance with the dispossessed English dynasty, and asked for Margaret's hand, which he obtained, in Thurgot's conventional phrase, 'by the will of her kinsfolk rather than her own, or rather, by the ordinance of God'.[14] Malcolm was already a wily and experienced campaigner who had overthrown the intrusive dynasty of Moray with English help, consolidated his position throughout Scotland, and been freed from dependence on the English by the events of 1065–6. He was to rule for a further twenty-three years, demonstrating that he knew how to negotiate and temporise as well as to fight, until in the end he was killed by the treachery of his own friends.[15]

Although there were clear political advantages in Malcolm's marriage to Margaret, Thurgot makes it clear that their relationship was affectionate. He touchingly describes how the illiterate king would 'handle and gaze upon' her favourite books, and would commission jewellers to decorate them so that he could give them to her as presents.[16] He accompanied the queen in her devotions, and even joined her in serving banquets to the poor during Advent and Lent.[17] But Thurgot's most charming picture of their relationship comes when he describes, as an eyewitness, how Margaret would occasionally steal some of the king's coins or property, and distribute it to the poor. Either Malcolm would try to ignore this 'pious theft', of which he secretly approved, or, if her action was too obvious to be ignored, would seize her hand and bring her before Thurgot, her chaplain, 'for judgement, saying in jest that she was a thief.'[18] They had at least eight children, which must say something about their relationship.[19]

It is worth bearing in mind that Malcolm and Margaret had some experiences in common. Malcolm too had lost his father in political turmoil when he was young, and he too had been a political exile at the court of Edward the Confessor. He had learned English there, so from their first meeting he and Margaret were able to converse fluently. Bearing in mind that her mother's native language was Magyar, and that she was first thrust into an English-speaking environment when she was somewhere between eight and twelve, one can imagine that Margaret appreciated Malcolm's command of English when she began her second exile.

It is an interesting question whether Margaret acquired Gaelic during her twenty-five years in Scotland. Thurgot's statement that she needed the king to interpret for her at her reforming council might be taken to imply that she never mastered Gaelic; on the other hand, he states that she 'very often visited with her presence and conversation' the hermits of Scotia, who would have been Gaelic speakers. The only such conversation which has been independently recorded was with the *clerici* of Laurencekirk, and it only survives in a Latin text;[20] but it is hard to believe that Gaelic was not the language used. It is hard to believe, indeed, that Margaret can have lived at Malcolm's court for so long without acquiring the language of the court.[21] So it may be that some parts of Thurgot's portrait of Margaret have to be used with caution.

There are more subtle difficulties as well. At the great ecclesiastical council at which she allegedly reformed abuses of the Celtic church, Margaret is portrayed almost as an imperious bully, delivering a 'Sermon on the Mound' worthy of a twentieth-century politician with a handbag. But at the same time, claims Thurgot, she invited churchmen to reproach her faults, because 'she sought censure as helping her advancement in virtue'.[22] And the impact of her reforming zeal may have been slightly lessened if she did indeed require her husband King Malcolm to interpret for her. Thurgot describes him as 'her chief helper' in her attempts at reform; he does not add the obvious truth, that Margaret could have achieved little without his support. It may even be questioned how much actually was achieved by Margaret's reforming councils; some twenty years after her death Thurgot himself, now 'bishop of the Scots', was in receipt of papal letters from Paschal II complaining that some of the same practices which were discussed and condemned at Margaret's councils (e.g., concerning Easter communion and the observance of Lent) were still prevalent.[23]

It may be that her strictures against Celtic Christianity were less severe in practice than Thurgot claims. In a passage which has attracted considerable comment,[24] Thurgot describes how 'At that time in the kingdom of the Scots there were many living, shut up in cells in places set apart, by a life of great strictness, in the flesh but not according to the flesh; communing, indeed, with angels upon earth.'[25] He goes on to describe how the queen 'venerated and loved Christ in these men', frequently visiting them and requesting them to pray for her; and when she could not persuade them to accept an earthly gift from her, asked them to impose some work of charity on her instead, whereby she could relieve poverty or suffering. Apart from its implications regarding the question of whether or not Margaret could speak Gaelic, this suggests a receptiveness to Celtic ways which is not totally consistent with other parts of Thurgot's portrayal.

Not all the churches which the queen visited refused her gifts. Thurgot describes how when he himself was prior of the church in which her marriage was celebrated (Holy Trinity, Dunfermline), 'she adorned it with many kinds of precious gifts... vessels of pure solid gold for the holy service of the altar... also a cross of matchless value, having on it an image of the Saviour covered with gold and silver and studded with gems'.[26] He also mentions 'a very beautiful crucifix' which she erected in the cathedral kirk of St Andrews, and describes how the queen established a ferry at Queensferry to facilitate the pilgrim traffic coming to St Andrews; but half a century later St Andrews still had many Celtic features, and a degree of secularisation as well.[27]

Professor Barrow has complained that we would like to know more about these hermits and holy men casually and vaguely mentioned by Thurgot.[28] But in fact we do know of several examples of Queen Margaret's generosity towards native ascetics in remote parts of Scotland. Orderic Vitalis describes how 'among other things... she rebuilt the abbey of *Eoa*... and she gave the monks fitting revenues for the work of the Lord, and restored it.'[29] No part of the queen's restoration work at Iona can now be identified, but it may be partly to her credit that there was a thriving Celtic monastic community there in the mid-twelfth century. This was not, however, a recognisable cloister of Benedictine monks, but a thoroughly Celtic community, containing a *sacart mór, fer léginn, dísertach*, and head of the *Céli Dé*.[30] Not until more than a century after Margaret's death was there a serious attempt to transform Iona into a Benedictine monastery, and that met with opposition from the Columban houses of Ireland.[31]

Among the Lochleven *notitiae* is a notice of a grant by Malcolm and Margaret to the *Céli Dé* of Lochleven. This has none of the characteristics of a feudal charter, but looks more like the continuation of a tradition of land grants of the kind found in the *Book of Deer*, in these Lochleven *notitiae* copied into the *Register of St Andrews Priory*, and in Irish MSS such as the *Book of Kells*. This grant states simply that 'King Malcolm and Queen Margaret of Scotland have piously granted the *vill* of Balchristie to God Almighty and the *Céli*

Dé of Lochleven, with the same liberties as [they had] before.'[32] The association of the queen with her husband in the grant is nothing new, since Gruoch ingen Boidhe had been associated with her husband Macbeth in their grant of Kirkness to Lochleven 1040 × 1057.[33] Similarly the grants to the church of Deer sometimes associate the spouse of an aristocratic donor with her husband in the making of a grant.[34] It is not certain that Margaret was regularly associated with Malcolm in records of his grants, or that there was anything unusual in this practice.[35]

But by far the most interesting account of Queen Margaret's generosity to a religious house in the Celtic part of her kingdom is that told in a late-eleventh-century *vita* of St Laurence of Canterbury by Goscelin of St Bertin, a Flemish monk living at Canterbury.[36] The story might otherwise be dismissed as legend, but it is in fact very closely contemporary, and was written either while Margaret was still alive or very soon after her death. It is of such interest and so little known[37] that it is worth quoting Goscelin's passage about Laurencekirk and Queen Margaret's visit there in full.

'Since Gregory, the admirable writer of sacred books, ascribes to Augustine and his companions the way of life and miracles of the apostles,[38] let us hear some other undeniable miracles of St Laurence, which learned and religious men have extracted for us from memory from the reading of his *vita*.

'So then: the eagle of God, spreading his wings from England into Scotland,[39] came to a place where his passage was hindered by an arm of the sea. While he was staying at a nearby hill, which is still called Laurence's Hill throughout that region,[40] awaiting a ship, he saw a sailor and besought him that he would take him across. But the man refused the suppliant's prayers, being far removed from divine and human pity. But heaven's indignation soon swallowed up the impious man and his ship, not merely in the jaws of the sea, but by fire from heaven. When he saw this, the athlete of God, filled with faith and the Holy Spirit, no longer waited for a ship, but entered into the terrifying deep as if it was a field, like as if he saw Christ going before him with Peter; and after making the sign of the cross, he trod down mountainous waves under his feet as if they were solid ground, and was brought to the other shore in miraculous fashion.

'After this crossing on foot of the stormy sea, the Lord's champion Laurence came to a village where he found no-one who would take in the messenger of Christ and bearer of the gospel of the Lord's peace; rather they put him out with curses, so that he rested under a hedge that night. Heavenly grace shone round about the witness of the Lord, and the splendour of the sun's brightness poured from the heavens, visible far and wide, and night was turned into day; the brightness of heaven revealed how far the heavenly man had been rejected by earthly darkness. A bolt of lightning, suddenly cast down from the heavenly throne, burnt up the village of that wicked people who drove out the messenger of salvation, with everyone in it, and reduced the whole place to a desert for ever, like Sodom or Babylon. Thus the Lord, the judge of all, divided light from darkness; so that by the element of fire in the night-time he might in starry glory illuminate the child of light who had been rejected by the children of darkness, and destroy the impious in terrible flames while at the same time making their unwelcoming land uninhabitable forever.

'Then the priest of the Lord went on and was received in another town, called Fordoun; he was heard there by many, sweetly teaching the joys of heaven. He found there a good and noble host, although he was not yet Christian, and stayed with him for some time.

'Meanwhile his fame flew across the sea, for 'a light upon a lamp-stand and a city upon a hill cannot be hid'.[41] St Ternan, Archbishop of Ireland, came to him,[42] a man of such great sanctity that he is said to have resuscitated three dead men. He heard St Laurence discoursing on the observation of Easter and other apostolic institutions, which they discussed together, and gave his assent to the truth. [Ternan's] disciples were indignant that such a holy man should be subject to this foreigner; but he brought them into the way of truth by his example, together with his whole people.[43]

'When Laurence returned to his lodging, he found that his host's son was dead, and his father and mother and the whole household in sorrow. The parents cried out to him, 'O holy Laurence, revive our child, so that we may more faithfully believe in the Christ whom you preach!' What more [need I say]? The godly priest prayed, then said to the boy, 'Rise up, in Christ's name!' and straightway he stood up. He swore vehemently that he was being dragged by dreadful demons to the flames of hell, but at the prayers of St Laurence he was restored to his body by brightly shining angels of God. So he was baptised by the bishop, together with his father and mother and their household and all their relatives, and given the name Gille-Labhrain, which means 'Laurence's lad'.[44] His son moreover was called Mac Chéli;[45] it is said that afterwards he wrote down the *vita* of his father St Laurence.[46]

'This high priest of the Lord went from place to place, filling them with wonders and life-giving teaching. Among other things, by his holy prayers he produced a spring of water in a dry region of [the land of] Alba,[47] which has flowed unfailingly ever since, satisfying all with its sweet taste and also imparting health to those who believe.[48]

'After he had passed in triumph to the heavens,[49] the affectionate residents founded in the town of Fordoun a church in honour of St Laurence,[50] which among other evidences of its power was distinguished with this sacred privilege: that no woman might ever enter into it.[51] Margaret queen of Scotland, however, most honourable descendent of the kings of England and beloved of God, filled with religious piety, brought thither wax candles and other holy offerings, desiring to enter.[52] The canons met her at the entrance to the enclosure[53] and begged her not to transgress this holy law and custom, lest she should incur the wrath of the patron ruling there. But she replied rather that she would honour and exalt this sacred place, and pressed ahead. Accordingly, she had barely entered the enclosure when suddenly she was seized by severe pains in her whole body, and she said to her retainers, 'Quick, get me out of here! I'm dying!' Quickly they brought her outside,[54] and she begged the clerics to intercede for her, and blamed herself for not having heeded them when they had warned her.[55]

'When they sang psalms on her behalf, the queen recovered her health, and rewarded them with joyful celebrations; she adorned the church with a great silver cross and a beautiful chalice, and with other royal gifts,[56] summoning to herself the proven, true and pious father Laurence by continual veneration, to whom she could not approach in the flesh.'[57]

The author of this story is a well-documented and prolific hagiographer of the second half of the eleventh century. 'Goscelin the Monk' was born probably in the diocese of Thérouanne (dép. Pas-de-Calais), and entered the Benedictine monastery of St Bertin at St Omer. He joined the household of Herman, bishop of Ramsbury (or Wiltshire), who was staying there at the time, and returned with him to England in or soon after 1058. He seems to have served for a time as chaplain to the nunnery of Wilton, a centre where many aristocratic young women were sent for their education (including at a later date Edith, daughter of Malcolm and Margaret, and future wife of

Henry I).[58] After Herman's death in 1078 Goscelin quarrelled with his successor and left Wiltshire. For a number of years he made his living travelling among the Benedictine monasteries and nunneries of England, compiling many *vitae* of local saints from locally available materials. C. 1090 he came to St Augustine's, Canterbury, where over the next few years he compiled *vitae* of the major Canterbury saints, including a longer and a shorter *vita* of St Augustine of Canterbury, a *Liber de miraculis* and a *Historia Translationis* of St Augustine, and *vitae* of Augustine's successors Laurence, Mellitus, Justus, Honorius, Deusdedit, Theodore, and a number of others. Goscelin was still alive in 1107, and probably died round about that time or soon after.[59]

The *Vita Sancti Laurentii* belongs to a series written in the early 1090s. In 1091 there was a major translation of the relics of the saints of Canterbury following the rebuilding of St Augustine's under the direction of Abbot Wido, and Goscelin's new *vita* was one of a group probably commissioned in connection with this occasion.[60] In other words, the story about Queen Margaret is a contemporary account written while the queen was still alive or very shortly after her death; although written in distant Canterbury, and perhaps suitably exaggerated for hagiographical purposes, its primary authority cannot be doubted.

The *vita* of St Laurence is contained in two MSS, both now in the British Library.[61] Both are early twelfth-century MSS of Canterbury provenance, and contain lives of Canterbury saints. There is no complete printed edition of this *vita*. Migne, among his collection of Goscelin's writings, put together an *Elogium Historicum Sancti Laurentii*, drawn from Bede, *HE*, ii, 4–6, and quotations from Goscelin's *Historia Translationis Sancti Augustini*; but it is not based on the MSS of the *vita*, even though he knew of its existence and knew that it contained material independent of Bede.[62] In largely ignoring the *vita* he was following the Bollandists.[63] Hardy identified it in his *Descriptive Catalogue* in the Rolls Series, and thought poorly of it: he remarks of the Scottish material that 'these additions are of no importance' and that 'the miracles ... are very vague and declamatory'.[64] The Bollandist *Bibliotheca Hagiographica Latina* cited Hardy's entry, and clearly looked no further.[65] A O Anderson did not mention it in his *Scottish Annals from English Chroniclers* or *Early Sources of Scottish History*; insofar as the Scottish material has been noticed at all,[66] it is through a late medieval paraphrase attributed to John

Capgrave. Goscelin's *Vita Sancti Laurentii* has recently been edited, however, with a full collation of the two MSS, in an unpublished University of Groningen thesis by Mr Wynzen de Vries, who has drawn my attention to it.[67] The Scottish material has recently been edited by me, and a complete critical edition of the *corpus* of Goscelin's work is presently being prepared at the University of Oxford.[68]

The material does deserve attention from Scottish historians, however, because it undoubtedly comes from a Scottish source. Goscelin states that *eruditissimi et religiosi uiri nobis memoriter de lecta eius excerpsere uita*, 'learned and religious men have extracted [these miracles] for us from memory from the reading of his *vita*'. This suggests that he was told these stories by Benedictine monks (Goscelin could hardly have applied the term *eruditissimi et religiosi uiri* to anyone else) relying on their recollection of a *vita* which they had heard or read. The passage claims that the son of an early Scottish convert called Gilli Laurentius (for Gaelic *Gille Labhrain*) wrote a *vita* of St Laurence; we may question how early they are, but certainly these miracles are characteristic of Scottish hagiography of the eleventh and twelfth centuries, and quite out of character with the rest of Goscelin's *vita* of St Laurence. There is some evidence of topographical knowledge: the source knew of St Laurence's kirk beside Fordoun, with its *atrium*,[69] staffed by a community of *clerici* or *canonici*;[70] and of St Laurence's Well.[71] He also knew of a hill called *Collis Laurentii* (perhaps for *Cnoc Labhrain*, or something similar) overlooking an arm of the sea, possibly the Firth of Tay.[72] Perhaps more significant are the two Gaelic personal names which Goscelin quotes: *Gilli Laurentius* (i.e., *Gille Labhrain*) and *Filius Cheli* (presumably for Gaelic *Mac Chéli*, 'servant's son'). He also mentions (in the genitive) *Albania ciuitas*, 'the city (or monastic community) of Alba', mistaking the Gaelic name of the kingdom for the name of a town. Goscelin himself presumably did not know Gaelic; if he was, as has been argued, the author of the *Vita Ædwardi Regis*, he could not master Macbeth's name, calling him only *rex Scottorum nomine barbarus*.[73] Only a Scottish source connected with Laurencekirk would have been interested in recording the foundation legend; and we can accept the *vita* as evidence for the existence of a community of *clerici* or *canonici* there in the eleventh century. The story about Queen Margaret would have been of wider interest, but must also have originated at Laurencekirk. It certainly does not reflect

Goscelin's attitude to women: he had been a nunnery chaplain, had warm relationships with many religious and lay women and wrote *vitae* of several female saints.[74]

It has been remarked that Goscelin's *vitae* are 'usually based on earlier material';[75] that certainly seems to be the case with this passage. One might perhaps speculate that the monks of Canterbury heard this anecdote about Queen Margaret, which must have been circulating in the 1080s or early 1090s, *via* the monks of Holy Trinity Dunfermline.[76] Goscelin is perhaps more likely to have referred to these as *eruditissimi et religiosi uiri*, rather than the simple *clerici* of Laurencekirk. Perhaps, indeed, there were Benedictine monks among the queen's retainers when she visited Laurencekirk; Thurgot implies that clerics travelled with the queen on occasion.[77] But the anecdote itself, and the foundation legend and miracles, can only have originated at Laurencekirk. However Goscelin came by these stories, there can be no doubt about their place of origin or their cultural *milieu*.

The foundation story is of little help in trying to determine the date and motivation of a dedication to St Laurence of Canterbury in Mearns. Its intrinsic interest is, however, much greater than has previously been recognised, and a number of other points are worth making. For a start, Laurence is a historical personage, and, by the standards of historical personages of the sixth and seventh centuries, fairly well and reliably documented. But the foundation legend owes nothing to Bede, and recounts instead a series of extremely derivative and unoriginal miracle stories without any basis in fact. We cannot, for example, have any confidence that Laurence really did travel in Scotland and visit Fordoun. This tells us something about how saints' *vitae* of this period were put together, and should caution us against relying too heavily on them as historical sources for the saints themselves. On the other hand, dedications and *vitae* appear usually to relate to people who did in fact exist in some shape or form, howsoever distorted they may have become.

The anecdote about Queen Margaret is of great interest, and may suggest that the traditional view of her as an intolerant and assertive colonial improver (as Thurgot portrays her) may stand in need of modification. Professor Donaldson correctly pointed out that 'Queen Margaret, though critical of much else, had evidently no criticism to make of Scottish orders or organisation'.[78] Her generosity to Iona, St Andrews, Lochleven, and Laurencekirk does not seem to have resulted in fundamental changes to the character and organisation of these houses. Her attempt to ignore the traditions of Laurencekirk, at least, allegedly resulted in a humbling and chastening experience for her. Surviving court poetry from the reign of Malcolm III, such as the fine verse history *Duan Albanach*,[79] likewise suggests the continuance of existing traditions rather than wholesale cultural innovation.[80]

One MS belonging to Queen Margaret has apparently survived. The only miracle which Thurgot tells concerning Queen Margaret describes how a person who was carrying her favourite gospel-book dropped it into a river while he was fording it, and how when it was eventually recovered from the stream it was found to be undamaged, apart from the outermost folios at either end and the loss of scraps of silk which covered the illuminations. According to Thurgot, the book had 'figures of the four evangelists decorated with painting, interspersed with gold, and the capital letters glowed all in gold'.[81]

The Bodleian Library holds an early eleventh-century English gospel-book 'of the Canute period' which certainly matches this description. In itself that tells us nothing, but the MS contains the following poem on a fly-leaf at the front in a twelfth-century hand:

Christe tibi semper grates persoluimus omnes,
Tempore qui nostro nobis miracula pandis:
Hunc librum quidam interse iurare uolentes
Sumpserunt, nudum, sine tegmine, nonque ligatum.
Presbyter accipiens, ponit sinuamine uestis,
Flumine transmisso, codex est mersus in amnem.
Portitor ignorat librum penetrasse profundum,
Sed miles quidam, cernens post multa momenta,
Tollere iam uoluit librum de flumine mersum;
Sed titubat subito, librum dum uidit apertum,
Credens quod codex extoto perditus esset.
At tamen inmittens undis corpus cumuertice, summo
Hoc euangelium profert de gurgite apertum.
O uirtus clara cunctis! O gloria magna!
Inuiolatus enim codex permansit ubique,
Exceptis foliis binis, que cernis utrinque
In quibus ex undis paret contractio quedam.
Que testantur opus Christi procidite sancto,
Hoc opus ut nobis maius mirabile constet,
De medio libri pannum lini abtulit unda.

Saluati semper sint rex reginaque sancta,
Quorum codex erat nuper saluatis abundis;
Gloria magna Deo, librum qui saluat eundem.

('All give thee thanks always, O Christ, who showest us miracles in our own times. Some men, wanting to swear [oaths] among themselves, took up this book, bare, uncovered and unbound. A priest received it and placed it in the fold of his clothing; while crossing a river, the volume fell into the stream. The bearer did not know that the book had fallen into the deep, but a knight, seeing it after some time, wanted to bring up the submerged book from the river; but suddenly drew back, seeing the book lying open, thinking the volume would be completely lost. Then, turning back, he plunged his body into the waves, and brought up the open gospel-book from the stream. O power clear to all! O great glory! The volume remained undamaged throughout, except for two folios which you see at either end, in which there appears a little shrinkage from the waves. These bear witness that the work of Christ is holy. That this event might seem more miraculous to us, the waves had drawn from the middle of the book a linen cloth. May the king and the holy queen be saved for ever, whose volume was recently completely saved; great glory be to God, who has preserved this book.')[82]

This book does show English cultural influence at Malcolm and Margaret's court, although there was nothing particularly innovative about Queen Margaret in the last quarter of the eleventh century owning a gospel-book of the second quarter of the same century. Probably imported books were not uncommon. If the Gospel MS *Book of Deer* is a typical native production of the late dark-age period, its poor quality in text and illumination suggest the need for quality imports.[83]

In spite of Thurgot's portrait, we have to remember that Margaret, for all the strength of her personality, and for all of King Malcolm's affectionate support, was a political exile, a foreigner, a member of a dispossessed dynasty which was entirely dependent on the generosity of the Scottish court, and a woman; all of these factors seriously limited her power and influence. It may be that we cannot fully accept Thurgot's picture of her as an assertive colonial improver; she emerges as a more attractive character as a result.

NOTES

1. *Vita Margaretae Reginae* is edited in J Hodgson Hynde, *Symeonis Dunelmensis Opera et Collectanea* (Surtees Soc., 1868)(hereafter *VMR*). Although it has been questioned, there is really no reason to doubt Thurgot's authorship; cf. Anderson, *ESSH*, ii, 59, n.
2. Quoted in *Chron. Fordun*, lib. v, caps 35–49.
3. G W S Barrow, *David I of Scotland (1124–1153): the Balance of New and Old* (1985).
4. For contrasting views of Margaret's achievement, cf. G W S Barrow, *The Kingdom of the Scots* (1973), chapter 6; and G Donaldson, *Scotland: Church and nation through sixteen centuries* (1960); see also his *Scottish Church History* (1985), chapter 2.
5. *VMR*, cap. 8 (the Surtees Soc. edn capitulation).
6. D Baker, "A Nursery of Saints': Queen Margaret of Scotland reconsidered', in *Medieval Women: Studies presented to Rosalind M T Hill*, ed. D Baker (1978), 119–142, at 130–32, demonstrates that the shorter version of the *vita* was composed 1093 x 1095, and the longer version 1100 x 1107.
7. *VMR*, cap. 3.
8. Ibid., cap. 7.
9. Ibid.
10. On the Hungarian background, cf. K Nagy, *St Margaret of Scotland and Hungary* (1973); A J Wilson, *St Margaret, Queen of Scotland* (1993), caps. 1–3.
11. R L G Ritchie, *The Normans in Scotland* (1954), 8 n; Baker, 'Nursery of Saints', 134 n.; *ODCC*, s.n., gives 'c. 1045'.
12. *ASC*, s.a.
13. Nagy, *St Margaret*, 15–18; Wilson, *St Margaret*, cap. 5. *Chron. Fordun*, v, cap. 14, states that Edgar intended 'to return to the country where he was born'.
14. *VMR*, cap. 3.
15. Anderson, *SAEC*, 110–111.
16. *VMR*, cap. 6.
17. Ibid., cap. 6, 10.
18. Ibid., cap. 9.
19. I say 'at least', because we do not know if others died in infancy. Six sons and two daughters survived to adulthood.
20. See below, p 216ff.
21. The poem *Duan Albanach* (see below, p. 222 and n. 79) is proof, if any were needed, that the court was essentially Gaelic speaking.
22. *VMR*, cap. 9.

23. D Bethell, 'Two Letters of Pope Paschal II to Scotland', *SHR*, xlix (1970), 33–45. The point is made in Baker, 'Nursery of Saints', 136–7.
24. Barrow, *Kingdom of the Scots*, 190.
25. *VMR*, cap. 9.
26. Ibid., cap. 4.
27. Ibid., caps 4, 9. In the mid-twelfth century St Andrews Cathedral had a bishop and his household, a hospitaller, and five lay *personae*; there was also a community of hereditary *Céli Dé* who had a side altar in the church. *Chron. Picts-Scots*, 188–9; A Macquarrie, 'Early Christian Religious Houses in Scotland: foundation and function', in J Blair and R Sharpe, *Pastoral Care before the Parish* (1992), 120–1.
28. Barrow, *Kingdom of the Scots*, 190.
29. Orderic Vitalis, *HE*, viii, 20.
30. *AU*, s.a. 1164.
31. *AU*, s.a. 1204; A Macquarrie and E M MacArthur, *Iona through the Ages*, (2nd edn 1992), 13–14
32. A C Lawrie, *Early Scottish Charters to AD 1153* (1910), no. viii.
33. Ibid., no. v.
34. Jackson, *Gaelic Notes in the Book of Deer*, 31–2; nos. iii, iv, vi.
35. For example, see the possible record of a grant by 'King Malcolm' (presumably Malcolm III) to the church of Monymusk, discussed in *RRS*, i, 162–3.
36. Found in two MSS: London, BM, Cotton Vespas. B XX, f. 197r ff, and Harley 105, f. 227v ff. It has been edited by Wynzen de Vries of the University of Groningen, who has drawn the passage here quoted to my attention. The translation is my own, from my own edition of the Scottish portion of the text in *Innes Review*, xlvii (1996), 95–109, at 105–7.
37. Writers who have referred to it include J Robertson, *Concilia Scotiae* (Bannatyne Club, 1866), i, pp. xxi-xxii nn.; W Moir Bryce, *St Margaret of Scotland and her chapel in the Castle of Edinburgh* (1914), 14–15; Wilson, *St Margaret*, 68. All of them know of the passage only through an abbreviated paraphrase in the late medieval English compilation which is known by the name of 'Capgrave', as quoted in *AASS, Feb.*, i (1863), 296–7.
38. Pope Gregory the Great. He heard that Augustine and his companions were working miracles, and likened this to the power of the apostles: *MGH, Epp.* ii, 305–8; partly quoted in *HE*, i, cap. 31.
39. *Ab Anglis in Scothiam*, literally 'from the English into Scotland'. Perhaps read *ab Anglia*?
40. *Collis Laurentii*. I have not been able to identify this hill. Perhaps the Firth of Tay is meant here rather than the Firth of Forth; the events that follow are set in Mearns.

41. Matt. 5, 14–15.
42. St Ternan is commemorated at Banchory Ternan and at Arbuthnott, among other places in Scotland. His feast-day is 12 June. He is also commemorated in the Irish martyrologies, on 12 June, as Torannán; he is said to have been a 6th-cent. saint from Scotland, an older contemporary of Columba (in which case he cannot in fact have been contemporary with Laurence, who arrived in Britain in 597). His relics were preserved at Banchory until the 16th cent. Cf. Watson, *CPNS*, 298–300. Cf. also *Chron. Fordun*, lib. iii, cap. 9; *Chron Bower*, lib. iii, cap. 9; *Aberdeen Breviary*, 12 June.
43. Presumably a reference to the archbishops of Canterbury's claim to metropolitan authority throughout the British Isles.
44. *Gilli Laurentius*. This is a latinisation of Gaelic *Gille Labhrain*, whence the later surname MacLaren. Goscelin's translation is correct.
45. *filius Cheli*. I take this to represent a Gaelic name, probably *Mac Chéli*, 'servant's son'.
46. Apart from extracts of it presumably included here, this *vita* has not survived and is otherwise unknown. We have seen that Goscelin claimed that the extracts were told to him from memory by 'learned and religious men' who had heard it read aloud.
47. *In arentibus locis Albaniæ ciuitatis*, literally, 'in dry places in the city of Alba'; presumably the author did not know that Alba is the native name of the kingdom, and mistook it for the name of a town or monastery.
48. 'St Laurence's Well' is beside Edzell kirkyard: Black, *Surnames*, 417–8. Edzell was, he says, 'dedicated to St Laurence the martyr'; it is more likely that the dedication was the same as that at Laurencekirk, to St Laurence of Canterbury. The Scots surname Lawrie seems to have been common in this area: Black, loc. cit.
49. Laurence died on 2 February 619; *HE*, ii, 7.
50. The 'church of St Laurence in the *vill* of Fordoun' is now Laurencekirk, which is dedicated to St Laurence of Canterbury. Fordoun evidently at one time covered a greater area than that of the present parish of Fordoun; there is a Fordoun Water in the present Laurencekirk parish, which flows into the Luther Water about 2 km west of Laurencekirk town. The dedication of Fordoun itself is to St Palladius. In the Middle Ages Laurencekirk was known as Conveth.
51. This does not reflect Goscelin's attitude to women. See below, p 221.
52. Margaret may have been still alive when this *vita* was written (c. 1091); Goscelin seems here to be recording a contemporary anecdote about her. In the *Historia Translationis* (1097; *PL*, clv, col. 20) he describes it as having happened *nuper*. This story seems to confirm Thurgot's portrait of the queen as a patron of local cult centres in the Celtic part of her husband's kingdom.

53. *Ad portam atrii.* I take *atrium* here to mean the enclosure, with a small church standing in its centre. Apparently Margaret never got as far as the church, and thus the sanctity of Laurencekirk was preserved.

54. *Elata foras*, literally 'outdoors'; but probably we should understand that they brought her out through the entrance of the enclosure, which would not have been covered.

55. The clergy serving at Laurencekirk are described here once as *canonici* and once as *clerici*. In the *Historia Translationis* they are referred to as *clerici* (*PL*, clv, col. 20). One is reminded of the term *clerici* being applied to the clergy of Old Deer in David I's reign, which is the one religious house about which we have any very substantial information in this period. Probably we should envisage that St Laurence's church was attended by a staff of secular clerks in the 11th cent. On the nature of such communities, cf. I B Cowan, 'The Development of the parochial system in medieval Scotland', *SHR*, xl (1961), 43–55, reprinted in I B Cowan, *The Medieval Church in Scotland* (1995), 1–11; A Macquarrie, 'Early Christian religious houses in Scotland: foundation and function', in J Blair and R Sharpe (eds.), *Pastoral Care before the Parish* (1992), 110–33.

56. Cf. the gifts which Queen Margaret gave to Holy Trinity Dunfermline mentioned by Thurgot: 'vessels of pure solid gold for the holy service of the altar... also a cross of matchless value, having on it an image of the Saviour covered with gold and silver and studded with gems.' Similarly she gave to St Andrews cathedral (now St Rule's church) 'a very beautiful crucifix'. *VMR*, cap. 4.

57. The remainder of the *vita*, just under half the total length, contains a lengthy homily on the subject of miracles, and a little material relating to Laurence's later life, death, burial (including Bede's account of these), and posthumous miracles. It contains nothing further of Scottish interest.

58. Edith/Matilda was at Wilton from c. 1086 until the year of her parents' death, so her sojourn there did not overlap with Goscelin's. She also seems to have been unhappy there. Cf. Baker, 'Nursery of Saints', 123–4.

59. The above paragraph is largely drawn from the account of his life and writings in Barlow, *The Life of King Edward the Confessor*, pp. xliv-li, 91–111, although Professor Barlow is cautious about his authorship of the *Vita Ædwardi Regis*. There is a list of printed editions of his writings in *ODCC*, 2nd edn, s.n. (though it contains errors), and a notice by T A Archer in *DNB*.

60. *Historia Translationis Sancti Augustini*, in *PL*, clv., cols. 14–46. See the historical note in ibid., cols. 13–14. Cf. also *William Thorne's Chronicle of St Augustine's Abbey, Canterbury*, ed. and trans. A H Davis (Oxford

1934), 59–61.   On the architectural details of the new building, which confirm a late-11th-century date, cf. P Collinson, N Ramsay and M Sparks, *A History of Canterbury Cathedral* (1995), 459–60 and nn.

61. See n. 36 above.

62. *PL*, clv, cols. 115–20. In a historical note in ibid., col. 11, while commenting that the *vitae* of Augustine's successors are drawn mainly from Bede's *HE*, is added: *In vita S Laurentii auctor longa digressione facta, fide sui temporis miraculis conciliare nititur.*

63. *AASS, Feb.* i, 296–7; the passage quoted here is from 'Capgrave', not from Goscelin's original.

64. T D Hardy, *Descriptive Catalogue of Material relating to the History of Great Britain and Ireland* (Rolls Series, 1862–71), i, pt i, no. 587, pp. 217–8.

65. *Bibliotheca Hagiographica Latina,* ed. Société des Bollandistes (Brussels 1898–1901), ii, 707 (no. 4741).

66. See above, n. 37.

67. W de Vries, Goscelin of St Bertin's Vita Sancti Laurentii Cantuariensis (BHL 4741) (Groningen, 1990).

68. *Innes Review,* xlvii (1996), 95–109.

69. I take *atrium* to be the enclosure, and *porta atrii* to be the entrance of the enclosure, which could presumably be secured in some way.

70. On the significance of these terms, cf. I B Cowan, 'The Development of the parochial system in medieval Scotland', *SHR,* xl (1961), 43–55, reprinted in I B Cowan, *The Medieval Church in Scotland* (1995), 1–11; A Macquarrie, 'Early Christian religious houses in Scotland: foundation and function', in J Blair and R Sharpe (eds.), *Pastoral Care before the Parish* (1992), 110–33, at 127–32.

71. Beside the kirkyard of Edzell; Black, *Surnames,* 417–8. Black states, loc. cit., that the dedication of Edzell is to St Laurence the Martyr; it is more likely, though, that it is the same as that of Laurencekirk.

72. Unidentified.

73. Barlow, op. cit., 42. The author of *Vita Ædwardi Regis* has no such difficulty with Gruffydd of Wales, whom he calls Griphinus. On the authorship of this, see ibid., pp. xli-lix; R W Southern, 'The First Life of Edward the Confessor', *EHR,* lviii (1943), 385–400, favouring Goscelin's authorship.

74. See Barlow, op. cit., 94–8. Goscelin's very personal *Liber confortatorius,* addressed to a former nun of Wilton, is edited by C H Talbot in *Studia Anselmiana,* xxxviii(1955), 1–117. He also wrote a number of *vitae* of female saints: cf. Barlow, op. cit., 109–10. There is, on the other hand, a story of women being denied access to a saint's shrine in the *Historia Minor Sancti Augustini,* Migne, *PL,* cl.

75. *ODCC,* 2nd edn, s.n. Goscelin, p. 583.

76. Holy Trinity Dunfermline was a daughter-house of Holy Trinity or Christ Church, Canterbury, a near neighbour of Goscelin's house of St Augustine. Queen Margaret's friendly relationship with Lanfranc, Archbishop of Canterbury 1070–1089, is well documented. Cf. Lawrie, *Early Scottish Charters*, no. ix; Barrow, *Kingdom of the Scots*, Chapter 5, passim, esp. 167.

77. The rank of the person carrying her favourite Gospel-book who dropped it into a river is not stated by Thurgot; *VMR*, cap. 11. However, in the 12th-century (?) verses prefaced to this book describing the incident, he is described as a presbyter. Oxford, Bodleian Library, MS Lat. Liturg. f. 5, fol. 2r; see below, pp. 222–3.

78. Donaldson, *Scottish Church History*, 24.

79. *Chron. Picts-Scots*, 57–64; critical edition by K H Jackson in *Celtica*, iii (1956), 149–67; edition with historical notes in *SHR*, xxxvi (1957), 125–37.

80. The aristocrats to whom this poem was read exercised their time-honoured right of 'electing' Malcolm's successor on his death; and their choice, in typical Celtic fashion, fell on his brother Donald. Cf. Anderson, *SAEC*, 117–8.

81. *VMR*, Cap. 11.

82. Oxford, Bodleian Library, MS Lat. Liturg. f. 5, fol. 2r; W Forbes-Leith, *The Gospel Book of St Margaret ... facsimile Reproduction* (1896), fol. 2r.

83. Jackson, *Gaelic Notes in the Book of Deer*, 7ff., 'hand apparently of the ninth century'.

Conclusions

In hoc periculossum et profundum narrationis sanctae pylagus, turgentibus proterve gurgitum aggeribus, inter acutissimos carubdes per ignota aequora insitos, a nullis adhuc lintribus ... ingenioli mei puerilem remi cymbam deduxi. ('I have brought the toy rowing-boat of my feeble intellect into the deep and dangerous sea of hagiography, with mountainous swellings of violent waters among jagged rocks and scattered whirl-pools, never previously sailed by any ship.')[1] Thus Muirchú, in the preface to his *vita* of St Patrick (c. 680), comments on the dangers and difficulties of writing the lives of saints. If the task of hagiography was difficult enough for the medieval writers themselves, how much more so for the modern scholar to try to bring calm for an audience of twentieth-century rationalists out of the swirling oceans of medie-val hagiography; he will often feel, with Muirchú, that his intellect is insufficient and that his vessel is no better than a toy rowing-boat.

The main problem is, of course, that we today sail upon a different ocean in very different boats, and in many ways these are the wrong surroundings in which to try to make sense of those medieval legends. Only if we can try to insinuate ourselves sympathetically into the minds of medieval hagiographers, only if we can try (if I may make one final use of Muirchú's metaphor) to set sail ourselves on their ocean and in their ships, will we be able to understand what these writers were trying to achieve and how far they succeeded.

The earliest saints' lives written in Celtic Britain belong to the middle of the seventh century. The earliest survivors are Cogitosus' *Vita Sancti Brigitae* and the slightly earlier *vita prima* of St Brigit.[2] Already the pattern for later *vitae* seems to be established. The writers had continental models which they admired and imitated, and from which they quarried freely: the favourites were Sulpicius' *Life of St Martin*[3] and Evagrius' translation of Athanasius' *Life of St Antony*.[4] For the most part, hagiographers fell quickly into a pattern set by these examples. Most *vitae* contain the same elements set within the same framework: the saint's birth, surrounded by miracles and often preceded by divine portents or angelic messages; a series of miracle stories, sometimes showing the saint passing from youth to maturity, but often with little chronological sequence;[5] the saint's death, usually predicted in advance and often accompanied by supernatural phenomena; and sometimes some posthumous miracles connected with the saint's relics. Ultimately, the model is biblical: Moses and Samuel are so treated in the Old Testament, and the gospels of Matthew and Luke are New Testament examples. Of the *vitae* considered in this book, Adomnán's *Vita Columbae* is the apparent exception, treating Columba's miracles in thematic groups rather than chronological sequence; but even here we have seen that Book iii does follow the chronological pattern described above.[6]

Although the Bible and earlier saints' lives are the most obvious sources for the structure of Celtic *vitae*, many of the episodes themselves belong to a *genre* of mythology which is found also in Celtic secular tales. When St Serf resuscitated a dead pig which had been slaughtered for his refection, he was repeating the action of Manannán, whose herd was slaughtered nightly to feed the *Tuatha Dé Danann*;[7] when repeated efforts at execution failed to kill St Teneu, we are reminded of the semi-divine figures of Irish tales (e.g. Muirchertach Mac Erca), who were so powerful that it required simultaneous multiple deaths to kill them.[8] Many of the picturesque tales in *Vita Kentigerni*, such as the *seanchaid*'s demand for fresh fruit at midwinter and the finding of the queen's ring in a salmon's mouth, are clearly folk-tales which would be equally at home in secular literature.[9] Even *Vita Columbae* is not free from folk-tale influence: Adomnán makes Columba predict a triple death (by piercing, falling and drowning) for Aed Dub mac Suibne, and there are probably folk-tale origins for the stories of the deaths of Guaire mac Aedáin and of Colcú mac Aedo Draigniche, among others.[10] It has even been suggested, though I am not convinced about this, that there is a likeness between Columba's parting from his horse and the death of Cú Chulainn.[11]

These elements remind us that sacred literature and secular tales cannot be rigidly separated, as they mostly are in modern times. The Celtic people delighted in storytelling. The secular legends like the *Táin* were full of exaggeration and supernatural phenomena, visitors from the otherworld, and a striking level of violence, torture and suffering. So it was only natural that stories of saints, the new heroes of Christianity, should be in a similar vein. Saints pray, fast, and mortify the flesh on a heroic scale. They recite the entire Psalter while plunged up to the neck in an icy torrent, then go to bed in a stone coffin. They battle against dragons and demons with supernatural weapons provided by angelic supporters. When they die, after un-naturally long life spans, they patiently endure torments and sickness which would discourage the most steadfast of ordinary men. The stories were intended to edify and terrify, to encourage visits to shrines, veneration of relics, respect for rights and property, and the giving of alms; but they were also intended to entertain. The Celts were master storytellers, who delighted in blending fact with legend, the homely with the supernatural. Their legends were certainly intended to be enjoyed.

One striking feature is the quite fantastic level of the miraculous in some *vitae*; although this element is always present, it seems to become more outlandish as time goes on, and later hagiographers sometimes felt the need to apologise for or tone down particularly silly miracles. Thus Jocelin's 'Scottish' source in *Vita Kentigerni* makes its hero levitate at the *Sursum Corda*, while Jocelin reduces this to saying only that Kentigern lifted up his own heart while exhorting others to do the same.[12] Likewise Goscelin of St Bertin, when he grafts the foundation legend of Laurencekirk onto Bede's sober account of Laurence in the *Ecclesiastical History*, feels the need to offer an *apologia* for these stories (walking on water, calling down fire from heaven, raising the dead, *et cetera*), in the form of a long homiletic defence of miracles.[13]

At a rather less edifying level, the degree of violence is also sometimes quite striking, nowhere more so than in the anonymous *Historia Beati Kentigerni* written for Bishop Herbert.[14] The graphic description of Teneu's rape followed by her other tribulations seems to dwell on female victimisation in a way that many people nowadays would find distasteful. But again cruelty and violence, often quite arbitrary, are a stock feature of Celtic secular literature, as in *Togail Bruidne Dá Derga* and other tales. The victimisation of women is also a feature of some Irish tales; Teneu's eventual deliverance is good fortune compared with the fate of Deirdre.

One feature of saints' lives is that they often attempted to establish relationships and alliances. Foundation legends frequently name a secular aristocrat as benefactor of a saint, donor of the site of his first church; sometimes, though not always, the donor has to be frightened into making the grant by a curse upon himself, his family, or his livestock. The point of these stories is that they establish a relationship between the church, personified by its reputed founder, and a secular dynasty, personified by a named king or nobleman. No clearer or more typical example could be found that the foundation legend of Deer in Buchan, which describes how Columba and Drostán mac Coscreig came to the place later known as Deer; 'and it pleased Columba.... He begged the mormaer [of Buchan, Bede Cruithnech] that he should give it to them; and he did not. And a son of his took a sickness, after the clerics had been refused, and was all but dead. Then the mormaer went to beseech the clerics that they should make a prayer on behalf of the boy, that health might come to him; and he gave them land.... They made the prayer, and health came to him.'[15] Obviously this is, at one level, an assertion of the powers of the church over the laity; but it is also an acceptance by the church that they have certain obligations to the founder and his family. Most of our *vitae* have at least one story of this kind, establishing links between, for example, Ninian and the family of a king called Tudwal (probably of Dumbarton), between Kentigern and the family of Rhydderch Hael of Dumbarton, between Serf and the house of Bridei f. Derile, king of Picts, or between St Drostán's monastery of Deer and the Mormaers of Buchan. *Vita Columbae*, an exception in this as in so many other ways, has no such stories; although the stories set at the court of King Bridei f. Maelchon near Inverness are similar in character, and the same slightly menacing miraculous atmosphere pervades other stories set in Pictish lands, in the Great Glen and Skye.[16] The Iona annalists knew that *Conall mac Comgaill … obtulit insolam Iae Columbe Cille*,[17] but Adomnán does not use any of these stories to assert relationships between Iona and the lay aristocracy of the Picts or the Dál Riata. There is something very unworldly about Adomnán's work.

Vitae also served to establish relationships between two churches or *parochiae*. If one saint is claimed as the disciple of another, that establishes a relationship of subordination between his church(es) and that or those of his master. For example, the *Aberdeen Breviary* lections for St Conval of Inchinnan, quoting from a lost *vita*, assert that he was a disciple of St Kentigern of Glasgow, a claim which was also made in the (mostly lost) *Historia Beati Kentigerni*; this helps, among other things, to provide a terminus for the lost *vita* of Conval, since Glasgow's claims to Inchinnan were abandoned c. 1150.[18] Glasgow had more success a few years later in its claims over the great minster church of Govan, perhaps helped by the spurious claim made in Jocelin's *Vita Kentigerni* that St Constantine was the son of King Rhydderch's barren queen, born in response to St Kentigern's prayers.[19]

Sometimes the claim was an assertion of independence. *Vita Sancti Servani* describes a meeting between St Serf and St Adomnán, in which Adomnán concedes to Serf the area to be occupied by his *familia* (i.e., the *parochia* of Culross?): *Habitent terram Fif, et a monte Britannorum usque ad montem qui dicitur Okhel.* Was there an ancient agreement between the *familiae* of Serf and Columba, allowing Culross an independent *parochia* in Fife? An Irish tract of uncertain date remembered the lands 'held' by St Serf: *Cuillennros hi Sraith Erenn hi Comgellaibh eter Sliabh nOcel* [7] *Mur nGiudan* ('Culross in Strathearn in *Comgellaig*, between the Ochil Hills and the Firth of Forth').[20] One is reminded of the concession made by Armagh in *Liber Angeli*, allowing the church of Kildare its *parochia* in Leinster, which is similarly couched in terms of a meeting between St Patrick and St Brigit, 'the pillars of the Irish'.[21]

It is sometimes said, with justice, that Celtic hagiographers had a scant regard for chronological accuracy; certainly it cannot be denied that they frequently arranged meetings between people who lived at very different times. Thus the twelfth-century *Vita Niniani* makes Ninian a contemporary of St Martin of Tours (d. 397), but also of a North British king called Tudwal (probably meaning Tudwal of Dumbarton, who may have died c. 560). Jocelin's *Vita Kentigerni* makes Kentigern a disciple of St Serf and contemporary of Rhydderch Hael (fl. 570–600), and sets him just a few years after Ninian's mission; this would be impossible if Serf really was, as his *vita* asserts, a contemporary of Adomnán (d. 704), but the problems are just as grave if one accepts the chronology of the *Historia Beati Kentigerni* and the *Aberdeen Breviary*, which make Serf a disciple of St Palladius (fl. 431).[22] The problems become surreal when we add in the claim in the *Aberdeen Breviary* lections for St Baldred of Tynninghame (d. 756) that Baldred was a disciple of Kentigern who wrote his first *vita*.[23] It might be consistent to make Kentigern a disciple of a Serf who flourished c. 700 and teacher of a Baldred who died in 756; but this would throw our received chronology, which is based on an *obit* for Kentigern in the *Annales Cambriae* c. 614, into confusion.[24] Vast numbers of saints are sent off to Rome to seek consecration at the hands of Pope Gregory the Great, and some of them demonstrably belonged to a different age.

But many of these chronological claims are carefully constructed and made for well thought out reasons. In medieval thinking, antiquity was equated with primacy: the older something was, the more authority it had. If Columba was a contemporary of Rhydderch Hael, as Adomnán asserts,[25] then those who set out to convince Bede of the primacy of Ninian made their hero a contemporary of Tudwal, Rhydderch's father; that way they could assert that he lived 'a long time before' Columba.[26] There may be good reasons for believing that Ninian was active in the first half of the sixth century; but the chronology proposed by hagiography is not much help. At the end of the day, to say that a saint was a disciple of Palladius, or a contemporary of St Martin of Tours, may be little more than an assertion of his antiquity, and therefore his priority over certain other saints. But to throw Palladius, or Martin, or Serf, or Tudwal, into a saint's narrative is probably not as arbitrary as it at first sight appears.

Perhaps the most obvious purpose in many *vitae* is to make assertions of property and title. *Vita Sancti Servani* is a particularly good example here: Serf goes from Culross, his first foundation, and travels round Lochleven, Dysart, Tullibody, Tillicoultry, Alva, Airthrey and Dunning, performing a miracle in each. This defines the *parochia* of Culross as clearly as any set of title-deeds could. Jocelin's *Vita Kentigerni* has stories set in Hoddom, Borthwick and other far-flung parts of Glasgow's *parochia* as well as stories relating to the immediate area, including the kirks of the Ramshorn, Govan and St Mungo in the East, and the lands of Partick and Gorbals.[27] In this as in most *vitae*, these scenes of miracles are claimed for the saint's *parochia*. Again the exception here is *Vita Columbae*: Adomnán does not include any territorial claims in his narrative.

We have seen that the majority of Celtic saints for whom *vitae* were composed lived between c. 500 and 700 AD; only a few fall outside these dates, and they not by more than half a century. This is true not only of the saints of major churches whose *vitae* have survived *in extenso*, but also for those whose *vitae* have not survived except as cryptic abbreviations in the *Aberdeen Breviary*. Before this 'age of saints', the sixth and seventh centuries, had come to an end, the art of hagiography was already well established, and we can be certain or reasonably confident that the *vitae* of Ninian, Kentigern and many others were first written down in the late seventh or eighth centuries.

There is little evidence, however, of hagiographic activity during the period of the Viking raids. In 825 Blathmac, a monk of Iona, was martyred by Vikings because he refused to divulge where the shrine of St Columba was hidden; but he was not made the subject of a *vita*.[28] In about 850 there was a major translation of Columba's relics to Dunkeld; but no *vita* commissioned for this important occasion has survived. A generation later the kirk of St Constantine was built at Govan, and at some stage probably in the tenth century a magnificent tomb-shrine was carved to hold the holy relics or royal bones of a Constantine; again, no *vita* commissioned for this occasion has survived, and there is no evidence that one ever existed.[29] These examples contrast with the foundation of the kirk of St Andrews (likewise with a great eighth-century shrine or tomb), where a foundation legend associated with Onuist f. Urguist (c. 730–761) survives in two versions.[30] Whether as a result of a change of fashion from the mid-eighth century, or the cultural shock of the Viking raids from the 790s, hagiographic literature seems to have stagnated for a period thereafter.

When the revival came is not certain. In Ireland vernacular saint's lives were being written in the tenth century, and it may be that stories like the vernacular foundation legend of Deer belong to this period.[31] The 'Scottish' source for the life of Kentigern, edited and toned down in Jocelin's *Vita Kentigerni*, and abbreviated in the *Aberdeen Breviary*, is probably eleventh century at latest.[32] This may be the period in which the miracles become ever more spectacular, declamatory and absurd; perhaps we can tentatively suggest that such assemblages as *Vita Sancti Servani*, the foundation legend of Laurencekirk, and many of the *vitae* mentioned and abbreviated in the *Aberdeen Breviary* but not otherwise known, belong to the tenth and eleventh centuries. Research is coming to suggest that where the lections in the *Aberdeen Breviary* acknowledge an earlier *vita*, that *vita* is likely to be twelfth century at latest, and in some cases earlier;[33] but these tentative conclusions will need to be further investigated.

In the eleventh and twelfth centuries Latin hagiography became fashionable again, with the polished *vitae* of Kentigern, Serf, Ninian, Queen Margaret and St Waldef, and Ailred's *Lamentatio* on the death of King David. If the last three of these are sober products of Anglo-Norman culture, the first three still look back to a heady age of fantastic storytelling; and the same is true of the foundation legend of Laurencekirk and of many of the stories preserved in the *Aberdeen Breviary*.

There seems to have been little addition to Scotland's hagiographic output after the twelfth century. The late medieval chronicles of Fordun, Wyntoun and Bower make extensive use of earlier materials, and the vernacular Scots verse *Lives* once attributed to Barbour do contain interesting lives of St Ninian and St Machar, but they are unique.[34] There are small amounts of material in liturgical MSS and fragments, but most of the immediate sources of the *Aberdeen Breviary* have been lost.[35] Where the compilers of the *Breviary* had sources to draw on, we have seen that these appear probably to be mostly twelfth-century and earlier; but the compilers themselves must have composed new lections for the many saints for whom they had no sources, and this counts as Scotland's greatest achievement of late medieval hagiography.[36]

Looking at these medieval *vitae* through modern eyes, what value are we to attach to them? It is clear that as historical documents about the people whose lives they purport to describe, they have to be used with caution; but used with experience and judgement, they can tell us much of historical value that we would not otherwise know, especially about the subsequent history of the churches where the saints were buried. They also have entertainment value, in that we can enjoy their unusual blend of the homely and the supernatural. In spite of their total disregard for any modern concept of cause and effect, they are not without intellectual interest: the author of *Vita Sancti Servani*, for instance, wrestled with genuine theological problems when he put into the Devil's mouth the question, 'Where was God before He made heaven and earth and before all His creation?' And St Serf's answer, 'He was in himself; for He is not localised and cannot be held or constrained in one place, nor is He subject to the movement of time, but He is all and everywhere', would have satisfied St Augustine himself.[37] And they are religious documents. Who is not moved by Muirchú's description of Patrick's growth in faith, trust and power, or by Adomnán's touching account of Columba's last days and hours?

And there is a universal quality to these documents. If men are striving to be good, they need examples of goodness to be set before them. The Bible sets out the lives of Moses, Samuel and Christ to teach and inspire; other faiths present other 'mediators', Zoroaster,

Buddha, Krishna, Muhammad.[38] Their lives have similarly become encrusted with legends, and many of them are similar in type to the legends of medieval hagiography. The fact that legends have been attracted to these great figures does not detract from their greatness; perhaps the legends surrounding our Celtic saints do not make them any less saintly. Whatever other motives they may also have had, the writers of saints' lives portrayed their heroes above all as good and holy men; and their holiness and goodness can still inspire us.

NOTES

1. Muirchú's *Vita Sancti Patricii*, in *St Patrick: his writings and Muirchú's Life*, ed. A B E Hood (1978), Preface, p. 61; also edited by Bieler in *PT*.
2. *AASS, Feb.*, i (1658),135–41;*Vita prima* is ed. J Colgan in *Trias Thaumaturga* (1647).
3. Copied into the *Book of Armagh* and echoed throughout insular hagiography. Of the *vitae* considered in this book, *Vita Sancti Servani* owes most to it; the continental *Vita Kaddroe* also quarries freely from it.
4. Used, for example, by Adomnán in the two prefaces and final chapter of *Vita Columbae*.
5. Muirchú's carefully constructed narrative is the clearest exception here; cf. L Bieler, 'The Celtic Hagiographer', *Studia Patristica*, v (1962), 243–65, at 253–6.
6. See above, Chapter 4,p. 164; J Marsden, *The Illustrated Columcille* (1991),143.
7. See above, Chapter 6, p 147.
8. See above, Chapter 5, p 124; for the death(s) of Muirchertach Mac Erca, cf. F J Byrne, *Irish Kings and High-Kings* (1973), 100–101; and 97–102 in general.
9. See above, Chapter 5, p 135; Jackson, 'Sources', passim.
10. *VC*, i, 36; i, 47; i, 17. See the notes in the Andersons' edition and Dr Sharpe's translation; also J M Picard, 'The strange death of Guaire mac Aedáin', in *Sages, Saints and Storytellers: Celtic Studies in honour of Professor James Carney*, ed. D O Corráin et al. (1989), 367–75.
11. *VC*, iii, 23.
12. See above, Chapter 5, p. 126.
13. See above, Chapter 10, pp. 216–8.
14. See above, Chapter 5, pp. 119–20.
15. K H Jackson, *The Gaelic Notes in the Book of Deer* (1972), 30, 33.
16. *VC*, i, 33, 37; ii, 26, 27, 32, 33, 34, 35, 42; iii, 14.
17. *AU*, s.a. 574.

18. Cf. A Macquarrie, 'Lections for Strathclyde saints in the *Aberdeen Breviary*: some problems of sources', *RSCHS*, xxvi (1996) (forthcoming).

19. See above, Chapter 5, p 134.

20. See above, Chapter 6, p 138.

21. In *PT*, 188–91; translation in K Hughes, *The Church in early Irish society* (1966), 279.

22. All of these sources are discussed in Chapters 5 and 6 above, pp 122ff., 148.

23. For his death, cf. Anderson, *SAEC*, 56; *Aberdeen Breviary*, PH, 6 March.

24. See above, Chapter 5, p 117.

25. *VC*, i, 15

26. See Chapter 3 above, p 57.

27. See above, Chapter 5, pp. 132–3, 136.

28. R Sharpe, *Medieval Irish Saints' Lives* (1991), 10. Walafrid Strabo's poem on his death is edited in *MGH, Poetae Latini Aevi Carolini*, ii , 299–301; translation in Anderson, *ESSH*, I, 263–5.

29. On Govan, cf. A Macquarrie, 'Early Christian Govan: the historical context', *RSCHS*, xxiv (1990), 1–17; A Ritchie, *Govan and its early medieval Sculpture* (1994); A Macquarrie, 'Lections for St Constantine's Day (11 March) in the *Aberdeen Breviary*', *Annual Report of theSociety of Friends of Govan Old*, v (1995), 25–32, arguing that these are not apparently based on any earlier *vita*.

30. See above, Chapter 8, p 181–2.

31. See above, p 233.

32. See above, Chapter 5, p 126–7, 139.

33. Cf. Macquarrie, 'Lections for Strathclyde saints in the *Aberdeen Breviary*' (forthcoming).

34. *Legends of the Saints*, ed. W M Metcalfe (Scottish Text Society, 1st ser., 13, 18, 23, 25, 1887–92); C Horstmann, *Altenglische Legenden* (Heilbronn, 1881).

35. See above, Introduction, p 7–10.

36. A Boyle, 'Some Saints' Lives in the Breviary of Aberdeen', *Analecta Bollandiana*, xciv (1976), 95–106.

37. A Macquarrie, '*Vita Sancti Servani*: the life of St Serf', *IR*, xliv (1993), 122–52, at 141, 149.

38. J Macquarrie, *The Mediators* (1995), esp. 131ff.

Bibliography

1. Primary and secondary works: books, theses, and articles cited in footnotes

Airlie, S, 'The View from Maastricht', in Crawford, B E, ed., *Scotland in Dark Age Europe* (1994), 33–46

Alcock, L, 'A Survey of Pictish Settlement Archaeology', in Friell, J G P, and Watson, W G, eds, *Pictish Studies* (BAR, British Series, cxxv, 1984), 7–41

Alcock, L, *Arthur's Britain* (1971)

Alcock, L, 'Pictish Studies: present and future', in Small, A, ed. *The Picts: a new Look at old Problems* (1987), 80–92

Alcock, L, *Survey and Excavation at Forteviot, Perthshire, 1981* (University of Glasgow Dept of Archaeology, 1982)

Allen, J R, and Anderson, J, *Early Christian Monuments of Scotland* (1903, reprinted 1993)

Ammianus Marcellinus, *Rerum Gestarum Libri* (Loeb, 1935–9)

Amours, F J, ed., *Andrew of Wyntoun, The Orygynale Cronykil of Scotland,* (Scottish Text Society, 50, 53, 54, 56, 57, 63, 1903–1914)

Analecta Bollandiana, lxxix (1961), 343–5

Anderson, A O, *Early Sources of Scottish History, AD 500–1286* (1922; new edn 1990)

Anderson, A O, *Scottish Annals from English Chroniclers, AD 500–1286* (1908)

Anderson A O and M O, eds, *Adomnán's Life of Columba* (1961; 2nd edn 1991)

Anderson, A O and M O, eds, *Chronicle of Melrose* (1936)

Anderson, M O, *Kings and Kingship in Early Scotland* (1973; 2nd edn 1980)

Anderson, M O, 'St Andrews before Alexander I', in Barrow, G W S, ed., *The Scottish Tradition: Essays in Honour of R G Cant* (1974), 1–13

Anderson, M O, 'The Celtic Church in Kinrimund', in MacRoberts, D, ed., *The Medieval Church of St Andrews* (1976),1–10

Arnold, T, ed., *Symeon of Durham's Historia Ecclesiae Dunhelmensis* (RS, lxxv, 1882)

Athanasius, 'Apologia contra Arianos', in Migne, *Patrologia Graeca*, xxv

Athanasius, 'Historia Arianorum', in Migne, *Patrologia Graeca*, xxv

Baker, D, "A Nursery of Saints': St Margaret of Scotland reconsidered', in D Baker, ed., *Medieval Women: Studies presented to Rosalind M T Hill* (1978), 119–41

Baker, D, 'Legend and Reality: the Case of Waldef of Melrose', *Studies in Church History*, xii (1975), 59–82

Bannerman, J W M, Appendix to K Hughes, 'The Church and the World in early Christian Ireland', *Irish Historical Studies*, xiii (1962–3), 113–16

Bannerman, J W M, '*Comarbe Coluim Chille* and the Relics of Columba', *Innes Review*, xliv (1993), 14–47.

Bannerman, J W M, *Studies in the History of Dalriada* (1974)

Barlow, F, *The Life of King Edward the Confessor* (1962)

Barrow, G W S, *David I of Scotland (1124–1153): the Balance of New and Old* (1985)

Barrow, G W S, *Regesta Regum Scottorum*, i; *the Acts of Malcolm IV* (1960)

Barrow, G W S, 'The Childhood of Scottish Christianity: a Note on some Place-name Evidence', *Scottish Studies*, xxvii (1983), 1–15

Barrow, G W S, *The Kingdom of the Scots* (1973)

Barrow, G W S, 'The Royal House and the Religious Orders', in Barrow, G W S, *The Kingdom of the Scots* (1973)

Barrow, G W S, 'The Sources for the History of the Highlands in the Middle Ages,' in Maclean, L, ed., *The Middle Ages in the Highlands* (1981), 11–22

Bernard, J H, and Atkinson, R, ed., *The Irish Liber Hymnorum* (Henry Bradshaw Society, 1898)

Bethell, D, 'Two Letters of Pope Paschal II to Scotland', *Scottish Historical Review*, xlix (1970), 33–45

Bieler, L, ed., *Libri Epistolarum S Patricii Episcopi* (1961)

Bieler, L , ed., *The Patrician texts in the Book of Armagh* (Scriptores Latinae Hiberniae, x, 1979)

Bieler, L, ed., *The Works of St Patrick* (Early Christian Writers, 1953)

Bieler, L, Review of *Vita Columbae* (1st edn), in *Irish Historical Studies*, xiii (1963), 175–84

Bieler, L , 'The Celtic Hagiographer', *Studia Patristica*, v (1962), 243–65

Binchey, D A, ed., *Scela Cano meic Gartnáin* (Dublin Institute for Advanced Studies, Medieval and Modern Irish Series, vol. 18, 1963)

Binchey, D A , 'St Patrick and his Biographers, ancient and modern', *Studia Hibernica*, ii (1962), 7–173

Black, G F, *The Surnames of Scotland* (1946; reprinted 1993)

Blair, P H, 'The Bernicians and their Northern Frontier', in N K Chadwick, ed., *Studies in early British History* (1954), 137–72

Boece, Hector, *Murthlacensium et Aberdonensium Episcoporum Vitae* (New Spalding Club, 1894)

Bollandus, J, et al., eds, *Acta Sanctorum* (1643–1910)

Boyle, A, 'Notes on Scottish Saints', *Innes Review*, xxxii (1981), 59–82

Boyle, A, 'Some Saints' Lives in the Breviary of Aberdeen', *Analecta Bollandiana*, xciv (1976), 95–106

Boyle, A, 'The Birthplace of St Patrick', *Scottish Historical Review*, lx (1981), 156–60

Bray, D, 'Some Aspects of Hagiography in the Celtic Church', *Records of the Scottish Church History Society*, xxi (1982), 111–26

Breeze, D J, *Roman Scotland: a guide to the visible remains* (1979)

Breeze, D J, 'The Imperial legacy – Rome and her neighbours', in Crawford, B E, ed., *Scotland in Dark Age Europe* (1994), 13–19

Breviarium Aberdonense (Edinburgh, 1510; reprinted, Spalding and Maitland Clubs, 1854)

Bromwich, R, *Trioedd Ynys Prydein* (1961; 2nd edn 1978)

Brooke, D, *Wild Men and Holy Places* (1994)

Broun, D, 'The Literary Record of St Nynia: Fact and Fiction', *Innes Review*, xlii (1991), 143–50

Bryce, W M, *St Margaret of Scotland and her Chapel in the Castle of Edinburgh* (1914)

Bury, J B, *The Life of St Patrick* (1905)

Bute, Marquess of, ed., *Breviarium Bothanum* (1900)

Byrne, F J, *Irish Kings and High-Kings* (1973)

Byrne, M E, and Dillon, M, eds., *Táin Bó Fraích* (Dublin Institute for Advanced Studies, Medieval and Modern Irish Series, v, 1933)

Campbell, J, et al., *The Anglo-Saxons* (1982)

Carney, J, *Studies in Irish Literature and History* (1955)

Carney, J, *The Problem of St Patrick* (1961)

Chadwick, H, *The Early Church* (1967)

Chadwick, N K, 'Early Culture and Learning in North Wales', in Chadwick, N K, et al., *Studies in the early British Church* (1958), 29–120

Chadwick, N K, et al., *Studies in the early British Church* (1958)

Chadwick, N K, 'Intellectual Life in West Wales in the last Days of the Celtic Church', in Chadwick, N K, et al., *Studies in the early British Church*, 128–58

Chadwick, N K, 'St Ninian: a preliminary Study of Sources', *Transactions of the Dumfriesshire and Galloway Natural History and Antiquarian Society*, 3d ser., xxviii (1951), 9–53

Chibnall, M, ed., *Orderic Vitalis' Historia Ecclesiastica* (1969–1980)

Clancy, T O, 'Iona, Scotland and the *Céli Dé*', in Crawford, B E, ed., *Scotland in Dark Age Europe*, 111–130

Clancy, T O, and Márkus, G, *Iona: the earliest Poetry of a Celtic Monastery* (1995)

Claudian, 'On the Consulship of Stilicho', ed. in *Monumenta Germaniae Historica*, x (1892)

Close-Brooks, J, 'Dr Bersu's Excavations at Traprain Law, 1947', in O'Connor, A and Clarke, D V, eds, *From the Stone Age to the 'Forty-Five: Studies presented to R B K Stevenson* (1983)

Close-Brooks, J, 'Pictish and other Burials', in Friell, J G P, and Watson, W G, eds, *Pictish Studies* (BAR, 125, 1984), 93–121

Coens, M, 'Le Premier Tome du légendier de Saint-Hubert', *Analecta Bollandiana*, vii (1939), 109ff

Colgan, J, *Trias Thaumaturga* (1647)

Colgrave, B, and Mynors, R A B, eds, *Bede's Ecclesiastical History of the English People* (1969)

Colgrave, B, ed., *Eddius' Life of Wilfrid* (1927)

Collinson, P, Ramsay, N, and Sparks, M, *A History of Canterbury Cathedral* (1995)

Constantius, 'Vita Sancti Germani (Life of St Germanus)', *Monumenta Germaniae Historica*, vii (1920)

Cowan, I B, and Easson, D E, *Medieval Religious Houses: Scotland* (1976)

Cowan, I B, 'The Development of the parochial System in medieval Scotland', *Scottish Historical Review*, xl (1961), 43–55

Cowan, I B, *The Medieval Church in Scotland* (1995)

Cowan, I B, *The Parishes of medieval Scotland* (Scottish Record Society, 1967)

Craig, D, 'The early medieval Sculpture of the Glasgow Area', in Ritchie, A, ed., *Govan and its early medieval Sculpture*, 73–90

Crawford, B E, ed., *Scotland in Dark Age Britain* (1996)

Crawford, B E, ed., *Scotland in Dark Age Europe* (1994)

Cross, F L, and Livingstone, E A, eds., *Oxford Dictionary of the Christian Church*, 2nd edn (1974)

Cumont, F, *The Mysteries of Mithra* (1956)

Curle, A O, *The Treasure of Traprain: a Scottish Hoard of Roman silver Plate* (1923)

Davies, W, 'The Latin Charter Tradition in Western Britain, Brittany, and Ireland in the early Medieval Period', in Whitelock, D, et al., eds, *Ireland in early Medieval Europe: Studies in Memory of Kathleen Hughes*, (1982), 258–80

Davis, A H, ed., *William Thorne's Chronicle of St Augustine's Abbey, Canterbury* (1934)

de Bhaldraithe, E, *The High Crosses of Moone and Castledermot* (Bolton Abbey, 1987)

de Bruyn, T, *Pelagius's Commentary on St Paul's Epistle to the Romans* (1993)

de Paor, M and L, *Early Christian Ireland* (1958)

de Vries, W, Goscelin of St Bertin's Vita Sancti Laurentii Cantuariensis (BHL 4741) (unpublished thesis, University of Groningen, 1990)

Dictionary of National Biography (1885–1900)

Dierkens, A, *Abbayes et Chapîtres entre Sambre et Meuse* (1985)

Dillon, M, *The Cycle of the Kings* (1946)

Dilworth, M, 'Iona Abbey and the Reformation', *Scottish Gaelic Studies*, xii (1971–1976), 77–109

Dilworth, M, *The Scots in Franconia* (1974)

Dio Cassius, *Dio's Roman History* (Loeb, 1914–27)

Diplomatarium Norvegicum (1849–1919)

Donaldson, G, *Scotland: Church and nation through sixteen centuries* (1960)

Donaldson, G, 'Scotland's earliest Church Buildings', *Records of the Scottish Church History Society*, xviii (1973), 1–9

Donaldson, G, *Scottish Church History* (1985)

Douglas, W, 'Culross Abbey and its early Charters, with Notes on a fifteenth-century Transumpt', *Proceedings of the Society of Antiquaries of Scotland*, lx (1925–6), 67ff

Dumville, D, 'Gildas and Uinniau', in Lapidge, M, and Dumville, D, eds., *Gildas: New Approaches* (1984), 207–14

Duncan, A A M, 'Bede Iona and the Picts', in R H C Davis and J M Wallace-Hadrill, eds, *The Writing of History in the Middle Ages: Essays presented to R W Southern* (1981), 1–42

Duncan, A A M, *Scotland: the Making of the Kingdom* (1975)

Dunlop, A I, et al., eds, *Calendar of Scottish Supplications to Rome* (1934-)

Durkan, J, 'The Bishops' Barony of Glasgow in Pre-Reformation Times', *Records of the Scottish Church History Society*, xxii (1986), 277–301

Edwards, N, 'The South Cross, Clonmacnois', in J Higgitt, ed., *Early Medieval Sculpture in Britain and Ireland* (BAR, British Series 152, 1986), 23–48

Enright, M J, 'Royal Succession and abbatial Prerogative in Adomnán's *Vita Columbae*', *Peritia*, iv (1985), 83–103

Evans, R F, *Pelagius: Inquiries and reappraisals* (1968)

Falkus, M E, and Gillingham J B, eds., *Historical Atlas of Britain* (1981)

Fisher, I, 'The Govan cross-shafts and early cross-slabs', in Ritchie, A, ed., *Govan and its early medieval Sculpture*, 47–53

Forbes, A P, ed., *Lives of SS Ninian and Kentigern* (Historians of Scotland, v, 1874)

Forbes-Leith, W, *The Gospel Book of St Margaret ... facsimile Reproduction* (1896)

Forsyth, K, 'The Inscription on the Dupplin Cross', in *From the Isles of the North: Medieval Art in Ireland and Britain* (1995), 237–44

Frend, W H C, 'The Christianising of Roman Britain', in Barley, M W, and Hanson, R P C, eds, *Christianity in Britain, 300–700* (1968)

Galbraith, J D, The Sources of the Aberdeen Breviary (Aberdeen University, M.Litt. Thesis, 1970)

Garmonsway, G N, *The Anglo-Saxon Chronicle* (1953)

Gibb, A, *Glasgow: the Making of a City* (1983)

Goodall, W, ed., *Scotichronicon ... Walteri Boweri* (1759)

Goscelin of Canterbury, 'Historia Translationis Sancti Augustini', in Migne, *Patrologia Latina*, clv

Goscelin of Canterbury, 'Historia Minor Sancti Augustini', in Migne, *Patrologia Latina*, cl

Grosjean, P, 'Les Pictes Apostats dans l'Epître de S Patrice', *Analecta Bollandiana*, lxxvi (1958),354–78

Hanson, R P C, *St Patrick* (1968)

Hardy, T D, *Descriptive Catalogue of Material relating to the History of Great Britain and Ireland* (Rolls Series, 1862–71)

Henderson, I, 'Early Christian Monuments of Scotland bearing Crosses but no other Ornament', in Small, A, ed., *The Picts: a new Look at old Problems* (1987), 45–58

Hennessy, W M, and MacCarthy , B, eds., *Annals of Ulster* (Dublin, 1887–1901)

Hennessy, W M, ed., *Chronicon Scotorum* (RS, 1866)

Henry, F, *Irish Art during the Viking Invasions*, (new edn, 1967)

Henry, F, *Irish Art in the Early Christian Period* (1940)

Henry, F, *Irish High Crosses* (1964)

Herbert, M, *Iona, Kells and Derry* (1988)

Herity, M, 'The Context and Date of the High Crosses at Disert Diarmata (Castledermot), Co. Kildare', in *Figures from the Past: Studies in Honour of Helen M Roe*, ed. E Rynne (Dublin, 1987), 111–30

Hill, P, et al., *Whithorn Excavation Reports* (1987-)

Hood, A B E, ed., *St Patrick: his Writings and Muirchú's Life* (1978)

Horstmann, C, *Altenglische Legenden* (1881)

Hughes, K , *Early Christian Ireland: Introduction to the Sources* (1972)

Hughes, K , *The Church in early Irish Society* (1966)

Hynde, J H, ed., *Symeonis Dunelmensis Opera et Collectanea*, (Surtees Soc., 1868)

Innes, C, and Chalmers, P, eds., *Liber S Thome de Aberbrothoc* (Bannatyne Club, 1848)

Innes, C, ed., *Registrum Episcopatus Glasguensis* (Bannatyne and Maitland Clubs, 1843)

Innes, C, ed., *Registrum Monasterii de Passelet* (Maitland Club, 1832)

Jackson, K H, 'Duan Albanach', *Celtica*, iii (1956), 149–67

Jackson, K H, 'Duan Albanach', *Scottish Historical Review*, xxxvi (1957), 125–37

Jackson, K H, *The Gaelic Notes in the Book of Deer* (1972)

Jackson, K H, *The Gododdin* (1969)

Jackson, K H, 'The Pictish Language' in Wainwright, F, ed., *The Problem of the Picts* (1955; reprinted 1980), 129–60

Jackson, K H, 'The Sources for the Life of St Kentigern,' in N K Chadwick et al., *Studies in the early British Church* (1958), 273–357

Jerome, 'Liber Interpretationis Hebraicorum Nominum', in *Corpus Christianorum*, ser. lat., lxxii (1959)

Jobey, G, 'Traprain Law: a Summary', in *Hillforts: later prehistoric Earthworks in Britain and Ireland*, ed. D W Harding (1976)

Johnson, S, *Later Roman Britain* (1980)

Jones, P F, *Concordance to the Historia Ecclesiastica of Bede* (1929)

Kelly, J N D, *Jerome: his Life, Writings and Controversies* (1975)

Kelly, J N D, *Oxford Dictionary of Popes* (1986)

Keppie, L, *Scotland's Roman remains* (1990)

Kirby, D P, 'Strathclyde and Cumbria', *Transactions of the Cumberland and Westmoreland Antiquarian and Archaeological Society*, n.s. lxii (1962), 77–94

Kirk, J, ed., *Stirling Presbytery Records, 1581–1587* (SHS, 1981)

Labbé, P, *Sacrosancta Concilia* (1671–3)

Lamont, W D, 'Hinba once more', *Notes and Queries of the Society of West Highland and Island Historical Research*, xii (1980), 10–15

Lamont, W D, 'Where is Adomnán's Hinba?', *Notes and Queries of the Society of West Highland and Island Historical Research*, vii (1978), 3–6

Lapidge, M, and Dumville, D, eds, *Gildas: New Approaches* (1984)

Lawrie, A C, *Early Scottish Charter prior to 1153* (1905)

Mac Airt, S, and Mac Níocaill, G, eds, *Annals of Ulster* (1983)

Mac Airt, S, ed., *Annals of Innisfallen* (1951)

Mac Cana, P, *The Learned Tales of Medieval Ireland* (1980)

Macalister, R A S, *Corpus Inscriptionum Insularum Celticarum* (1945)

Macbain, A, *Etymology of the Principal Gaelic National Names, Personal Names and Surnames, to which is added a Disquisition on Ptolemy's Geography of Scotland* (1911)

Macfarlane, L J, *William Elphinstone and the Kingdom of Scotland, 1431–1514* (1985)

MacIvor, I, *Dumbarton Castle* (n.d.)

MacKay, W R, 'Hinba again', *Notes and Queries of the Society of West Highland and Island Historical Research*, ix (1979), 8–17

Mackey, J P, ed., *An Introduction to Celtic Christianity* (1989)

MacNeill, E, *St Patrick* (1934, reprinted 1964)

Macquarrie, A, 'An Eleventh-century Account of the Foundation Legend of Laurencekirk, and of Queen Margaret's Pilgrimage there', *Innes Review*, xlvii (1996), 95–109

Macquarrie, A, *Cille Bharra: the Church of St Finnbarr, Barra* (1984)

Macquarrie, A , 'Early Christian Govan: the historical Context', *Records of the Scottish Church History Society*, xxiv (1990), 1–17

Macquarrie, A, 'Early Christian Religious Houses in Scotland: Foundation and Function', in J Blair and R Sharpe, eds., *Pastoral Care before the Parish* (1992), 110–33

Macquarrie, A, 'Kings, Lords and Abbots: power and patronage at the medieval monastery of Iona', *Transactions of the Gaelic Society of Inverness*, liv (1984–1986), 355–75

Macquarrie, A, 'Lections for St Constantine's Day (11 March) in the Aberdeen Breviary', *Annual Report of the Society of Friends of Govan Old*, v (1995), 25–32

Macquarrie, A, 'Lections for Strathclyde saints in the Aberdeen Breviary: some problems of sources', *Records of the Scottish Church History Society*, xxvi (1996) (forthcoming)

Macquarrie, A, Review of *Vita Columbae* (2nd edn), *Scottish Historical Review*, lxxii (1993), 213–5

Macquarrie, A, *Scotland and the Crusades* (1985)

Macquarrie, A, 'The Career of St Kentigern of Glasgow: *Vitae, Lectiones* and Glimpses of Fact', *Innes Review*, xxxvii (1986), 3–24

Macquarrie, A, 'The Date of St Ninian's Mission: a Reappraisal', *Records of the Scottish Church History Society*, xxiii (1987), 1–25

Macquarrie, A, 'The Historical Context of the Govan Stones', in Ritchie, A, ed., *Govan and its early medieval Sculpture* (1994), 27–32

Macquarrie, A, 'The Kings of Strathclyde, c. 400–1018' in Grant, A, and Stringer, K J, eds, *Medieval Scotland: Crown, Lordship and Community: Essays presented to G W S Barrow* (1993), 1–19

Macquarrie, A, '*Vita Sancti Servani*: the Life of St Serf', *Innes Review*, xliv (1993), 122–52

Macquarrie, A, and Macarthur, E M, *Iona through the Ages* (2nd edn, 1992)

Macquarrie, J, *The Mediators* (1995)

MacQueen, J, 'A lost Glasgow Life of St Thaney (St Enoch)', *Innes Review*, vi (1955), 125–30

MacQueen, J, 'Myth and the Legends of Lowland Scottish Saints,' *Scottish Studies*, xxiv (1980), 1–21

MacQueen, J, 'Reply to Professor Jackson' in *Transactions of the Dumfriesshire and Galloway Natural History and Antiquarian Society*, xxxvi (1959), 175–83

MacQueen, J, *St Nynia* (1961; 2nd edn., 1990)

MacQueen, J, 'The Dear Green Place: St Mungo and Glasgow, 600–1966', *Innes Review*, vliii (1992), 87–98

MacQueen, J, 'The Name Molendinar', *Innes Review*, viii (1957), 67–9

MacQueen, J, 'Yvain, Ewen, and Owain ap Urien', *Transactions of the Dumfriesshire and Galloway Natural History and Antiquarian Society*, xxxiii (1956), 107–31

MacQueen, J, and MacQueen, W, 'Vita Merlini Silvestris', *Scottish Studies*, xxix (1989), 77–93

MacQueen, W, 'Miracula Nynie Episcopi', *Transactions of the Dumfriesshire and Galloway Natural History and Antiquarian Society*, 3d ser. xxxvii (1960), 21–57

MacRoberts, D, 'A Legendary Fragment in the Scottish Record Office,' *Innes Review*, xix (1968), 82–5

MacRoberts, D, *Catalogue of Scottish Liturgical Books and Fragments* (1953)

MacRoberts, D, 'The Death of St Kentigern of Glasgow', *Innes Review*, xxiv (1973), 43–50

Mann, J C, and Penman, R G, *Literary Sources for Roman Britain* (1978)

Mansi, J D, *Sacrorum Conciliorum Nova et Amplissima Collectio* (1759)

Marsden, J, *The Illustrated Columcille* (1991)

Mayr-Harting, H, *The Coming of Christianity to Anglo-Saxon England* (1972)

Meckler, M, 'Colum Cille's ordination of Aedán mac Gabráin', *Innes Review*, xli (1990), 139–50

Metcalfe, W M, ed., *Legends of the Saints*, (Scottish Text Society, 1st ser., 13, 18, 23, 25, 1887–92)

Meyer, K, and Nutt, A T, eds., *The Voyage of Bran* (1895)

Meyer, K, ed., *Cáin Adomnáin* (1905)

Miller, M, 'Historicity and the Pedigrees of the Northcountrymen', *Bulletin of the Board of Celtic Studies*, xxvi (1976), 255–80

Miller, M, 'The disputed historical Horizon of the Pictish King-Lists', *Scottish Historical Review*, lviii (1979), 7–34

Mohrmann, C, *The Latin of St Patrick* (1961)

Morris, J, ed., *Nennius: British History and the Welsh Annals*, (1980)

Morris, J , *The Age of Arthur* (1973)

Moss, H St L B, *The Birth of the Middle Ages* (1935)

Munro, R W, ed., *Donald Monro's Western Isles of Scotland and Genealogies of the Clans* (1961)

Murphy, D, ed., *Annals of Clonmacnoise* (1896)

Musset, L, *The Germanic Invasions* (1975)

Nagy, K, *St Margaret of Scotland and Hungary* (1973)

National Museums of Scotland, *The Treasure of Traprain* (National Museums of Scotland Information Sheet, no. 7, 1980)

Nicholson, M F, 'Celtic Theology: Pelagius' in Mackey, J P, ed., *Introduction to Celtic Christianity* (1989), 386–413

Nicolaisen, W F H, *Scottish Place-Names* (1976)

Ní Dhonnchadha, M, 'The Guarantor List of Cáin Adomnáin', *Peritia*, i (1982), 178–215

O'Donovan, J, ed., *Annals of the Four Masters*, (1856)

Ó Fíaich, T , 'Irish Monks on the Continent', in Mackey, J P, ed., *An Introduction to Celtic Christianity* (1989), 101–39

O'Rahilly, T F, *Early Irish History and Mythology* (1946)

O'Rahilly, T F, *The Two Patricks* (1942)

Ó Riain, P (ed.), *Corpus Genealogiarum Sanctorum Hiberniae* (Dublin Institute for Advanced Studies, 1985)

Ó Riain, P, 'Towards a Methodology in early Irish Hagiography', *Peritia*, i (1982), 146–59

Origen, 'Homilies on Ezekiel', in Migne, *Patrologia Graeca*, xiii

Paschoud, F, ed., *Zosime, Histoire Nouvelle* (Universités de France, 1971–89)

Phillimore, E, '*Annales Cambriae* and Old Welsh Genealogies from Harleian MS 3859', *Y Cymmrodor*, xi (1888), 141–83

Picard, J M, 'The Purpose of Adomnán's *Vita Columbae*', *Peritia*, i (1982), 160–77

Picard, J M, 'The strange death of Guaire mac Aedáin', in Ó Corráin, D, et al., eds, *Sages, Saints and Storytellers: Celtic Studies in honour of Professor James Carney* (1989), 367–75

Plummer, C, ed., *Venerabilis Baedae Opera Historica* (1896)

Plummer, C, ed., *Vitae Sanctorum Hiberniae* (1910)

Prinz, F, *Frühes Mönchtum in Frankenreich* (1965)

Pryde, G S, *The Burghs of Scotland* (1965)

Purser, J, *Scotland's Music* (1992)

Radford, C A R, and Donaldson, G, *Whithorn and Kirkmadrine* (1953)

Radford, C A R, 'Early Christian Monuments at Govan and Inchinnan', *Transactions of the Glasgow Archaeological Society*, n s xv (1966), 177–88

Radford, C A R, 'Whithorn excavation reports', in *Transactions of the Dumfriesshire and Galloway Natural History and Antiquarian Society*, 3d ser., xxxiv (1957), 85–126, and ibid., xxxvii (1960), 131–94

Raine, J, ed., *The Historians of the Church of York* (RS, lxxi, 1879)

Rees, B R, *Pelagius: a reluctant heretic* (1988)

Reeves, W, *On the Céli-Dé, commonly called Culdees* (1860)

Reeves, W, *The Culdees of the British Islands* (1864)

Richards, J, *The Popes and the Papacy in the early Middle Ages* (1979)

Ritchie, A, ed., *Govan and its early Medieval Sculpture* (1994)

Ritchie, A, *Picts* (1989)

Ritchie, G and A, *Scotland: Archaeology and early History* (1981)

Ritchie, R L G, *The Normans in Scotland* (1954)

Robertson, J, ed., *Concilia Scotiae* (Bannatyne Club, 1866)

Royal Commission for the Ancient and Historical Monuments of Scotland, *Inventory of the Monuments of Fife and Clackmannan* (Edinburgh, 1933)

Royal Commission on the Ancient and Historical Monuments of Scotland, *Inventory of Argyll*, v: *Iona* (1982)

Scott, A B, 'Nynia in Northern Pictland', *Scottish Historical Review*, ii (1905), 278–88

Sellar, W D H, 'Warlords, Holy Men, and Matrilineal Succession', *Innes Review*, xxxvi (1985), 29–43

Sharpe, R, 'Armagh and Rome in the seventh Century', in Ní Chatháin, P and Richter, M, eds, *Irland und Europa: Die Kirche im Frühmittelalter* (1984), 58–72

Sharpe, R, ed., *Adomnán of Iona, Life of St Columba* (1995)

Sharpe, R, 'Gildas as a father of the Church', in Lapidge, M, and Dumville, D, eds, *Gildas: new approaches* (1984), 193–205

Sharpe, R, *Medieval Irish Saints' Lives* (1991)

Sharpe, R , 'Saint Mauchteus, *discipulus Patricii*' in Bammesberger, A, and Wollmann, A, eds., *Britain 400–600* (1990), 85–93

Sharpe, R, 'St Patrick and the See of Armagh', *Cambridge Medieval Celtic Studies*, iv (1982), 33–59

Sharpe, R, 'The Life of St Columba in Latin Verse by Roderick MacLean (1549)', *Innes Review*, xlii (1991), 111–32

Sheldon-Williams, I P, et al., eds., *Johannes Scotus Eriugena, Periphyseon or De Divisione Naturae*, (Dublin Institute for Advanced Studies, 1968-)

Skene, W F, and Reeves, W, eds., *Adomnán's Life of Columba* (Bannatyne Club, 1874)

Skene, W F, ed., *Chronicles of the Picts: Chronicles of the Scots* (1867)

Skene, W F, ed., *Johannis de Fordun Chronica Gentis Scottorum*, (Historians of Scotland, i, 1871)

Skene, W F, 'Notice of the early ecclesiastical Settlements at St Andrews', *Proceedings of the Society of Antiquaries of Scotland*, iv (1860–2), 300–21

Smyth, A P, 'The earliest Irish Annals: their first contemporary entries, and the earliest centres of recording', *Proceedings of the Royal Irish Academy*, lxxii (1972)

Smyth, A P, *Warlords and Holy Men: Scotland, AD 80–1000* (1984)

Société des Bollandistes, ed., *Bibliotheca Hagiographica Latina* (1898–1901)

Southern, R W, 'The First Life of Edward the Confessor', *English Historical Review*, lviii (1943), 385–400

Steer, K A, 'Two unrecorded early Christian Stones', *Proceedings of the Society of Antiquaries of Scotland*, ci (1968–9), 127–9

Steer, K, and Bannerman, J W M, *Late Medieval Monumental Sculpture in the West Highlands and Islands* (1977)

Stevenson, R B K, 'Pictish Art', in Wainwright, F T, ed., *The Problem of the Picts* (1955; reprinted 1980)

Stokes, W, ed., 'Annals of Tigernach', *Revue Celtique*, xvi (1895), 374–419, xvii (1896), 6–33, 116–263, 337–420, xviii (1897), 9–59, 150–303, 374–91

Stokes, W, ed., *The Tripartite Life of St Patrick* (RS, 1887)

Stone, J, ed., *Illustrated Maps of Scotland from Blaeu's Atlas Novus of the 17th Century* (1991)

Strecker, K, ed., 'Miracula Nynie Episcopi', in *Monumenta Germaniae Historica, Poetae Latini Aevi Carolini*, iv (1923), 943–62

Sulpicius Severus, 'Chronica', in *Corpus Scriptorum Ecclesiasticorum Latinorum*, i (1866)

Talbot, C H, ed., 'Goscelin of Canterbury's *Liber confortatorius*', *Studia Anselmiana*, xxxviii (1955), 1–117

Tertullian, 'Adversos Iudaeos', in *Tertulliani Opera*, ii, *Corpus Christianorum*, Ser. lat., ii (1954)

Thomas, A C, *Christianity in Roman Britain* (1981)

Thomas, A C, 'The Evidence from North Britain', in Barley, M W, and Hanson, R P C, eds, *Christianity in Britain, 300–700* (1968), 93–121

Thomas, A C, *Whithorn's Christian Beginnings: the Whithorn Lecture 1992* (1992)

Thomson, E A, 'St Patrick and Coroticus', *Journal of Theological Studies*, n.s. xxxi (1980), 12–27

Thomson, T, ed., *Liber Cartarum S Andree in Scotia* (Bannatyne Club, 1841)

Thurneysen, R, *A Grammar of Old Irish* (new edn, 1980)

Todd, M, *Roman Britain: 55 BC-AD 400* (1981)

van Hamel, A G, ed., *Compert Con Culainn and other Stories* (Dublin Institute for Advanced Studies, Mediaeval and Modern Irish Series, iii, 1933, reprinted 1968)

'Vita Kaddroe', in *Acta Sanctorum, Mar.*, i (1865), 468–80

Wade-Evans, A W, 'Who was Ninian?', *Transactions of the Dumfriesshire and Galloway Natural History and Antiquarian Society*, 3d ser., xxviii (1951), 79–91

Walafrid Strabo, 'Life of Blathmac', in *Monumenta Germaniae Historica, Poetae Latini Aevi Carolini*, ii, 299–301

Wall, J, 'Christian Evidences in the Roman Period', *Archaeologia Aeliana*, 4th ser., xliii (1965), 201–25

Walsh, M, and Ó Croinín, D, eds., *Cummian's letter De controversia Paschali, etc.* (Toronto Pontifical Institute of Mediaeval Studies, Texts and Studies, 1988)

Watson, W J, *History of the Celtic Place-Names of Scotland* (1926; reprinted 1986)

Watt, D E R, ed., *Walter Bower's Scotichronicon* (1987-)

Watt, D E R, *Fasti Ecclesiae Scoticanae Medii Aevi* (Scottish Record Society, 1969)

Williams, A, Smyth, A P, and Kirby, D P, *A Biographical Dictionary of Dark Age Britain* (1991)

Wilson, A J, *St Margaret, Queen of Scotland* (1993)

Wilson, P A, 'St Ninian: Irish Evidence further examined', *Transactions of the Dumfriesshire and Galloway Natural History and Antiquarian Society*, xlvi (1969), 140–59

Winterbottom, M, ed., *Gildas: the Ruin of Britain (De Excidio Britanniae) and other works* (1978)

Wormald, C P, 'The Emergence of the *Regnum Scottorum*: a Carolingian Hegemony?' in Crawford, B E, ed., *Scotland in Dark Age Britain* (1996), 131–60

2. Manuscripts cited in footnotes

Dublin, Marsh's Library, MS Z 4.5.
Edinburgh, NLS, MS Adv. 34.7.3
London, BM, Cotton Vespas. B XX
London, BM, Harley 105
Oxford, Bodleian Library, MS Lat. Liturg. f. 5
Oxford, Bodleian Library, MS Rawlinson B. 488
Rome, Vatican Archives, Registrum Supplicationum

Index

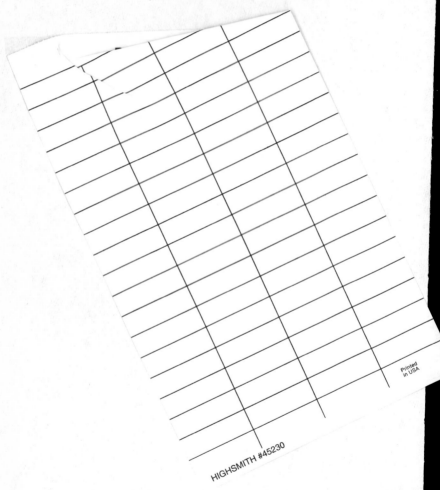

HIGHSMITH #45230

Printed
in USA